DATE:
ARTISTE:
daft punk
ALL AREAS
CREW
V.I.P.
GUEST
PHOTO/PRESS

DISCO POGO



Published by Disco Pogo Ltd. First Edition 2023.

discopogo.co
instagram.com/discopogo.co
facebook.com/discopogo.co
twitter.com/discoxpogo

ISBN: 978-1-3999-4619-3

Printed and bound by Everbest Printing Co Ltd.

# DAFT PUNK
# WE WERE THE ROBOTS
## A DISCO POGO TRIBUTE

NORMAL POSITION · TYPE I
JVC
AFI·60
60 AFI
DAFT PUNK
JVC
DATE 10th November
A
ON OFF
NOISE REDUCTION
ON OFF
B
- The NEW WAVE (PART I) - ≈ 5'05"
- The NEW WAVE (Part II) ≈ 7'00
- "ASSAULT" ≈ 5'40"
- ALIVE (New Wave finale) ≈ 5'
SONY
All-Round Audio Reproduction
HF
SONY
90
DAFT PUNK - (See Notice card)
N.R. ON
A

# DAFT PUNK
# WE WERE THE ROBOTS
## A DISCO POGO TRIBUTE

TR-909
ALESIS

VO

MAR-9 15:51 DE:DAFT TRAX 0142511354 A:041 353 0017 PAGE:01

04 of March 97

I, Thomas Bangalter, confirm that Daft Punk will be performing live at T in the Park on the 12th of July

daft punk

# CONTENTS

# ONE MORE TIMELINE

**01.05.93**
Melody Maker reviewer Dave Jennings calls the Darlin' tracks on the 'Shimmies in Super 8' EP (Duophonic) a "daft punky thrash".

**25.09.93**
Thomas and Guy-Man hand their demo to Stuart McMillan of Soma Records at Dance Europe Weekender at Euro Disney, Paris.

**01.04.94**
First DJ appearance as Daft Punk at Blues du Nord in Paris.

**20.01.97**
'Homework' album released on Virgin.

**03.02.97**
'Da Funk' single released on Virgin.

**11.02.97**
Daftendirektour world tour begins in Chicago.

**02.03.97**
Their first Essential Mix is broadcast on Radio 1.

**07.04.97**
'Around the World' single released on Virgin.

**24.05.97**
Daft Punk return to play Tribal Gathering at Luton Hoo, joining Kraftwerk and Orbital on the bill.

**15.09.97**
'Burnin'' single released on Virgin.

**05.11.97**
Daft Punk play two nights at London's Astoria.

**16.02.98**
'Revolution 909' single released on Virgin.

**02.05.98**
At the first Creamfields they curate The Daft Club arena featuring Roger Sanchez, Cassius and more.

**20.07.98**
Stardust's 'Music Sounds Better With You' single released on Roulé.

**16.08.98**
Daft Punk play live at V Festival in Leeds, UK and Chelmsford the following day.

**18.05.03**
'Interstella 5555: The 5tory of the 5ecret 5tar 5ystem' screened at Cannes.

**28.05.03**
'Interstella 5555: The 5tory of the 5ecret 5tar 5ystem' film released via Virgin.

**10.10.03**
'Face to Face' single released on Virgin.

**14.11.03**
'Something About Us' single released on Virgin.

**01.12.03**
Daft Club remix album released via Daft Club.

**21.06.04**
Franz Ferdinand's 'Take Me Out' (Daft Punk remix) released on Domino.

**13.09.04**
'Human After All' recordings start.

**09.11.04**
'Human After All' recordings end.

**14.03.05**
'Human After All' album released on Virgin.

**11.04.05**
'Robot Rock' single released on Virgin.

**14.06.05**
'Technologic' single released on Virgin.

**21.10.05**
'Human After All' single released on Virgin.

**03.12.10**
'Tron: Legacy' (Original Motion Picture Soundtrack) released on Walt Disney records.

**08.12.10**
'Derezzed' single from 'Tron: Legacy' released on Walt Disney records.

**05.04.11**
'Tron: Legacy Reconfigured' remix album released on Walt Disney records.

**16.09.11**
Soma release 1994 track 'Drive Unreleased 1994' on 'Soma Records 20 Years'.

**26.02.13**
Daft Punk's official website and Facebook announce they have signed to Columbia Records.

**03.03.13**
Teaser trailer with the riff from 'Get Lucky' pops up in the commercial break of 'Saturday Night Live'.

**24.03.13**
'Get Lucky' longer video teaser screened at Coachella featuring Pharrell Williams and Nile Rodgers.

**19.04.13**
'Get Lucky' released on Columbia.

**17.05.13**
'Random Access Memories' album released on Columbia.

**18.06.13**
Kanye West 'Yeezus' album features four tracks produced by Daft Punk.

**13.08.13**
'Lose Yourself to Dance' single featuring Pharrell Williams and Nile Rodgers released on Columbia.

**03.09.13**
'Doin' It Right' single featuring Panda Bear released on Columbia.

**21.06.17**
Parcels release the song 'Overnight' on Kitsuné, produced and co-written by Daft Punk - their last production.

**09.04.19**
Launch an art exhibition at the Philharmonie de Paris featuring various costumes, guitars, and other ephemera.

**22.02.21**
Daft Punk announce their split with a video entitled 'Epilogue' on YouTube.

**1993 - 2021**

**11.04.94**
'The New Wave'/'Alive' 12-inch released on Soma.

**15.05.95**
'Da Funk'/'Rollin' & Scratchin'' 12-inch released on Soma.

**28.08.95**
The Chemical Brothers' 'Life is Sweet' (Daft Punk remix) released on Virgin.

**30.9.95**
Play live to 500 people on the Renfrew Ferry at a Soma party in Glasgow.

**15.01.96**
I:Cube's 'Disco Cubizm' (Daft Punk remix) released on Versatile.

**29.01.96**
'Indo Silver Club' (Part One & Part Two) released on Soma.

**26.02.96**
Ian Pooley's 'Chord Memory' (Daft Punk remix) released on Force Inc.

**10.04.96**
Gabrielle's 'Forget About the World' (Daft Punk remix) released on Go! Beat.

**04.05.96**
Play live at Tribal Gathering, Otmoor Park, Oxford alongside The Chemical Brothers, Leftfield and Underworld.

**26.05.96**
First American live show at Even Furthur festival, Wisconsin.

**01.07.96**
'Musique' appears on the 'Source Lab 2' compilation.

**01.09.96**
Daft Punk sign to Virgin, licensing their tracks to the label through their production company Daft Trax.

**16.11.98**
Scott Grooves' 'Mothership Reconnection' (Daft Punk remix) released on Soma.

**27.11.98**
Daft Punk DJ and Thomas Bangalter plays live at Bugged Out!, Nation, Liverpool.

**01.01.99**
Daft Punk's second Essential Selection 'Special Edition Hotmix' broadcast on Radio 1.

**05.11.99**
Daft Punk DJ at Bugged Out! at the newly-opened fabric in London.

**28.03.00**
'D.A.F.T.: A Story About Dogs, Androids, Firemen and Tomatoes' video collection released on Virgin.

**13.11.00**
'One More Time' single released on Virgin.

**12.03.01**
'Discovery' album released on Virgin.

**28.03.01**
'Aerodynamic' single released on Virgin.

**11.06.01**
'Digital Love' single released on Virgin.

**03.08.01**
The first four episodes of 'Interstella 5555: The 5tory of the 5ecret 5tar 5ystem' are screened.

**01.10.01**
'Alive 1997' album released on Virgin.

**13.10.01**
'Harder, Better, Stronger, Faster' single released on Virgin.

**13.12.05**
'Touch It' by Busta Rhymes released. It's the first hip hop artist to sample Daft Punk ('Technologic').

**29.03.06**
'Human After All' remix album released in Japan.

**29.03.06**
'Musique Vol. 1 1993 - 2005 Anthology' released on Virgin.

**29.04.06**
Daft Punk reveal their 'Pyramid' live show in the Sahara tent at Coachella.

**21.05.06**
'Daft Punk's Electroma', their avant-garde science fiction film, released.

**16.06.06**
Headline Wireless festival in London's Hyde Park with Klaxons, LCD Soundsystem and more.

**17.06.07**
'The Prime Time of Your Life' single released on Virgin.

**15.10.07**
'Harder, Better, Faster, Stronger' (Alive 2007) released on Virgin.

**19.11.07**
'Alive 2007' live album released on Virgin.

**10.11.08**
Daft Punk join Kanye West at the Grammys to perform his track 'Stronger'.

**08.02.09**
'Alive 2007' wins Best Electronic/Dance album at the Grammys.

**16.10.10**
Daft Punk co-write and produce N.E.R.D's single 'Hypnotise U'.

**22.11.13**
'Instant Crush' single featuring Julian Casablancas released on Columbia.

**26.01.14**
At the 56th Annual Grammy Awards the duo win best Electronic Music/Dance album.

**31.01.14**
'Give Life Back To Music' single featuring Nile Rodgers released on Columbia.

**24.10.14**
Daft Punk co-write and provide backing vocals for Pharrell Williams' 'Gust Of Wind'.

**30.03.15**
Daft Punk join what they call 'The Avengers of Music' to launch Jay-Z's Tidal platform.

**24.06.15**
'Daft Punk: Unchained' – a documentary directed by Hervé Martin-Delpierre – is televised via Canal+.

**17.12.15**
Place 12th on Rolling Stone's 20 Greatest Duos of all time beating Steely Dan and the Righteous Brothers.

**16.04.16**
Junior Kimbrough's 'I Gotta Try You Girl' (Daft Punk edit) single released on Fat Possum.

**21.09.16**
The Weeknd's 'Starboy' single, which Daft Punk co-write and co-produce, is released on XO Republic.

**12.11.16**
The Weeknd's 'I Feel It Coming' – another Daft Punk co-write and co-production – released on XO Republic.

**11.02.17**
Daft Punk open a pop-up shop in Los Angeles, selling limited edition clothing and accessories.

**12.02.17**
Daft Punk's last performance is with The Weeknd at the Grammys.

# AROUND THE DAFT PUNK WORLD

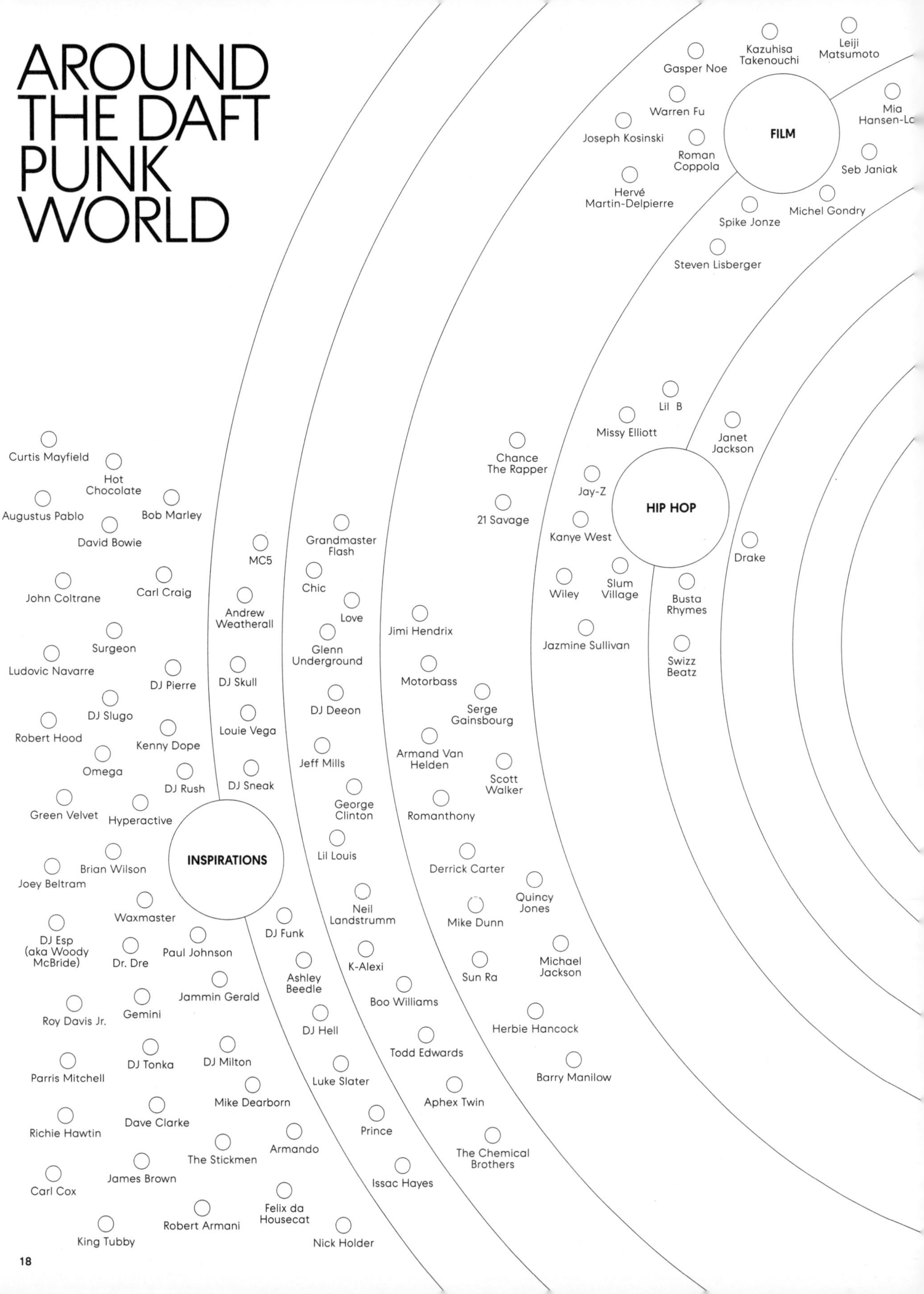

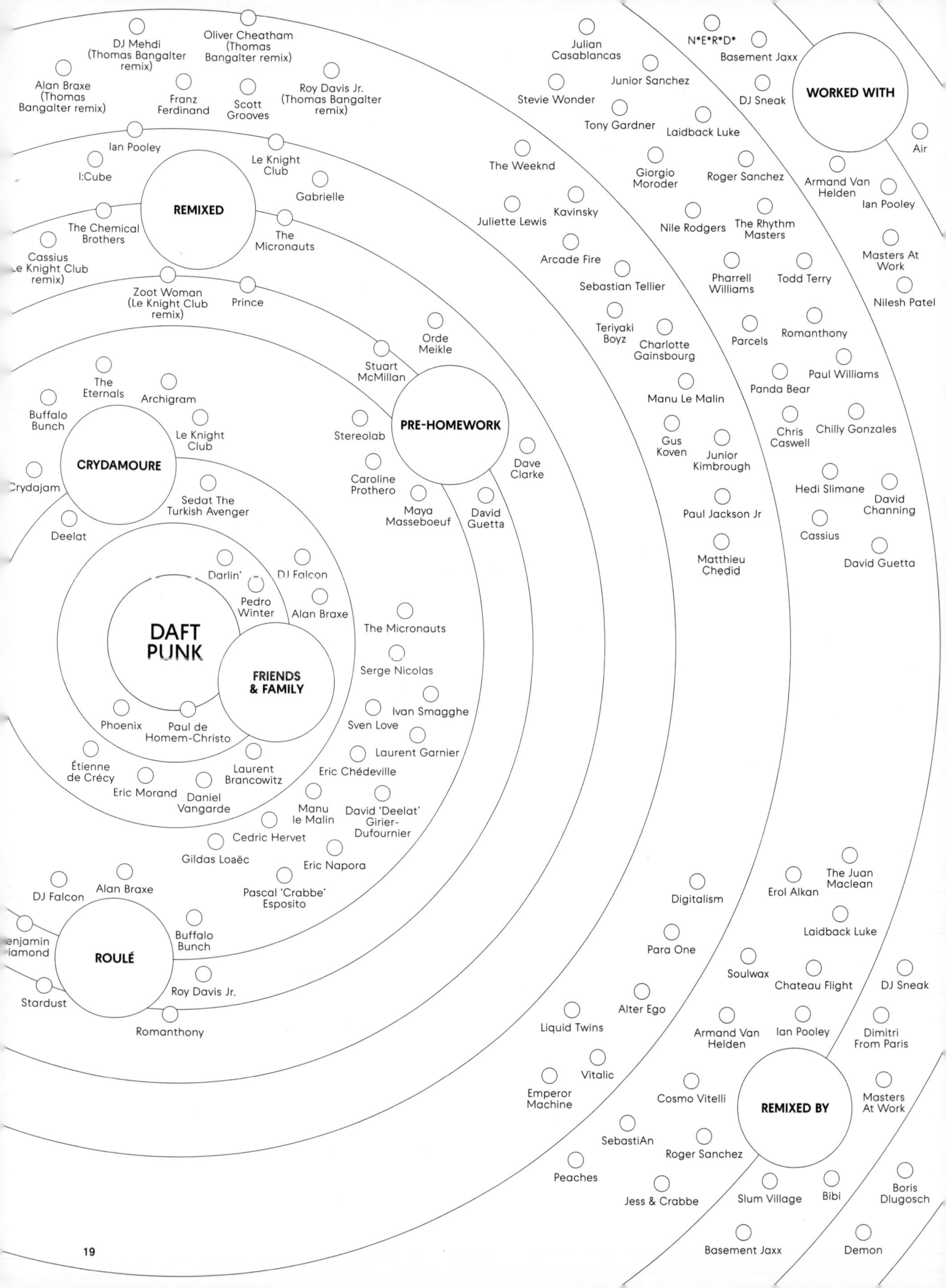
DAFT PUNK
FRIENDS & FAMILY
Darlin'
DJ Falcon
Pedro Winter
Alan Braxe
Phoenix
Paul de Homem-Christo
Étienne de Crécy
Eric Morand
Daniel Vangarde
Laurent Brancowitz
CRYDAMOURE
The Eternals
Archigram
Buffalo Bunch
Le Knight Club
Crydajam
Sedat The Turkish Avenger
Deelat
The Micronauts
Serge Nicolas
Ivan Smagghe
Sven Love
Laurent Garnier
Eric Chédeville
Manu le Malin
David 'Deelat' Girier-Dufournier
Cedric Hervet
Gildas Loaëc
Eric Napora
Pascal 'Crabbe' Esposito
PRE-HOMEWORK
Orde Meikle
Stuart McMillan
Stereolab
Caroline Prothero
Maya Masseboeuf
Dave Clarke
David Guetta
REMIXED
DJ Mehdi (Thomas Bangalter remix)
Oliver Cheatham (Thomas Bangalter remix)
Alan Braxe (Thomas Bangalter remix)
Franz Ferdinand
Scott Grooves
Roy Davis Jr. (Thomas Bangalter remix)
Ian Pooley
I:Cube
Le Knight Club
Gabrielle
The Chemical Brothers
The Micronauts
Cassius (Le Knight Club remix)
Zoot Woman (Le Knight Club remix)
Prince
ROULÉ
DJ Falcon
Alan Braxe
Benjamin Diamond
Buffalo Bunch
Stardust
Roy Davis Jr.
Romanthony
WORKED WITH
Julian Casablancas
N*E*R*D*
Basement Jaxx
Junior Sanchez
Stevie Wonder
DJ Sneak
Tony Gardner
Laidback Luke
Air
The Weeknd
Giorgio Moroder
Roger Sanchez
Armand Van Helden
Ian Pooley
Kavinsky
Juliette Lewis
Nile Rodgers
The Rhythm Masters
Arcade Fire
Masters At Work
Sebastian Tellier
Pharrell Williams
Todd Terry
Nilesh Patel
Teriyaki Boyz
Charlotte Gainsbourg
Parcels
Romanthony
Paul Williams
Panda Bear
Manu Le Malin
Gus Koven
Junior Kimbrough
Chris Caswell
Chilly Gonzales
Hedi Slimane
David Channing
Paul Jackson Jr
Cassius
David Guetta
Matthieu Chedid
REMIXED BY
The Juan Maclean
Erol Alkan
Digitalism
Laidback Luke
Para One
Soulwax
Chateau Flight
DJ Sneak
Alter Ego
Liquid Twins
Armand Van Helden
Ian Pooley
Dimitri From Paris
Vitalic
Emperor Machine
Cosmo Vitelli
Masters At Work
SebastiAn
Roger Sanchez
Peaches
Jess & Crabbe
Slum Village
Bibi
Boris Dlugosch
Basement Jaxx
Demon

# Cool Right From The Start

They were cool right from the start. We were in Year One of running Jockey Slut, it was still early days and the magazine was printed in black and white. The monochrome press photo of two teenagers, one smoking a cigarette, one in a tight tee that accompanied their first record instantly piqued our interest. In 1994, techno acts generally didn't look like this, they could've been an indie duo (which they had been the previous year), they didn't sport the ubiquitous ponytail barnet of the era or the scruffy, charmless look of electronic acts on the Megadog circuit. That they were called Daft Punk and their single was titled 'The New Wave' ticked two further boxes which made us pick up the phone to Soma and request an interview. Oh, the music was bloody good too, especially the B-side track 'Alive'. Co-editor Paul Benney secured what would be the first-ever Daft Punk interview in print, which you can read at the end of this introduction.

Months later we received a white label with 'Da Funk' written on it in biro. Records that don't sound like anything that predate them and remain without peer for the rest of existence don't come around that often, but Daft Punk nailed it with this second release. They were on a techno label at a time when patrons of the genre liked their beats set to plus 8 but they had opted for a 110bpm plodder that drew more on George Clinton than Jeff Mills.

There followed a run of remixes that kept their new fans sated while we awaited their debut long player (albums were still a rare commodity in techno back then). The reworks for The Chemical Brothers, I:Cube, Ian Pooley and - bizarrely - Gabrielle remained in record boxes while Soma teased us with a mysterious eponymous release called 'Indo Silver Club'.

In 1996, we offered them the cover of Jockey Slut. It would be their debut cover and one of the last to feature their faces. It was also going to be the first issue we printed in full colour.

Thomas Bangalter and Guy-Man de Homem-Christo were reserved, self-effacing chaps. On the same weekend as their cover shoot I had accompanied them to Nottingham for a DJ gig at Heavenly Records' club night The Social. The boisterous coach trip featured 50 or so Londoners dipping cigarettes into amyl nitrate and setting them ablaze - and there was a raffle for an ecstasy tablet. A song erupted from the rear - sung in a Scottish accent - which concluded with: "The front of the bus ye cannae sing for peanuts!" Daft Punk were at the front of the bus looking very disconcerted.

On the Sunday we booked one of the rooms in London's Embassy hotel for our photo shoot (this can be witnessed on YouTube in the trailer of 'Daft Punk Unchained' at 0:25). Thomas gamely threw shapes for the photographer RIP, but Guy-Man, perhaps still traumatised by Friday's coach trip, was less cooperative. When we looked over the contact sheets the cover choice was simple; there was only one shot of Guy-Man not scowling, so we went with that. Daft Punk seemed so dispirited by the experience that they took to wearing masks in all future photo shoots.

The first-ever press shot that accompanied 'The New Wave' release

Later that year our office received the promo vinyl double pack of 'Homework'. It was everything we hoped it would be; running like a collection of singles and remixes rather than a classically programmed album. There was an abundance of riches, every time you listened to it a different track would become your new favourite. It also felt like they were at the pinnacle of a new wave of house and techno that was pioneered by the artists featured on the track 'Teachers', most notably American artists DJ Sneak, Paul Johnson and Armand Van Helden. Their Parisian students had taken over. The 'Homework' sleeve broke away from electronic music cliché too as it featured a satin tour jacket. Inside, there was a range of teenage bedroom ephemera that included a Kiss tour poster and a naff compilation that featured a Barry Manilow track (who they later sampled on 'Superheroes'). They moved further from convention by employing first Spike Jonze and then Michel Gondry to direct the idiosyncratic videos for 'Da Funk' and 'Around the World'.

After cementing their club nous through 1998, when they concentrated on their own labels Roulé (Thomas) and Crydamoure (Guy-Man), the world was blind sided by what followed. I remember being in the back of a car listening to Pete Tong on Radio 1 on a Friday night in 2000, and hearing a track that sounded like it might be Daft Punk though I hoped it wouldn't be as it seemed so cheesy. Yes, it was 'One More Time' and like countless other fans I didn't warm to it initially or the autotuned vocal pioneered by Cher on her number one hit 'Believe'. Now (again, like many) it's one of my favourite tracks, the

breakdown being particularly audacious and affecting. When it came to reviewing the album that followed - 'Discovery' - the close contact we used to have with the band had long gone. I was summoned to Virgin to listen to it twice through in a room on my own with just a pen and notepad. It provoked a Marmite reaction depending on how purist you felt you were and if you wanted the same 'Homework'-style dance bangers rather than yacht rock and 80s pop which were now part of their aural arsenal. I loved it and despite the lack of access gave it top marks in Jockey Slut. The most surprising moves for me came early on - in particular 'Aerodynamic' with its Eddie Van Halen-style shredding guitar and 'Digital Love', the DJ Sneak co-write, that parked the boompty boomp house for which he was renowned for whimsical pop that could have been by 80s new wave duo The Buggles.

'Discovery' was a very different record to 'Homework' but also prescient as it was embraced by a new breed of DJs like 2manydjs and Erol Alkan who ushered in a sea-change in clubs the same year. Daft Punk were also bang on the zeitgeist again with their next album 'Human After All' pre-empting the gnarly, rough-and-ready sound adopted by fellow Parisians Justice and their Ed Banger brothers. Famously made in a few weeks it remains an experiment that didn't quite work and is their least-loved album.

Of course, without 'Human After All' there may have been no Pyramid show and their ensuing renaissance. Following the album's relative failure they needed to make a statement, finally accepting the (very good) financial offer from Coachella so they could create a groundbreaking live show. It now feels that when talk turns to Daft Punk at Coachella they must've been closing the main stage. In fact, they were in the 10,000 capacity Sahara dance tent with a show so shrouded in mystery even their manager Pedro Winter didn't know what to expect until the night. For better or worse their Pyramid shows influenced a lot of American producers as they attempted to equal or better it, resulting in a lot of EDM bluster. They were probably also culpable for the over use of autotune that also blighted the pop and dance landscape back then. I saw the Pyramid at

"They pioneered the banging club tracks album; mastered the album that reflected their salad days; attempted the knock-it-out-in-a-couple-of-weeks experiment and then the opposite."

Hyde Park in 2007 during the peak of new rave with Daft Punk topping a bill that featured LCD Soundsystem and Klaxons, plus a young Calvin Harris who seemed destined to be about as big as Mylo.

The next time they appeared at Coachella was with an advert for 'Get Lucky'. The build up to this release was genuinely thrilling and they cleverly used YouTube to ignite the spark, knowing that the teaser advert in the commercial break of 'Saturday Night Live' was going to end up on the platform - it ended up being shared millions of times on social media. A friend of mine looped the riff to infinity online so you could play it for as long as you wished so long as your device was powered (it had over a million views in 24 hours). The sound featuring Nile Rodgers' unique choppy-style of guitar playing signified that their next album was going to be much more produced than 'Human After All'. Like so many in the UK, I woke up that Saturday morning after Coachella - where the full video featuring Nile and Pharrell Williams had been played the night before on the festival's screens - to an excitable online frenzy. I loved 'Get Lucky', their successful attempt at a massive Britney-style pop record and the resulting album, particularly the bold, super indulgent track 'Touch' and the joyous robo-funk of 'Lose Yourself To Dance'. Of course it immediately had its voracious naysayers, as all their previous albums had (bar 'Homework') - usually from DJs and musicians who just couldn't shake their love for 'Homework'. It was an album made by wealthy men in their late-30s living in sun-soaked LA. Why would they want to keep making music they conjured up on a small bedroom floor in their early-20s?

Where could they have gone after 'RAM'? They'd pioneered the banging club tracks album; mastered the album that reflected the music of their salad days; attempted the knock-it-out-in-a-couple-of-weeks experiment and then the opposite: their final opus where they utilised their heroes, orchestras and the most expensive session musicians and studios. It left them with a legacy where everybody has a favourite version of Daft Punk; from studio boffs who studied the compression on 'Around the World' to their elevation of autotune on 'Discovery' to the pioneering electronic dance music live show with the Pyramid. Sure they could've been more prolific, but as artists they'd covered all bases within their genre without resorting to ill-fitting fads. Their demise came without warning, announced during a worldwide pandemic, amplifying global bad news for a day. It was sudden, shrouded in mystery and tantalisingly short on info. Very Daft Punk.

We approached them to be interviewed for this book back in 2021, they declined saying they didn't want to look back to their past at this point and they wanted to look to the future, but Thomas did wish us the best of luck. We look forward - as they are - to what they will both do next.

*John Burgess*

# The Real New Wave

By Paul Benney

The press release said 'French Teen Techno'. In reality they're both French, one of them is a teenager and the music's definitely techno. Hard, funky, white-hot, teutonic techno. You know, the best kind. Not only that but they're from Paris releasing their debut single 'The New Wave' on one of Scotland's finest record labels. It sounds good so far doesn't it?

"We were introduced to Stuart McMillan by a mutual friend at last September's Euro Disney [Dance Europe Weekender rave] as a surprise, as we had told him we liked his DJing," explains Thomas, the younger half of the duo. "We weren't even thinking of having it released on Soma. We just wanted Stuart to hear our music. But he liked it and so we did some more tracks and here we are."

Daft Punk have been making music for years but it's only in the past 12 months that their output has been of the sexy technological variety. In fact if you were wondering about their name it's in their pre-electronic, seedy rock days you should be looking.

"We used to be in a rock band and we had a very bad review in the Melody Maker where they described our single as 'daft punk'. We thought it was funny so we used it."

So is the title of the single a dig at the weeklies' recent invention - the so-called New Wave of New Wave? Apparently not, as the single was named about eight months ago but a record like this is still a sharp poke in the eye for ageing hacks who refuse to acknowledge the real groundbreaking sounds. Unfortunately, these lads are far too sussed to get involved in a slanging match.

Daft Punk reckon they have no French contemporaries in the techno field but name-check the likes of Luke Slater, Weatherall, Richie Hawtin and CJ Bolland as people they respect and possible clues to influences on the French duo's sound. They're planning to spend some time in Glasgow in the near future laying down some tracks in Soma's studio and experiencing some Scottish hospitality Slam-style. In the hands of that lot it's more likely to be a hospital they experience. Let's hope they get a chance to make some music first. Not as daft as punk '94 style, but miles more fun.

DAFT PUNK
FRENCH! TEEN!
TECHNO!
SOMA QUALITY RECORDINGS
Soma
THE
REAL
NEW WAVE
OUT 11th APRIL

darlin'©
CINDY, SO LOUD (demo)
DARLIN 2
GUY-MANUEL
THOMAS
LAURENT
darlin'© Plays Soul Music
stereo
write 2 : daniel dauxerre - 51 place saint-charles - 75015 paris

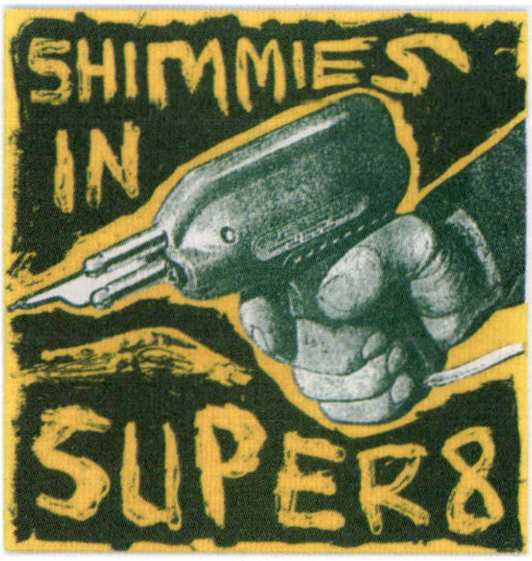
SHIMMIES IN SUPER8

WHITE
SIDE 1
HUGGY BEAR
TRAFALGAR SQUARE
GODZILLER
MORE MUSIC FROM BELLS
SNOW WHITE, ROSE RED
SIDE 2
DARLIN'
CINDY SO LOUD
DARLIN'
GREEN
SIDE 3
COLM
SOUNDTRACK
000466
SIDE 4
STEREOLAB
REVOX!
MADE IN ENGLAND
DUOPHONIC SUPER 45'S
C/O MARTIN - 19 BRAMBLING ROAD
HORSHAM - WEST SUSSEX RH17 6AX
DS 45
05 & 06

COLM
SOUNDTRACK!
RECORDED IN JUNE 92 - ENGINEERED BY AMADOU -
COLM'S 45 AVAILABLE NOW ON DISTORTION. INTERESTED PEOPLE
WRITE TO: TRAFIC RESTREINT 4 RUE TARBE 75017·
PARIS FRANCE
DESIGNED BY GUY-MANUEL

Above: The original DAT tape that Thomas and Guy-Man gave to Soma. It became Daft Punk's first release, 'The New Wave'. Right: 'Drive 1994', which sat in a drawer for over 20 years before being included on Soma's 25th anniversary compilation, 'Soma25'. Left: The 'Shimmies in Super 8' compilation, released on Duophonic in 1993, featuring Darlin', alongside Huggy Bear, Colm and Stereolab. Some copies included a Darlin' insert (main image) and a Colm insert, which was designed by Guy-Man.

# Here Comes The New Wave

A young Thomas and Guy-Man enjoying some Scottish hospitality at the old Soma office. From left to right: Jamie Cloughley (Desert Storm), Felix da Housecat, Dave Clarke, Melanie Clarke, Calvin Bush aka Stuart Goldberg (crouching), Orde Meikle (at back), Glenn Gibbons, Thomas and Guy-Man

## The Cast

### Calvin Bush

Freelance music journalist and the press officer for Soma Records until 1995, including for the first two Daft Punk singles.

### Dave Clarke

Managing Director of Soma Records, promoter of Slam club nights and manager of DJ duo Slam.

### Jim Muotune

Founding artist and director of Soma.

### Richard Brown

Press and promotions for Soma from 1995 and then label manager up to the release of 'Homework' on Virgin.

### Stuart McMillan

One half of Slam (with Orde Meikle) and director of Soma.

**Stuart McMillan:** "Nicky Holloway (promoter and DJ) had this Euro Disney dance music festival which was quite ambitious at the time [1993]. Its main objective was to get people from the UK to come over to Paris, party a little bit at Euro Disney and have fun. We kind of made a bit of a holiday out of it and one of Thomas and Guy's friends got in touch because they knew that we had the label Soma. So all the time when we were hanging around in Paris there were these two guys in the group of people that we were with that didn't say a single word. I'm sure we'd been told that these guys made music, or these guys are producers, and we were like: 'Oh yes, it's just those two guys again.' When we came back from the Euro Disney rave we went up to someone's flat and we finally got to hear Daft Punk's music for the first time off cassette. We didn't expect much, because we had no idea who these two guys were. I think everybody just stopped and looked at each other because it was really quite different. At that point it sounded quite industrial, it sounded very raw."

**Dave Clarke:** "We had a couple of nights in Paris. I mean, there were all sorts of people there, Dave Beer (Back To Basics), Darren Emerson (Underworld), I seem to remember Slam were DJing at the Queen Club. We'd had a couple of nights to hang out in Paris and there was a guy who I think was a journalist at the time, called Serge Nicolas. I think he went on to do the artwork for 'Homework'. He knew us, we used to phone each other, and he knew we were coming to Paris. He said there were a couple of his friends who would like to meet us. He said they made some techno and were fans of 'Positive Education'. We went round to Serge's house before the weekend and we met Thomas and Guy. They were like: 'We're making tracks, do you want to come and meet us at the studio at my mum and dad's house and listen to the tracks?'"

**Stuart:** "They wanted to meet the guys who made 'Positive Education'. I don't think they knew much more than it was a record that they quite liked. I think their sound was initially supposed to sound like it came from Chicago or Detroit. But because they were from Paris, there was a whole different set of influences there. There's now a homogenisation of music due to the internet, but back then music was much more displaced and scenes were much more separated. So people from Cologne would make a different sound to people from Glasgow or people from Detroit. There's a very French element within the music that you can definitely hear. But I think in their minds, they wanted to make music like Cajmere or someone from Chicago like that."

**Jim Muotune:** "The thing was, when I first met them, I was immediately of the opinion these guys were fucking talented as hell. They were quietly confident and just supremely talented with their music. They had a real understanding of what they were, what they wanted to do."

**Dave:** "We offered them a deal there and then. That was it, off the cassette. What we heard became the first single ['The New Wave'], pretty much. We knew instantly we wanted to put it out. It just sounded fresh, different, powerful, raw. I'm sure Stuart and I were very enthusiastic at the time. We got back, they sent us over the DAT tape and I think the first one we got mastered. We always got stuff mastered at The Exchange, and a lot of the time the cutting engineer was Nils, who was known as the best. I remember every record after that, Daft Punk would get cut by Nils and they would go and attend the cut. And I'm pretty sure all their vinyl they got cut with him, even subsequent to Soma."

**Jim:** "I remember being in the kitchen in Thomas' house in Paris and his dad was there. We were talking about the different types of deals that we could do. They had this concept that they were producers, that they wanted to do something different in terms of record labels. They didn't need us to advance them money. They just needed us to release their music. So the idea was that they would produce the music and licence it to us for a certain amount of time, the amount of time that we thought we could exploit the recordings for."

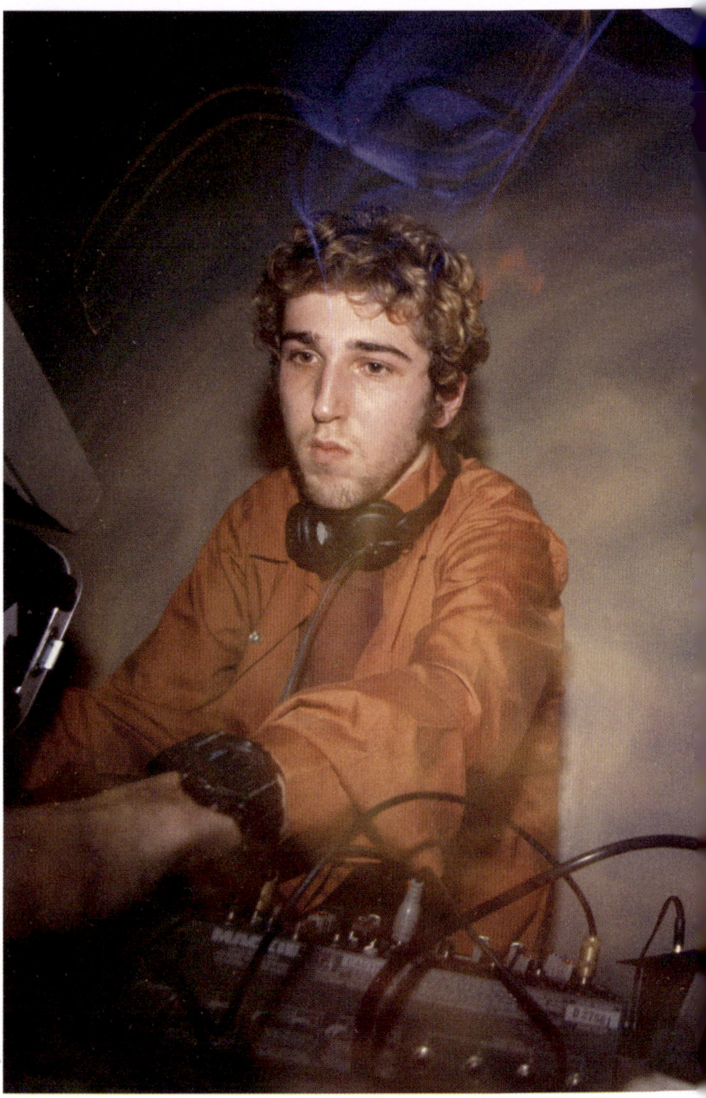

Performing at The Arches, Glasgow, January 1997

**Dave:** "I think it's safe to say that every big artist now has a similar deal – they pioneered that. And Thomas' father being a producer himself and part of the French music industry, he stood up for the rights of writers and producers against all the collection societies, and had really instilled this knowledge in them. We went to hang out with them in Paris in January and Thomas drove us down to Cannes and we got to speak a lot on the way. We met Thomas' father Daniel at Midem, the music conference, and he would always teach us something. He'd be like: 'Don't worry about the advance, make sure the

royalty's high and the deductions are low or non-existent. Don't give it away forever. Don't give it away for life of copyright.'"

**Jim:** "Thomas had these ideas as a producer about the purity of the sound, the purity of the Moog and the 909, and he wanted to use the best wires for the sounds to travel the least amount of distance before it was getting to the speakers."

**Calvin Bush:** "The brilliant thing was the first two singles sounded nothing like anything else on Soma. They really had attitude and they were sort of nasty but cool, and chic and dirty and raw. They had aspects of Chicago but it genuinely didn't sound like anyone else out there at that time."

**Stuart:** "I think it's definitely because they were in the band Darlin', which was the failed indie band. I think they had a certain rock element to their music as well, so you had a sort of hybrid of all those kind of techno, house records and indie tracks. They had all these other influences which they put into their music as well which made them unique."

**Jim:** "When we were making records we had quite a big desk and lots of inputs and stuff like that. But the thing that also made them stand out to me as being utterly unique and special was that literally 'Da Funk' was like four channels on their Mackie mixer and mixed onto this boombox. The idea was that they wanted it to sound really dirty and raw. They were so paranoid about something fucking up the boombox."

**Stuart:** "When I went to Thomas' mum and dad's house I said can you show me the studio? And I went in and there was like a couple of drum machines, a keyboard and a boombox sitting in the middle of the floor. They used to just sit on the floor and make music with this boombox. I think maybe that's just what they had grown up listening to music on, or maybe that was their point of reference for how music should sound."

**Jim:** "I also remember they went into a big studio and tried to do some stuff with an SSL desk and they thought it sounded shit. I think that's when they were convinced – we're going to do it on the boombox. That's what works."

**Stuart:** "They were big on compression. They were one of the first to drop out the kick drum, they were over-compressing so that when the kick dropped out, the music would rise, which you're not supposed to do with compression. That's the wrong use of compression. But they crafted the sound via compression, by over-using it and by breaking the rules. Personally that's what I loved about them, because they didn't follow any traditional path. It's like maybe they didn't know exactly what they were doing and then they came across this sound. It was a happy accident somehow."

**Dave:** "They came and visited us in Glasgow just on a kind of holiday and they stayed at my house. Me and Stuart had a flat at the time, they just had the living room to crash out in. They met a couple of other young producers, the Desert Storm guys. They were maybe three or four years younger than us. We were all in our 20s, they were very young 20s, probably 19, 20 when we met them and 20, 21 when they came over. They came and hung out at the Arches. Felix da Housecat had played and him and Tyrone Palmer were in town. I remember we had a party after the club and the Brand New Heavies were in one room. They must have had a gig in Glasgow. We were a bit up all night in those days but people like Felix didn't drink at the time either. It was kind of each to their own. But yes, they had a good time and I guess that forged this kind of bond between us."

**Stuart:** "They came over to Glasgow to hang out with us, without playing or anything. They came to hang out at the club and I remember they came back to my flat. And they were just looking at everybody, as if we were these fucking mad people. But they came to the Arches and I think they loved it. They loved the vibe."

**Jim:** "We were kind of like the mad Jocks in the scene. I think we were lucky because we sat away from all sorts of other scenes, so we weren't in the Chemical Brothers scene or the Weatherall scene."

**Calvin:** "And they thought, this is a Scottish label who are well respected but not aligned to anyone. I think with the benefit of hindsight, they were very clever to understand that we would be the right label to release their single. We were quite proud to be very removed from the whole London music scene and doing our own thing."

**Dave:** "Thomas actually said they deliberately chose to be removed from the French scene because they didn't want to just be another French act. They wanted to be international, and somehow by coming to Scotland it made them not part of that scene but an international prospect in their own country."

△

**Dave:** "'The New Wave' EP came out in April 1994. It was a slow burner. In those days, especially with the success of 'Positive Education', we were regularly selling 5,000 copies on vinyl. I think 'Positive Education' sold 20,000 to 30,000 vinyl. But the Daft Punk single, people wrote about it, DJs played it but it only sold about 2,000 copies. Which was promising but it wasn't a flyaway success and didn't put their name on the map in any way. Then they were kind of doing the odd DJ thing in Paris. I think they did a live gig for one of their friends. Then we wanted to put them on live in Glasgow."

**Calvin:** "The press release for the first single was a homage to 'Never Mind the Bollocks', we did it as a newspaper cut out. It was a bit of a dig at all that New Wave of New Wave nonsense in the NME which was just dreadful. People were getting really excited about that and this was the time when, certainly in the mainstream press, like Melody Maker, NME, you couldn't get much coverage for techno and house artists. So it was a bit of a dig at all that. I think it just said: 'French Teen Techno, The Real New Wave.' They had their own press photos. When we signed them, they said, here's the photo you have to use."

**Dave:** "They did the artwork, they did the logo, they attended the cuts."

**Jim:** "They'd taken complete control."

**Stuart:** "It might not sound unusual now but back then to have those assets in place at that point in time was very unusual. Most teenagers, artists in

# "They didn't want to just be another French act. They wanted to be international, and somehow by coming to Scotland it made them... an international prospect in their own country."

their early 20s, they needed to be guided by a manager."

**Jim:** "They complemented each other perfectly. In a lot of duos you have the creative, ideas guy and the guy that's kind of holding in some of that [in order] to put out something that's very palatable. But they were just kind of perfect together."

**Calvin:** "They were great to interview but it was basically just Thomas for three hours and Guy-Manuel didn't answer any questions at all."

**Dave:** "He could understand every word of English but he wasn't as confident speaking. But I think that he was quite happy to let you think he didn't really speak any English. Once you got to know Guy-Man, he would have a one-on-one conversation on the side but it took a while."

**Calvin:** "The first two singles went down really well. Jockey Slut covered it and I think Melody Maker might also have done something. But I would say the reaction was mainly on the club side, rather than the press side. The first two singles definitely had an impact and people were intrigued. But I would say it wasn't until 'Da Funk' that it really kicked off, press-wise.

**Richard Brown:** "My first Daft Punk Soma memory is working in the record shop near the club, then Dave came in with a test pressing of 'Da Funk' and I remember thinking: 'Fucking hell, I love it.' Then very soon after, I was moving to London. I'd been offered a couple of things down south but I didn't take them. Then Jim and everyone offered me a role at Soma. We were just getting on to 'Da Funk'. We pressed up 3,000 copies with a bright orange sleeve. And then we couldn't sell them."

**Dave:** "It didn't even blow up when 'Da Funk' came out. On that trip to Midem that Jim and I were on, when we got back to Paris, Thomas played us an early version of 'Da Funk'. He also played us 'Rollin' & Scratchin'', which was quite an abrasive techno record and felt more like a follow-up to the first single, but 'Da Funk' really stuck in my head in particular. It was so different. When we got back to Glasgow, they sent us over 'Rollin' & Scratchin'' with this other track called 'Drive' (which materialised years later on the Soma 25th anniversary compilation. It was called 'Daft Drive' originally I think. It was basically sat in a drawer in the office which never came out in the end. We said to them, look, this never came out. They said, release it, but as part of your album and just put 'Drive 1994', so it dates it, it's not a new Daft Punk record.) So we got these two similar tracks and I'm on the phone going: 'What about the funky one? What happened to the funky one?' And they're like: 'Oh, do you like that? Do you like that one?' And I often wonder, would that have come out or did they just think they'll do something else with that? So they sent over 'Da Funk' and 'Rollin' and Scratchin'' on the other side."

**Richard:** "The tipping point was Annie Nightingale's radio show. She played 'Da Funk', and it literally took off from that minute, and we were pressing like 500 or 1,000 a week. It was bonkers."

The ARCHES
H523 DRO

The Arches, Glasgow, January 1997

**Stuart:** "At the time, if Radio 1 played your record, everybody heard it. We used to go to the office and the phone started going a little bit crazy after maybe one or two releases. The phone started going, I think, when we put 'Da Funk' out. The first release was like: 'Who the fuck are these guys? They're quite interesting.' I remember this guy Paolo (Sedazzari) who used to run a night in London said to me: 'I want to book these guys for New Year's Eve' a year later. Because I think he knew at that point they were going to be big. But we didn't know. But then 'Da Funk' came out and we got so many phone calls in the office that Richard used to answer the phone jokingly, instead of saying 'Hello, Soma Records', he'd pick up the phone and go: 'Hello, 'Da Funk'.'"

**Dave:** "I think it was a double A, and that was their choice and they did the art. Even in those days, they chose the colour of the sleeve it went in, which was a kind of orangey colour, it was the same as the black sleeves. It didn't have artwork on it. They did their own artwork for the labels. It was a kind of a blue and an orange. So they were always in control. They knew what they wanted, and they attended the cut with Nils at the Exchange. It was a kind of slow burner. After a few months, I mean, it had maybe sold 2,000-3,000 copies. We noticed that Richie Hawtin had reacted on it and said: 'I really love this, this is fucking wild.' And Dmitry from Deee-Lite in New York, he got back, saying he was playing this record. It was one of those records, Stuart was like: 'I can't play that, because I can't mix that in. I'm going to play 'Rollin' & Scratchin'', I can fit that in.'"

**Stuart:** "I remember a lot of DJs playing it, especially 'Da Funk'. It was quite an awkward record to play. The Chemical Brothers and Richie Hawtin were supporters, that's when you knew back then a record was going to be big. You couldn't mix that record, it's impossible to mix simply for the fact it is quite slow. And at that point people were playing 127-130bpm-plus. So you had to stop your set to play the record. And that's exactly what I heard Kevin Saunderson do at Back to Basics. And I heard Richie play it. So the record had stood out anyway but because you had to go through that whole process to play the record, it did get people's attention."

**Dave:** "People would just kind of stop the record they were playing and put it on. It really grew and snowballed exponentially. I can remember people from Island Records getting in touch. All the main A&Rs, the majors were getting in touch. A lot of that came just before and just after that In The City gig, because people were getting hyped about it, going: 'What is this?' Everyone wanted to get hold of them eventually, but it was months, maybe six months after 'Da Funk' came out. I've got 11 April 1994 for the 'The New Wave' EP, and 15 May 1995 for 'Da Funk'. And obviously we would promo it for quite a while in advance of it going on sale. So I think by September you can see that's a good few months after DJs had it, by the time it was snowballing. And then 'Indo Silver Club' which was Soma 35, 'Da Funk' was Soma 25 and the first one was Soma 14. 'Indo Silver Club' was 29 January 1996. They actually chose not to use the Daft Punk name for the 'Indo Silver Club' release. They wanted to give us the third single, because we'd always spoken about this kind of three-single agreement. They ended up using 'Indo Silver Club' (Part Two) on 'Homework', and they would have used both tracks, but one of them, they couldn't clear the sample. 'Da Funk' went from struggling to sell the first 3,000 to doing 25,000 until it was stopped and deleted, deliberately."

**Richard:** "We did a party with Dave Beer at In The City. That's when we finally got a contract signed. We didn't have a contract before that."

**Dave:** "We didn't have a written contract, you know, it was those kind of days. When we sat down with Thomas, obviously we'd had this relationship with his father as well, learning about the music industry. When we worked out the deal, the lawyer said it was the most honourable deal he'd ever been party to in the music business."

**Dave:** "The next time they came back to Glasgow they played the Never Get Out The Boat Party, which again was '95."

> "It's so exciting to have a record label and to have something that everybody wants to talk to you about, everybody wants to play... It was a whirlwind two years - it was unbelievable."

**Calvin:** "They actually played Ministry of Sound the night before, on the Friday, and I think they had one gig in France before they came over, a practice thing."

**Dave:** "I'm actually looking at the flyer for the 1995 first UK tour and Bugged Out! is there on 13 October. So a couple of weeks after the first date, they seem to come over. It's pretty much anyone we knew that had a club, we just phoned up. They did Ministry of Sound. I can't remember which way the dates went, but certainly Glasgow wasn't the first day on the tour. I'm pretty sure they might have done Kelvin Andrews' club night. It was just all people we knew in the UK. I've actually got a recording of the live set. It was a 32-minute live set which featured 'Da Funk'. It was when they just had the 303, the 909, the sampler, the little desk, very raw, and there is an early 'Da Funk' and 'Rollin' & Scratchin'' is on it, as well as the tracks off 'The New Wave' EP. That was probably their second time in Glasgow when they were actually playing live and people still didn't really know who they were."

**Stuart:** "Daft Punk on the Renfrew Ferry was probably one of their first gigs – one of those ones people say they went to and you know they didn't."

△

**Richard:** "I think they were always absolutely clear that we weren't getting the album."

**Dave:** "Thomas' father said if you want to sell a major amount of records, you have to work with a major record label."

**Richard:** "At the time I was speaking to Daniel Miller (Mute) and to Martin Mills (Beggars Banquet/XL), who obviously had done it themselves but it wasn't on the table that we would be able to do that sort of thing. But on a positive note, it's so exciting to have a record label and to have something that everybody wants to talk to you about, everybody wants to play, everybody wants to put on live, everyone wants to licence. It's like it was a whirlwind two years – it was unbelievable."

**Dave:** "I think the deal with Virgin was a five-year licence and I know that they didn't want a big advance. They just wanted to be able to create and have fun and spend their money on what they'd created and have the ownership of it. So yes, that was all very much a learning curve for all of us. We had that kind of relationship with them where they were teaching us as much as we were teaching them. The relationship there was interesting, because Maya (Masseboeuf), who was one of the A&Rs at Virgin France, had already licensed some Soma tracks for compilations in France. She was a fan of what we did. So she kind of found out about Daft Punk almost through Soma, and they're both from Paris. They did talk to the various majors, including Island in London, but eventually they felt that they could get what they wanted with Virgin and they had the right creative people there, people that understood how they wanted to market it. I think it was her boss that signed them but she was the person that knew about them first. It was a case where they could come up with their own marketing ideas – everything they did was their own idea. I think they just wanted a major company to distribute their music. They insisted on the Soma logo on their album and they personally brought us the gold disc from the first 100,000 sold in France. And they played the very first Slam tent (at T in the Park) for a handshake. Thomas just sent a fax (see page 14) in his own handwriting saying that Daft Punk would play and that was good enough for us and the people behind T in the Park."

**Stuart:** "I don't think they were ready to lose that connection that had built them up. They weren't ready to lose that completely on 'Homework'."

**Dave:** "As part of the agreement they said, we're going to do a remix for Soma, which ended up being another massive investment to the label, because it was the record Scott Grooves from Detroit brought to us when he worked with Funkadelic's live recordings. Because there was a situation with George Clinton where – I mean, he's one of the most sampled artists ever, you know, you'll hear Funkadelic on so many hip hop artists. But he never got paid for any of that because he was unrecouped with whatever major label he was on. So although these samples were always declared, the money would never end up in George Clinton's pocket. But Scott Grooves had got friendly with someone at a recording studio in Detroit and they had live recordings that were owned by George Clinton. So the record we put out was made from samples of Funkadelic playing live and all the money that was made went to George Clinton. Daft Punk loved the idea of working on that. It was an even nicer touch that we knew the money was going back to George Clinton as well as to Scott Grooves, a Detroit producer, and to Soma, the Glasgow label. So Daft Punk, through their success and making a brilliant remix, it was a bit of a payback again to people that I guess don't always get what they deserve."

## "I had Bob Sinclar booked to DJ and I cancelled it. I was like: 'I don't want you to come. You've messed my mate about.' I remember telling Thomas' mum and she's like: 'Yes, sticking up for my boy.'"

**Dave:** "They also said they would do a few more gigs, so they DJed at the Arches just before 'Homework' came out. I think it was Daft Punk samplers, machines and turntables or something. There were queues round the block. I'm not sure how the recording leaked out, I think someone stole it from my flat one night, but you can find the recording of that online, the Daft Mix from Glasgow. They also played for us in Miami at one of the Soma label parties. So they definitely kept trying to give us a leg up, and helping us out. They liked being part of what we did, even though they were moving in different circles at that point, probably spending a bit of time in Hollywood and whatever. They felt like they'd made an investment into our label because we made some money out of it, but they also had the freedom to do what they wanted, artistic freedom and most importantly, they owned their masters. We went one stage further and we got the metal plates from the pressing plant and we sent them over to Paris as a gift. So we actually gave them the means of production of their original three vinyl releases, so no one could ever press it again other than them."

**Dave:** "We pretty much invested the money we made from the Daft Punk records in the label. We probably did more debut albums for artists than most. We were a place where you could come with some ideas and we'd put some time, effort and a little bit of money into what you were doing and try and get you a few gigs along the way or hook you up with an agent. So yeah, it gave us the freedom to continue doing that."

**Dave:** "They're very authentic, very ethical, loyalty is important. I was proud of them and I always wanted them to succeed and I'd always stick up for them. I remember when Bob Sinclar did that 'Gym Tonic' record with Thomas and they couldn't clear the sample with Jane Fonda. I can remember it was a bit upsetting to Thomas. I had Bob Sinclar booked to DJ at The Arches and I cancelled it. I was like: 'I don't want you to come. You've messed my mate about.' I remember telling Thomas' mum and she's like: 'Yes, sticking up for my boy,' you know. So I guess that was my kind of relationship with them, always had their back. Not that they needed it much."

**Stuart:** "I think they became as influential as a band like Kraftwerk were for another generation. I often compare the two although the music is completely different. But the influence that they had on other bands and other electronic acts, and the anonymity they had with disappearing into the robots, there are similarities."

**Dave:** "I emailed Thomas when they split. I didn't ask them anything about it. I just said: 'Oh, it's been great, eh? Well done, good work.' He sent me a lovely message back, saying: 'I really need to thank you and everyone at Soma for being there for us at the very beginning. Sometimes we think if we hadn't given you that cassette, what might have happened?' He also said something along the lines of: 'I feel like we've done something, we finished it, now I can almost go back to the underground if I wanted.' A bit of freedom from the weight of being in Daft Punk, perhaps."

**Dave:** "I'm sure they must have a lot of music because the previous time I'd seen him, they had released the last album and he said they were in a situation where they weren't in a record deal, and he and Guy-Manuel were working with an engineer they liked in a studio in Paris. They had no pressure to release anything and they were just having fun in the studio. They have probably got music they've done together that's never seen the light of day, and I've no idea what they're going to do with it. It'll be quite interesting. He said something about returning to the underground, and somehow we are still underground, so maybe I'll tap him up for a couple of tracks!"

# THE YOUNG PARISIANS

Daft Punk, the 'teen techno sensation from Paris' of yesteryear, have both entered their 20s chased by every record company in town due to the success of the huge mutant disco of 'Da Funk', their alter ego Indo Silver Club and cool Roulé label. **John Burgess** meets up with them after a heavy weekend in Britain to find that stardom is not their trip.

Daft Punk are not amused. They've spent much of Friday night and Saturday morning on a coach, not able to sleep because of the sights, sounds and smells you might expect from an excursion with the Heavenly Social crew. The fug of amyl nitrate is ever present which worsens when one hapless chap dips a fag into the seedy stuff and almost sets his face alight on ignition.

Earlier, to the bewilderment of our Parisian friends, there is a raffle for an E: they do not buy a ticket. "I think from what we've seen people are getting more stoned here than in France," they mention later.

The back of the bus – historically the perfect place for adolescent japes like mooning and singeing your eyebrows with amyl fags – is naturally where most of the fun originates. "The front of the bus they cannae sing, they cannae sing, they cannae sing, the front of the bus they cannae sing, they cannae sing for peanuts!" they chorus.

Daft Punk are at the front of the bus. Thomas Bangalter and Guy-Manuel de Homem-Christo are probably wondering why they were asked to DJ at the Nottingham Heavenly Social and at the Social-inspired 'London After Midnight' the following night during this working weekend in England.

The Heavenly Social helped make stars out of The Chemical Brothers, will make Richard Fearless and Jon Carter household names, and usually feature pop icons like Tim Burgess and Tricky on the decks. Earl Brutus, who play live on the same bill as the Punks, are so desperate to be stars that they drop their trousers during their set hoping to shock some sales out of the Socialites.

Daft Punk, with their pop-friendly name, acid funk and media hype as the 'Next Chemical Brothers' should slot in quite nicely with this motley crew of characters. Except they don't. Daft Punk don't want to be stars.

House music, in all its mutations, has matured to the extent that people are now hungry to know about the characters behind the tunes. The genre is no longer 'faceless'. It's all tour buses as well as Technics these days. Dave Angel and Goldie are currently on the road, Lionrock and Underworld both have front men with guitars slung over their shoulders and John Peel and the wonderful One FM recently broadcast from Dave Clarke's house. Elsewhere, Leftfield and the Chemical Brothers have sold more albums than most Britpop bands, Larry Heard and Kenny Larkin want to break the lucrative R&B market in the States, you'd recognise Mike Paradinas and Richard James in Sainsbury's if they left their studios for five minutes, and Jeff Mills is about to embark on a DJing tour of Britain sponsored by über-corporation Sony.

Faceless techno? Bollocks! When a genius record comes out now, we want to know more about it than the information offered on the run out groove. We want to know more about Daft Punk.

Daft Punk currently have several major labels chasing them. They hope to ink a deal soon because Thomas says it will give them more freedom to live solely as musicians, recording and releasing music when they are happy with it rather than churning out release-on-release to pay the bills. Thomas met Steve Stoll in New York recently - he still works in a studio equipment store.

It is easy to see why chequebooks are being waved. Two Parisians fresh out of their teens who make records under the coolest name and are multi-faceted: they DJ, they play live, they have their own record label, Roulé, they are talented enough to work on solo projects in their spare time and their slightly oddball good looks make them instantly recognisable. They are on our front cover. Except they didn't really want to be.

Guy-Manuel explains that they want to reach a lot of people through their music, but adds: "We don't really want to be photographed." They have a French TV crew following them around London for the weekend to capture their antics for an arts programme, but Guy says: "We didn't really speak on the TV because it is dangerous. We don't especially want to be in magazines. We have a responsibility."

Guy-Manuel doesn't elaborate on who he has a responsibility to and nor does he smoke in photographs like he did two years ago. "I was young then," he explains. "It is a bad example..."

Guy-Manuel, long-haired and surly and Thomas, curly-thatched and smiley, met at school in 1987 when they were 13 and 12 respectively. Swiftly recognising that French pop music is historically about as important as the Sinclair C5, they both listened to more American grooves: "Jimi Hendrix and any good band from the 60s from soul to funk to rock. Motown, Stax, and everything."

No one else at their school really shared their tastes. "We were deeply into music and clothes and searching for records" adds Guy. House music only really reached them if it broke big in France. S-Express' wonderful 'Theme' being an introduction of sorts before they heard what the British hyped as 'indie dance'.

"We discovered the house scene through people like Andrew Weatherall, Primal Scream and the Orb," says Thomas. Weatherall's mix of the Scream's 'Loaded' was their dance Damascus.

"We found house was the real music for us. Rock won't die but house is younger, fresher" Thomas exclaims.

Daft Punk wanted to be pop stars in a previous life. They wanted to be in a band, go on the road and find girls. In their mid-teens in 1990 they formed a guitar band called Darlin'. Thomas played the bass and Guy sang and wrote music about girls.

"It was very clichéd" he shrugs. A couple of their "not-very-good" tracks ended up on Stereolab's Duophonic label. Supporting Stereolab earned them a review in the Melody Maker. Darlin' sounded like "daft punk" laughed the journalist.

The guitars, like childhood toys, were soon discarded, house music was embraced and Thomas received a sampler for his 18th birthday. Finding it hard to think of a name for their embryonic techno outfit in English they self-mockingly settled on Daft Punk.

"In France, to a lot of people, the name is empty of meaning."

In 1993, they met Glaswegians, Slam, at a Euro Disney rave. Though not particularly fans of their label Soma, Thomas and Guy did like 'Positive Education' and Slam's DJing, so they gave Stuart McMillan a demo tape featuring a track called 'Alive'. Six months later 'Alive', a now much sought after three minutes of hypnotic 909 action, was released backed by 'New Wave' - which poked fun at the British music press' preoccupation with the ridiculous New Wave of New Wave hype.

"We are the real New Wave!" they piped. A press campaign that screamed out 'new teen techno sensation from Paris!' was backed with shots of Thomas and Guy looking way cooler than a lot of the Brit techno bands on the Megadog circuit at the time. Apart from a short piece in Jockey Slut they were largely ignored until the summer of last year when a tentative 3,000 copies of 'Da Funk' were cut.

The crossover success of the mutant disco of 'Da Funk' - 15,000 on promo – brings us bang up-to-date to their weekend in London, the Heavenly Social, the television crews, the lunches with publishers, and front cover photographs. On the Saturday they played eclectic club London After Midnight which attracted a trendy crowd closer in age to 30 than 20, who chatted and danced to a soundtrack of La Funk Mob and Smashing Pumpkins. The room was candle lit, had a bar and was packed.

Upstairs, however, in a cavernous black room with no bar or seating were Daft Punk and, later, Dave Clarke. Despite them both being the main attractions the environment they played in meant Daft Punk's excellent set, drawing heavily on the music of Chicago and Detroit, attracted few people. Downstairs the DJ dropped 'Da Funk' and the crowd went wild.

The following Sunday evening in their hotel room I arrive to find Guy and Thomas hungrily waiting for room service. It is cramped and at the foot of their beds is a camp bed for a friend of theirs who smiles about as much as Guy. They are both tired, Guy having been up until nine in the morning at the club's after party.

When pressed as to what he was up to he shrugs and offers perhaps, existentialist reasons: "I was doing nothing. Not even drinking. I spoke to girls and sat in a chair waiting... for nothing."

Room service arrives – burger meals (burnt) and ice cream (left uneaten). It is quiet as they munch on our great British cuisine and the mood is far from jocular as the Dictaphone is clicked on. My first question about what they think about the comparisons with The Chemical Brothers elicits a weary, defensive response.

Thomas: "Maybe it's our link with the remix ('Life is Sweet') we did and now there's this hype. I think they like the stuff we are doing."

Guy: "There's no comparison between them and us. Not at all. Especially with what we're going to do next, there won't be any links. 'Da Funk' is more of a disco track than hip hoppy which is what they're doing. I think their sound is more rock using guitars. We may use guitars, but in a funkier way. We will be doing stuff in more categories so you can't say it sounds like The Chemical Brothers."

They never have sounded like The Chemical Brothers, or anyone else for that matter. Sure they use acid (of the Roland variety) and 'Da Funk' is big of beat and down of tempo, but generally the Daft Punk sound is more linked to the music of Chicago house and disco (of which there is a strong tradition in Thomas' family - his dad Daniel Vangarde wrote and produced the Gibson Brothers' 'Cuba').

As Guy points out, 'Da Funk' was partly inspired by American R'n'B and the pure precision of New Jack swing. Their apparent discomfort with the Heavenly Social freeform nutterdom and fear of the press distances them further from the Brothers. The only comparisons I can see is that there are two of them, they have past links to the world of rock, and their live shows are monstrous affairs, very house-driven, full of complex EQ action and chargin' crescendos.

Daft Punk as characters have more in common with the Detroit techno underground than any British dance stars. The only time they become really animated in conversation is when they are using the press to encourage others to follow

DJing at the Heavenly Social in Nottingham, 1996

their example and use music to escape the drudgery of everyday life. They, like Robert Hood and Mike Banks, seem more comfortable talking about politics and the subversiveness of party culture than any on-the-road antics.

"People in France are more into the music than the hype and the pictures in the papers," Thomas states. In The Face last year though, didn't you say: 'Techno should be about images and strong personalities. We want to put our faces to the music?'

"I didn't say quite that. It's more about a human thing than a star thing. If you like a track by a Detroit guy you like to know his face, the fact that sounds are generated by machines, you like to know there's a group of people running them. As a listener you are always curious of seeing people's faces. But I think it's quite ordinary people that make the music. The white label anonymous thing was fun at the beginning, but you have people thinking the music is all made by computers and not people."

So it seems they are quite happy to let their personality shine through the music, for people to go: 'Ah, look - there are those Daft Punk chaps.' But as far as the star trip goes, they're reluctant to get onboard. As Guy points out, when the TV cameras were on them the previous night they only talked about their music and how anyone could be in their position. A pure punk ethic.

Guy: "We began from nothing. You can make music from nothing. Anyone can do it. We will talk about music; we don't want to talk about us. We are trying to say that everyone should get involved. It is a time to move, for everyone to do something on their own."

Thomas: "You can make music in your bedrooms in France, Australia, Japan... more people should be doing demos. There's not much of a gap between wannabees and canbees."

Guy: "I think it's about sharing music with everyone. Now we are getting known it's got to be serious. When we were younger, we started music to find girls. Now music is more important, serious and deep. It's not just a record to dance to. It can bring people together like on the War Child project (the 'Help' album). That is very noble. The people who are 20 to 25 have a responsibility to do something for the next century. Music is one of the ways to make something good for the world. All the art is mixing now, and young people have a chance to do something in music, movies... There's a big energy when you see the festivals. I don't think we need any politics, it's just human beings trying to move things forward. Everything is getting on the edge; we've got to go the right way. We can decide."

With Guy coming down from a touch of millennium fever I ask if the conservative French government – famed for its nuclear testing – has clamped down on underground party culture? France has had a thriving underground culture in the past which erupted onto the streets in 1968 almost causing the fall of the government.

Thomas: "They are afraid. Especially if they can't control these young people having fun. They don't like people having fun, they try and make young people in the press look like they are all completely stoned out of their minds."

Guy: "It's frightening the governments. There are networks building that they cannot control. They are annoyed by these meetings (raves)."

Thomas: "There's a lot of pressure to cancel parties. It's impossible to open new clubs, only the old clubs can stay."

Guy: "The Right want to keep their supporters, who are conservative, who are old people, content. They want traditional things to please the electorate. To please them they say: 'We will fight drugs, we will keep your children safe.'"

Having only just left their teens behind, Daft Punk seem very serious young men. Everything is on the edge? Music is deep and serious? Do the duo like partying?

Thomas: "Yeah, we're into partying, but when you do a lot of DJing and you go into a lot of clubs for a long time you're probably not into the same kind of partying. Personally, I feel a bit bored in clubs, it's too loud on my ears. Unless there is a DJ, we really want to see we hang out at the bar. I prefer partying in apartments where there is less music and you can speak. But... yeah, we're into partying."

If they're happier at the bar a lot of other people will be ecstatic on the dancefloor when they hear Thomas and Guy's new material. Thomas' first release on Roulé, 'Trax on da Rocks', with its bar fly funk and Relief-style house was another crossover success, not just amongst the commercial and cutting-edge house DJs, it also invaded the future funk discotheques more used to dropping the likes of Howie B. Guy is currently working on the second Roulé EP. They've also recorded a 'secret' EP for Soma as the Indo Silver Club which has earned them even more respect.

"Indo Silver Club is more underground, melodic and minimal," Thomas says proudly.

Don't hold your breath for any new Daft Punk product. 'Da Funk' will receive a 'proper' release after the ink has dried on some chuffed label's contract and then work will resume on the album, which should be finished pretty rapidly if they continue to use their punk-ish attitude to recording.

"Just keep it simple, keep the right elements. If you make a track in an hour and it sounds right, you should leave it at that."

"Daft Punk is about what we like about all aspects of dance music," Thomas concludes. "Hard stuff to disco. Hip hop stuff to house and techno. It's very boring if all your tracks sound the same."

After soaking up Jimi Hendrix and Dave Clarke, expect Daft Punk to be anything but boring. But unlike their influences, Daft Punk don't want to be stars.

But they soon will be.

*Originally published in Jockey Slut, April/May 1996*

'DAFT PUNK'
KENRO

©Rip
(VELMA)
©Rip
©Rip
©Rip

DAFT PUNK.
APRIL 97 ISSUE
ODD'S
4.
KEN 160

DAFT PUNK
APRIL 97 ISSUE
LIVE / ODD'S
3.
-> Rip
KENRO
KEN 160

# The Great Rock'n'Roll Swindle

By Emma Warren

When Guy-Manuel de Homem-Christo speaks (and he does it rarely), you could write the entire works of Samuel Beckett during the many pauses. Words are dragged kicking and screaming from his mouth; slow, ponderous sentences moving with all the force and vitality of a corpse's drawl. You have to move up close to catch what he's saying. Listen carefully. And maintain your concentration across the yawning chasms of time which divide each small, mumbled block of words.

"I'm just quiet, that's all... Can be whatever I want... When I speak, I try to be nice... I think when maybe... when journalists are in front of some persons... they think they are some special people. (Long pause) Maybe I think more than I speak."

One writer has already described him in the past as 'surly'. An incident from that interview springs to mind. Daft Punk, on the road with the Heavenly Social crew, heading up to Nottingham for the Heavenly night at Deluxe. At the back of the bus, hedonistic chaos reigns. Pills are being auctioned off, booze swilled, substances consumed like nobody's business. In the front row, Guy-Manuel and his Punk partner, Thomas Bangalter, sit silently, oblivious to the chanting coming from the back: 'The front of the bus they cannae sing!' Alone, aloof perhaps. Uncertain of quite how they got there.

It must be something to do with that name of theirs. Let's face it. You're expecting mohicaned glue-sniffers with two fingers permanently stuck up the nose of society. Stage shows that stomp size-12 Doc Martens on the pimply faces of schoolboy swots and goody two-shoes. Snot and bile. Venom and anger. And then you meet them. Guy-Manuel, making Rodin's 'Thinker' look like a happy-go-lucky court jester. Thomas Bangalter, lean, skinny and thoroughly affable, but with a jovial determination and a business head that belies his 21 years. He even carries a briefcase, for goodness sake. Suffice to say, if Malcolm McLaren had caught this lot down the 100 Club in 1976, he'd have taken one look and run a mile.

Daft Punk. Neither daft. Nor punks. Just two ordinary French kids, 21 and 22 years old, with a mere three singles to their name. No gimmicks. No flashy outfits. Not even a Svengali manager to manipulate their careers. What a con, eh? Or, as John Lydon (née Rotten) famously said at the Sex Pistols' final ever gig: "Ever get the feeling you've been cheated?"

**NEVER MIND THE BOLLOCKS... HERE'S 'DA FUNK'**

Except... Well, the music, of course. The reason Daft Punk have spent the best part of a year at the centre of one of those classic industry 'Who's gonna snap 'em up?' whirlwinds has nothing to do with how they should or shouldn't look or how many nights a week they go out for a top caning session. For once, it's not even about an over-eager media. Which is just as it should be, really, if you think about it. Because Daft Punk simply make fantastic music.

So it doesn't translate too well onto the page, but if I were to hum you something like: 'ner, ner-ner-ner-ner, ner-ner-ner-ner ner-ner' like a stoned police siren, telling you to imagine the bastard son of Queen's 'Another One Bites the Dust' and Hardfloor's 'Acperience' with a hefty dose of 'Clash City Rockers'-era, Strummer and Jones thrown in, you'd be screaming 'Da Funk'! long before the tune's breakaway 303 mayhem even kicked in.

A tune so underground, it was originally only pressed up in a limited run of 2,000 copies and virtually ignored on release in the spring of 1995. Until, that is, those ever-perceptive Chemical Brothers picked up on its raw, stomping funk flavour and turned it into an anthem wherever they played. A remix of the Brothers' 'Life Is Sweet' followed. And before you knew it, you could barely step out for a bit of Saturday night amyl and breakbeat-fuelled fun without being guaranteed an airing of 'Da Funk' to blow the snot clean out your ears and spray your brain across the ceiling.

To date, it's sold over 30,000 copies, become a hardy perennial for everyone from Annie Nightingale to Athletico, been voted Number One single in France's top club magazine, Coda, with a whopping 33% of the vote, and ended up as a classic tune both of the times and for the times. Oh, and it's being re-released as the Punk's debut for lucky Virgin Records, who captured their signatures after a frenzied chase by every major on the block. Not bad for a tune Thomas and Guy-Manuel knocked off in a week and are rumoured to have been uncertain about whether to release or not.

As we lounge aboard the luxury of the very bloody fast TGV train, taking us from Paris to a warehouse party in Marseilles later that evening, Thomas takes up the story.

"The bass drum had already worked with 'Alive'. So we said: 'Ok, let's use it again'. And we'd been listening to some R'n'B stuff at the time. Tracks like Warren G's 'Regulate' and some Dr. Dre stuff they were playing on the radio. The original riff was actually a siren. But we wanted to make it more of a gangsta rap thing, more dirty, so we changed the sound a bit. The bassline itself was from a 303 I'd bought in 1993. I'd just made all these random patterns, so when we were looking for a bassline, we listened to some of those I'd already programmed and took the one that fitted best."

The rest, as they say, is history.

**THIS IS THE NEW WAVE**

"What about the new wave?/Did you think it would change things?" The Adverts' 'Safety in Numbers', August 1977

But there's far more to the Daft Punk story than just one solitary storming piece of punk funk.

In the autumn of 1993, another of those spurious journo terms was coined to lump together an obviously ill-begotten rag-bag of indie bands who shared little apart from a love of amphetamine sulphate, power guitars, searing pop harmonies and the back catalogue of The Clash. Most of them have disappeared into the bargain bin mists of time. These Animal Men. Smash. Shed Seven. The thing was, because of their obvious penchant for the late-70s post-punk era, they came to be called, in one of the great unwieldy name-tags of our time, The New Wave Of New Wave.

Around the same time, Daft Punk's debut single arrived on a select few DJs and journos' turntables. Coincidentally, it was called 'The New Wave'. Except that DP's version truly deserved the title. A ferocious blast of Djax-style rough techno, it was different because it had all the paint-stripping, brain-blistering power of a Jeff Mills record, but grooved at a more pedestrian house tempo. Here was something truly fresh, something to blow away the cobwebs of conformity with Hurricane Annie-strength winds of change. It was accompanied by a press release screaming, in cut-out newspaper letters: 'This is the real New Wave', and proclaimed Thomas and Guy-Manuel 'France's teen techno sensation'. The fact that they were actually 19 and 20 at the time had been somewhat overlooked.

And then there was the accompanying press shot. Thomas and Guy, lounging with attitude against a bare brick wall. Shot in grainy black and white, it made them look like the lost grandchildren of Jean-Paul Belmondo in 'Breathless' - ironically France's own hero of the cinematic New Wave. A fag dangling insouciantly from Guy's indifferent snarl, Thomas with his cutesy, ruffled, teen gamin appearance. Cool beyond belief really. It reeked of adolescent, fuck-you attitude. No wonder we fell for them.

Therein lies the beauty of Daft Punk. Everything about them speaks of La Nouvelle Vague (New Wave), a fresh start, the next generation to rule the nation. As we drive to the gig in Marseilles later that evening, Thomas is keen to stress how far they really are from the originators of house.

"We're still young," he insists. "We didn't grow up with this house revolution of 1987/1988. We can't claim to have bought all the original house music records. We didn't really even start going out to clubs until 1992. It's not like Laurent Garnier, who was there the first time round. We came much later."

In other words, Daft Punk really are the New Wave. Trace their musical roots and, like many kids their age, they grew up on indie, rock and classic pop. For them, Chicago house is the form of music they love the most, but they're not about to turn their backs on all those formative sounds of their school days. So how did they first get into house and techno?

Thomas: "I think it happened because it was so exciting going to clubs and listening to records you didn't already know. That was the difference. You'd go to a rock club and they'd have all these leaflets telling you the names of all the bands they played. You'd go to a house club and you would know maybe only three or four tracks all night."

Guy-Manuel: "With most rock gigs in Paris, you go to the gig, you don't dance, you don't speak too much, you're in the dark and then you go home. With dance stuff, you can meet people. It's a living life not a dead life."

Check the list of people they pay respect to on 'Homework'. Alongside the likes of Boo Williams, Curtis Mayfield and Joey Beltram you'll find Television, 13th Floor Elevators, Roxy Music and Brian Wilson. On Side 2, 'Rock 'N' Roll' even has a classic northern soul-type hand clap as its bedrock, while the short sketch, 'WDPK 83.7FM', pays homage to American FM radio.

"I really love that FM sound," Thomas admits enthusiastically. "It's totally different from Europe. You get into your car and the sound is brilliant. There's so much bass compression, it makes the voices go all deep and the sub-bass makes them go even lower."

We don't really need to dwell on the album here. Check the review and DJ reactions elsewhere in this feature. Just remember that it's a quote from legendary mad Beach Boy, Brian Wilson, which graces the inside sleeve. And that the duo's first ever band together, Darlin', took their name from a Beach Boys song. Which brings us, in a roundabout way, to how they actually received their Daft Punk moniker.

Thomas: "When we were about 17 or 18, we made this tape which was a cover of a Beach Boys song. We just recorded it at home with guitars and drum machine. No melody, just the chords. The band Stereolab were coming to Paris and we really liked them because they had these incredibly cool seven-inch singles. So we gave the tape to a girlfriend of ours who then passed it on to Laetitia from the band."

He continues: "Stereolab put it on a compilation single they made with bands like Huggy Bear, Colm and Stereolab themselves. Just 1,500 copies. It got a very bad review in Melody Maker, basically saying that Darlin' was 'a bunch of daft punk'."

## IF THE KIDS ARE UNITED

These are strange times for French youth. On the one hand, the French music scene appears to be thriving. Labels like Source, Yellow, BPM, Versatile, Solid and Bangalter's own Roulé are thriving. Artists such as Dimitri From Paris, Air, Zend Avesta (Arnaud Rebotini), DJ Cam, La Funk Mob, Motorbass et al have proven that sometimes not being first can be an advantage. There is also a wonderfully refreshing lack of purist snobbery and destructive self-consciousness that's blowing through the French club scene and the result is some of the finest music we've heard in the last couple of years.

Then, just when you're thinking that, yes, France always has had a reputation for placing far greater emphasis on the importance of cultural and artistic pursuits, along comes the recent case of NTM (the rap group imprisoned for cursing the police on stage) to destroy that hard-earned liberal facade. Just when you're applauding the French music scene for being an exemplary case of the multi-national, multi-cultural, multi-genre melting pot at its best, along comes Jean-Marie Le Pen's fascist Front Nationale party, with their growing support to make you wonder.

Add to this the fact that the French government is openly following its British counterpart in forming its own special anti-rave police squad and adopting similar measures to the Criminal Justice Act, and it's time to start worrying. Anyone who's seen the film 'La Haine' will know just how explosive the situation is becoming. Ask Daft Punk, placid to a fault, what they hate most about France, and they'll answer without hesitation. The police.

"Techno is becoming very political over here," explains Thomas. "You can't do one-off parties any more. You have to do everything in clubs. Also, you can't even open a new club. It's impossible. Right now, we've got some friends who are being charged with inciting people to take drugs. They weren't even selling anything. They were just having a party. But in France these days they're saying that having a party is encouraging people to take drugs, booking a DJ is encouraging people to take drugs. There's a lot of pressure."

What about NTM? Thomas is quick to point out that, despite differences in their music, he feels a strong sense of solidarity with the besieged rappers.

"I think that any creative person, regarding freedom of expression, would feel a sense of solidarity. It's like in Israel. There was a famous trance party where this guy had put on a rave. The police arrested everyone and convicted the drug dealers. But they also charged the guy who was doing the live PA. He is risking a seven-year prison sentence. And the government are saying they've got to stop not just the people who are drug dealers but also the people making the music."

The crazy truth is that Daft Punk, as we have already seen, are about as far removed from the whole British up-all-night, cane-the-chemicals club lifestyle as you can get. They are in this for the music, not the benefits that come with the fame and glory that's heading their way. Thomas says he doesn't do ecstasy because when he did experiment with the drug "it made me like every track. Ecstasy is very bad when you're trying to make music because it controls your musical tastes."

And yet, they could still face a possible jail sentence just for playing their music live if things keep on going the way they are. Scary stuff.

## TEENAGE RIOT... INSIDE MY HEAD

'Homework' rules. It's the album that Bis or Huggy Bear would just love to make, the kind of teenage freakbeat DIY wonder which comes on like DJ Sneak producing The Jackson 5 from the wrong side of the tracks. It reeks of teen spirit, that sense that you've got the whole world before you, but right now all you want to do is listen to your records, dodge school, read Batman comics, party with your mates 'til the police or your parents come and not have to give a fuck about tomorrow. The inside cover even has a photo of a typical teen bedroom, the desk littered with the iconography of youth. Graffitied school-books, matches, home-made tapes and old rock'n'roll magazines.

In actual fact, Thomas' teen years were probably a little different. After all, this is the kid whose dad wrote no less a classic than The Gibson Brothers' 'Cuba' (as sampled by Roger Sanchez). Oh, and Ottowan's equally massive

'D.I.S.C.O.'. As well as producing hundreds of other 70s records, many of them hits around Europe.

Sadly, we don't get to meet Bangalter Senior as he's away for the weekend. So I asked Thomas if he lived that classic 70s pop star lifestyle?

"No," he responds. "No, not at all. My dad was very inspired by the riots of 1968, so he's kind of left-wing. He has very liberal ideas. He's against a lot of institutions, like the police. And he's not into show business. In fact, he's totally apart from it, he doesn't like it at all."

Guess this means that the Village People weren't sneaking into the Bangalter bog for some crafty nasal powdering sessions then.

What Thomas' dad has clearly given the duo is the determination to keep what they call "the producer image, not the ego artist thing". That's why anyone who's caught their scorching live shows will have wondered why they look so inanimate, so focused on their machines, so detached from their surroundings. Despite being so young, Daft Punk are utterly unfazed by all that's going on around them.

**PSYCHOTIC REACTION**

1996 was the year Daft Punk exploded across the scenery of a static house scene like the tracer fire of an Exocet rocket. Their remix of Gabrielle ('Forget About the World') was sheer irreverent brilliance, sticking a ludicrous 3/4 house beat underneath a heavily distorted vocal and using a breakdown which sounded like the whole track was collapsing in on itself. They weren't trying to be clever, just not giving a damn. They even gave Go! Discs a choice of what price to pay. It's your conscience, not ours, they said in effect. Tops! They remixed I:Cube's 'Disco Cubizm' for free, but wouldn't let the label license their remix to anybody else. Bizarre! Then they finally released a single, the superb house-mania of 'Musique', and there were only 500 copies for the world to share. Damn!

And there's more. They blew us away at 1996's Tribal Gathering without even appearing to move on stage. Thomas' solo project, 'Trax On Da Rocks', released on his Roulé label, sold 13,000 copies worldwide and ended up bootlegged in Chicago. They set up their own distribution company to handle new Paris talent like the Versatile and Cassius labels. They've got Spike Jonze (of Beastie Boys, Björk and Weezer fame) to direct the video for 'Da Funk'. And they even negotiated to do their own artwork for 'Homework'.

1997 and the world lies before their feet, awaiting conquering. But, in a hotel room in Marseilles, two hours before they're due on the decks at an old school warehouse party, Guy-Manuel de Homem-Christo, the least punk character you could ever hope to meet, is lost in musing.

When was the last time you got really angry?

"Just now... In the shower... Some personal reasons. What makes me angry? A lot of people make me angry."

Long pause. We're not going to find out who those people are. Then the Cantona of house talks briefly of how, when he makes music, he's thinking only of other people. And not just when he's making music in fact. All the time.

"It's harder to be good than bad," he reflects and I wonder whether he's talking about himself or others. "I would prefer to be always laughing and smiling. But it's hard to be always like that."

Daft Punk. Neither daft, nor punk. Trouble funk on their minds, house magic deep in their souls. Vive their différence.

*Originally published in Muzik, February 1997*

# Da Punk Mob

By Alexis Petridis

Thomas Bangalter stares disconsolately at the floor. Even for a man blessed with a face that looks permanently bewildered – the sort of face you suspect girls want to mother – he looks particularly troubled at the scene before him.

The other half of Daft Punk, Guy-Manuel de Homem-Christo, is on his knees, scrabbling through a massive black holdall, chucking its contents over his shoulders. Masks of every conceivable shape and size are scattered around the room. Suddenly he stands up, waving what looks like a grotesque, deflated head at Thomas with a cheery flourish.

"Beavis and Butt'ead!" he enthuses.

"We 'ave already been Beavis and Butt'ead zis week," mutters Thomas, darkly. "Twice."

Guy-Man tuts petulantly, chucks the mask on the floor and goes back to his holdall. More masks go flying, more suggestions are flatly rejected. Dance music's latest sensation, two Parisian kids whose debut album has turned house music on its head and wedged ferocious jackin' grooves into the Top 5, are squabbling over masks. But no one else in the room so much as bats an eyelid.

Daft Punk have a reputation for being difficult that would shame Dave Clarke. They won't have their photograph taken unless their faces are obscured. They ooze a bored hauteur onstage, barely moving, never smiling. They stormed out of a press conference at the prestigious Transmusicales festival when someone asked them a "stupid" question. They sat in attitude-laden silence on the Heavenly Social tour bus, while the Chemicals and co got wasted and auctioned off pills. Another magazine described them as "surly". Their press officer tells me their last interviewer gave up and went home after 20 minutes of blank stares and monosyllabic answers.

Eventually, they settle on clown masks with protuberant red noses. They look at each other… and burst out laughing.

"Sometimes," sighs Thomas, "I think dance music is too cold, y'know? We don't really take it very seriously."

People will tell you there's nothing daft or punk about Daft Punk, that the name came from the Melody Maker's scathing description of an indie band they were once in. They're wrong. It's exactly what they are: daft, and punk.

Thomas and Guy-Man found themselves in the same classroom 10 years ago. They were 12, and, according to Thomas, "quite lazy". They started skiving off, hanging around record shops and cinemas, devouring old Beach Boys albums and "all kinds of movies: teen movies, horror movies, cult movies, Andy Warhol movies". Watching them together it's clear how their friendship lasted out the decade. Thomas is lanky and chatty, ambling about with that expression – "Huh?" – and a hopeless stoner's stroll.

Guy-Man is shorter, truculent, given to silly voices and kid's pranks. Thomas fusses over Guy-Man's clothes before the shoot like an older brother. Guy-Man pushes him over and laughs. They're knackered but having fun: like you would if you'd just made an incredible record and were zooming round the world with your best mate.

By the time they were 17 they'd formed Darlin', a ramshackle indie band that lasted six months and released one single: a pidgin English Beach Boys pastiche called 'Cindy So Loud'. Guy-Man, the singer, treats us to a mercifully brief screech of wobbly falsetto, then says he saw a copy in a collector's shop for £15. Thomas looks absolutely horrified.

Correctly guessing the world wasn't ready for a Gallic surf-pop combo, the pair started listening to The Orb and Andrew Weatherall and checking out the Parisian rave scene.

"The rock scene was slowing down in Paris," recalls Thomas. He was already exposed to the dancefloor via his songwriter dad, who inflicted Ottawan's 'D.I.S.C.O.' on the world. "This was more energetic; people were smiling. Then we discovered Detroit and Chicago stuff."

Taken as they were by the tunes rumbling from Laurent Garnier's turntables, Thomas and Guy-Man couldn't entirely forsake their love of rock. The two of them hatched a plan. What if they could combine everything they loved into one fierce, crazy, fucked-up noise? What if they made

tracks as influenced by 60s pop and 70s rock as they were by disco and DJ Sneak – what Guy-Man called "melting music"? What would that sound like?

Drop the needle in the groove of 'Homework', twist your ears round the slow burn of 'Da Funk' or the glitterstomp blitz of 'Rock'n'Roll' and you'll find out. Goodbye Darlin'. Hello Daft Punk.

And is it punk? Take every golden rule that house music's defined by. Then bend them, break them, turn them inside out. Do the opposite of what you're expected to. People think you deal in sharp, harsh, jack trax? Release a crawling, smouldering drag of a single like 'Da Funk' that sounds like G-Funk fed through creaking machines. People want pristine techno and beat-perfect sets? Drop Prince records and old handbag tunes, plunge clubs into silence and play fake radio ads. People are obsessed with technology? Record your album on synths older than you are. In your bedroom. That's punk.

"We're very keen on recording at home, not going into studios," says Thomas. "It was very seductive to do that with a major label, all the more if you're in the charts. But you can do some really lo-fi stuff with two drum machines and an old synth and put it out on a major label! That's seductive as well: playing with the rules. When we started, it was more economic, we didn't have the money, but now it's a reason in itself. We do it because we want to."

'We do it because we want to' could be Daft Punk's catchphrase. It's the fuck-you confidence of two kids, barely out of their teens, who've suddenly realised the mad musical plan they hatched while bunking off school not only works, but sounds – and sells – like the freshest noise on the block. When Thomas talks about their incredible DJ sets, which smash every shade and shape of music against a wall of 909 drum noise, he acts like it's the most obvious idea in the world.

"I'm surprised," he deadpans. "The live show we do is quite normal. I don't know why anyone hasn't done it like this before."

"We enjoy it inside. We might not smile, but we're enjoying it. Maybe we're not enjoying it like dancing or singing, but... we like the concept of doing it."

And, as you listen to Thomas, you remember any great artist after their debut album's exploded. You remember the effortless swagger of prime-time Stone Roses or Goldie, after 'Timeless', whispering: "It's just breakbeat". A perfect pop star pose, then, but one that's already been mistaken for stroppy petulance or snot-nosed arrogance. What about their full-on live performances, where a motionless, emotionless Daft Punk stare blankly at banks of knackered equipment in sharp contrast to the awesome, fizzing racket they produce?

"We enjoy it inside," says Thomas. "We might not smile, but we're enjoying it. Maybe we're not enjoying it like dancing or singing, but... we like the concept of doing it."

Daft Punk stood up for their rights on 'Homework''s 'Revolution 909', which flips an unrepentantly funky finger at the French government's brutal anti-rave clampdown. Thomas describes it as "mad and angry".

"In France they think techno and house is devil music with drugs," he explains. "Hopefully, if the music stands, it'll show the music isn't linked to drugs. It's becoming very big and we have the power to change things a little bit."

But despite the show of unity in their grooves, there's a sense that Daft Punk want little to do with the burgeoning French dance scene. They're full of praise for the likes of Air and Motorbass, who have been granted the first ever remix of a Daft Punk track, tackling 'Around the World', but Thomas complains that "people try to put us in a French sound and we don't want that."

Both Punks complain bitterly about the insular nature of the Paris scene, savaging the "purists" who've attacked their success.

"In Paris, there are people who complain about the shit that's in the charts, that there's no house music, that it's not big enough," snaps Thomas. "Then when it gets big, they spit on it. Purists think people don't deserve to listen to good music, they think you have to be clever or something. DJs in Paris will buy three or four copies of a record just because they don't want other DJs to get it. They think it will make a small difference between them and the next DJ. If people want to do that..." his voice trails off in disgust.

"We don't want to compromise ourselves," he sighs. "We just want to reach people. The ideas we have are totally against the keep-it-underground thing. People think once it's gone overground you lose control, it gets spoilt. We want to show that you don't lose anything."

And he leans back, looking quietly confident, like a man who's just recorded a Top 5 album in his bedroom, a man who knows that a multinational record company can't commission remixes, can't change the artwork, can't make him have his photo taken, can't do anything without his and Guy-Man's say-so.

"We didn't want a '97 remix of 'Da Funk'," he grins. "We're not The Nightcrawlers."

They're locking them out of Leeds' Back To Basics and it's not even midnight. Squeeze your way in and you'll find the crowd are screaming their praise of Ralph Lawson's dark, deep, liquid grooves. But when Daft Punk take to the decks – looking, as usual, like they'd rather be anywhere else – everything becomes a blur.

'Homework''s highlights get hacked into oblivion as the drum machine pounds and they grab and snatch at other people's tunes. The bassline from 'Disco's Revenge' lurches into life, the vocal from Lil Louis' 'Freedom' gets strung out and scratched into infinity; everything's tweaked and trashed and fucked up beyond all recognition. They drop 'Revolution 909' and when that megaphone voice drones: "Stop the music... stop the music and go home", they kill the sound for what seems like an age, only to kick back in twice as loud when the crowd reach squealing point.

Then, towards the end of their set, something weird happens. As Daft Punk shift seamlessly from a lone, sparse kickdrum into Prince's 'Raspberry Beret', a collective gasp of recognition comes from the floor. And one solitary bloke, dancing at the side, actually starts bashing his head against the wall in time to the music.

Now that's punk.

*Originally published in Mixmag, March 1997*

---

"THE TWO DARLIN' TRACKS ARE A DAFT PUNKY THRASH CALLED 'CINDY SO LOUD' (THAT'S THE TITLE AND THE SOLE LYRIC), AND A BIZARRE FUZZ-GUITAR READING OF THE BEACH BOYS' 'DARLIN'."

Dave Jennings/Melody Maker/1993

# JUST THE FAX»

The Fax pages in the 90s editions of Jockey Slut were a popular feature idiosyncratic to the times. It was a relatively easy way to get access to bigger artists who didn't have the time to meet us in person and it was something they could do at their leisure – perhaps on tour as The Prodigy were when they did theirs. The only stipulation was that it was faxed back prior to us going to press. Back then, as everything was typed in – no email in the mid-90s – we didn't even have to spend any further time on it, the designer just scanned the fax pages in and framed them.

It helped if the band/artist was decent at doodles and it further assisted us and the reader if their writing was legible. Aphex Twin either got bored with his missive or wasn't happy with his words or pictures so he spoiled the pages with heavy scribbling so not much was readable. He still faxed it back to us and – deeming it 'Very Aphex Twin' – we printed it.

It was always a cheap thrill for us when the fax machine kicked in in the office going fud-fud-fud-fud-fud as the pages reeled out and then ended up in a furled heap on the floor. And in March 1997 we received one from Paris. We're not sure whose handiwork the doodles are, but here in all its vintage none-more-90s glory is Daft Punk: The Fax.

# FAX

## DAFT PUNK

**Daft Punk are the funk phenomenon of '97. With their daft disco album, mad videos with blokes dressed up as daft dogs, genre bending daft DJ sets and daft masks they have invaded Britain with style, wit and top five bustin' tuneage. They are amongst the headliners at Tribal Gathering and will no doubt be 'droppin' their new single *All Around the World*. The kids love 'em, the government fear them . Viva le Revolution 909!**

**Introduce yourselves by way of a self portrait.**

**Which are your favourite masks?**

see above ↑ ↗

**Where did you get the idea for the 'Da Funk' video and who's in the dog costume?**

Spike did WHAT HE WANTED... HE KNOWS THE ACTOR (TONY!) (MUSTACHE ACTOR)

**Why do you think the British have taken you so heartily to their hearts?**

because we are a HEART-ATTACK!

**You are Presidents Punk de Daft for the day. What three things would you change?**

POVERTY ; IGNORANCE ; SUCKSESS, etc...

**What's your favourite conspiracy theory?**

we're already livin' in many ones...

06-MAR-97 16:02 DE:DAFT TRAX 0142511354 A:01619504217 PAGE:02

FROM : JOCKEYSLUTJOCKEYSLUTJOCKEYSLUT PHONE NO. : 01619504217 Feb. 27 1997 07:00AM P03

Illustrate what you think da funk looks like

If you could put on a fantasy club where would it be and who would you have DJing and playing live?

If you could ban one form of music what would it be?

MUSIC AND its FORMS are unbannable.

Name your all time top five favourite Beach Boys records.

GOD ONLY KNOWS; SURF'S UP; WOULD'NT IT B NICE; FIRE; OUR PRAYER.

Anyone else you'd like to include on 'Teachers'?

THE LIST IS NOW INFINITE, 2 MUCH TO MENTION, 2 MUCH GOOD MUSIC.

Please select one current record from each of the following genres currently rockin' your :

*House/Techno* DJ Gregory's 'PHANTOM'S FAITHFULL.

*Hip Hop* LL Cool J "ain't Nobody"!

*Drum 'n' Bass* AINT ARMAND AVOO

*Rock 'n' Roll* NO DOUBT'S "DON'T Speak"!

Draw the opening three frames from the forthcoming 'Daft Punk - The Movie'.

From performing at the fringes of music festivals to changing the face of electronic music, this is the oral history of 'Homework' by the people who witnessed history being made...

By Duncan Dick

# ACID HOUSE HIGH SCHOOL

## The Cast

### Caroline Prothero

Former Virgin Records' club promotions. Would help Daft Punk break the world before going on to do the same as David Guetta's manager

### Erol Alkan

DJ, super producer for the likes of Duran Duran, Ride and Mystery Jets, one half of Beyond The Wizards Sleeve, founder and resident of Trash (1997-2007)

### Joe Mount

Founder and creative force behind Metronomy

### Myles MacInnes

Aka Mylo, DJ and producer behind 2004's smash hit album 'Destroy Rock & Roll'

### Pedro Winter

Daft Punk manager and DJ/producer under the name Busy P

### Soulwax

Musicians, producers, DJs and remixers David and Stephen Dewaele. Also known as 2manydjs

### The Blessed Madonna

Kentucky-by-way-of-Chicago DJ legend and producer

**Mylo:** "I was aware of Daft Punk in the mid-90s, before 'Homework' came out, not that I was a cool kid – anything but. But some of my pals from the south end of Skye went to Glasgow after leaving school where they became Sub Club devotees, so I learned of them that way, through the Soma Records connection. Apparently, Thomas and Guy-Manuel attended an afterparty at the Skye boys' flat in West End Park Street whereupon Guy-Manuel threw up (White Lightning cider, I'm told) on the stairwell."

**Caroline Prothero:** "I was working at Virgin Records in 1996 and I was the club promotions person. So it was my job to give music to DJs. Back then, pre-internet, DJs were usually responsible for breaking club music and so it was through their hands that records got broken. Some music was dropped on my desk that had come from the French label by Ashley Newton, the A&R guy who had signed Massive Attack. He said: 'Can you have a listen to this? Apparently, this is hot.' So I took it home and I froze. As I'm talking to you now I'm getting goosebumps, just remembering the moment of putting it on and just like being totally transfixed. I'd never felt music like it. I've never heard music like it."

**Soulwax:** "In '96/'97 it's hard to describe now how powerful the music industry was. An artist didn't have much leverage. Being signed by a major label was like winning the lottery. And then you would have to go through this whole system and through the motions. Daft Punk's deal with Virgin, the creative control [that Daft Punk insisted upon] was featured heavily in the music press and everywhere. They had basically paved the way for the idea that you could do these things, but you didn't necessarily have to go along with the system that is the music industry.

"Even the two of them being anonymous was a powerful thing because it took them out of the equation of having to do a lot of interviews and doing a lot of the stuff that comes with contemporary music – especially in those days. A lot of what we did was a reaction to the superstar DJ culture of the late-90s. And they were so far ahead that they had already gone completely the other way. When we wore tuxedos and bags over our heads it was a bit less stylish than what they did! But we loved this idea of anonymity."

**Pedro Winter:** "Of course the Daft Punk boys were working and recording and producing the album before they signed to Virgin. That signature itself didn't change the creative process or the creative direction of the record. The music was done in total freedom as it always was with Daft Punk. So the signature with Virgin has different meanings. It meant that electronic music suddenly became something that interested major labels. It meant also that an independent label like Soma, for example, or an underground artist like Daft Punk could enter the big circle and the big game of the music business, have major labels invest and make sure they can reach the world.

"Because it's true that the arrival of Virgin into the Daft Punk history helped the band become what it became. Thomas and Guy-Man had always said that to change the system, you have to enter the system and I think Virgin was the perfect door to enter the system and slowly, but surely, change the game for electronic music. And a few years later we would realise they'd changed the face of pop music."

**Caroline:** "I was sent to a festival in Rennes called Transmusicales in December 1995. There I met up with a woman who was instrumental in them signing to Virgin Records called Maya Masseboeuf. And there they were: this little French act performing at 4 o'clock in the afternoon on the fringe of this big music festival, and it was cold and wet and grim. And she said you have to meet these guys and so it was a very brief meeting and then we watched them DJing."

**Soulwax:** "They opened doors for a lot of European acts and a lot of people who kind of lived in that sort of grey area between pop, rock and say maybe dance music. But there was also another aspect which was influential on so many levels. We thought it was very brave of them to sort of disregard their home country and say: 'We make music for the whole world' and that's something that we also felt. We definitely took it on, it's not like we are the biggest band in Belgium, but we have an international outlook and that's definitely something that we learned from Daft Punk. They were the first to have the balls to say: 'Fuck this, we're just going to do whatever we think is cool.'"

**Pedro:** "Thomas' father Daniel was and has been there since day one, first around the band, then of course around me, because I became suddenly the one in between the band and Daniel. He knew about success and also he was teaching Thomas and Guy-Man, sharing with them, trying to explain to them what was the right and what was the wrong direction. So Daniel was really helpful to me because I was 20 years old. I knew nothing about the music business. I had my graduation and I wanted to become a lawyer, so I went to law school for three months. To be honest, I didn't learn anything there. Daniel was definitely the best teacher I had, because he was really sharing with me all the keys of this business. Of course, you take the information, you digest it and keep what is needed. I know some people say that Daniel was the puppet master, but that's not how it worked with Daft Punk. In the end, Thomas and Guy-Man were only picking up what they wanted to know."

**Caroline:** "The creative all came from the band – the direction all came from the band. There was no record company directive as to what they could do or what they should do. They did what they wanted and we had to do as they saw fit. And they were right: they had precision, they had vision, they were uncompromising. This is the key thing; they directed every single move. You know, even down to which DJs got the tracks first. And in what order they went out. I was just really honoured to be a little channel to be able to take their stuff. But everything - everything - came from them."

**Erol Alkan:** "I think where I first heard anything from 'Homework', would have pretty much been 'Da Funk'. I first heard that on the Annie

Nightingale compilation, 'Annie On One'. It was alongside a load of big beat stuff, I think. So Death in Vegas and a Chemical Brothers track. I heard 'Da Funk' as part of that family. It just sounded like electronic music with a real alternative spirit. So I always equated that record with that moment. I was hearing things that were coming through that filter of a lot of UK DJs."

**Caroline:** "I was gifted the job of promoting the record to DJs. Pedro Winter had a very clear vision, as did the band, so we would pore over lists of DJs to introduce the music for the first time. The promos came and they were hand stamped and the copy on the white labels was handwritten in France and sent to us. The hardest part of my job was to cut the list to 25 first run and then 15 and it went against the grain of every kind of promotion that we did. Because in those days you sent out 2,000 copies of stuff.

"The internet existed but there was no way of sharing music that way. So it was a physical vinyl copy. So I was tasked with literally sending or hand-delivering these tracks to a list that the band, management and myself had come up with together. People like the Chemical Brothers and Justin Robertson, Stuart and Orde (Slam) obviously, Ross Allen, Jon Carter, Pete Tong and Annie Nightingale. Pete went off on a charge: Essential New Tune, Essential Mix. And he was one of the first and strongest champions. But it was the easiest thing, I just had to ring up and listen to people weep and wail about the reaction this record had had on the dancefloor."

△

**Pedro:** "If I had to choose one track from 'Homework', of course it has to be 'Da Funk', you know. There is no way to choose another one because I think it commenced the period, it's the perfect link between Soma and the Virgin era. I bought it when it was on Soma, I met the guys in a radio station in Paris when they were promoting it, and I was throwing my parties and we met like that: "Ok, you're doing a record. I'm doing parties. Do you want to come to… ?" Literally, it happened like that. That was in 1995. I'm still playing this song today."

**The Blessed Madonna:** "There was an event called Even Furthur in Wisconsin in the spring of 1996. This is how young we were: we decided to go to this rave and sleep in the car instead of going to a high school dance. It was eight or nine hours away from where I lived at the time, right out in the woods. You can't imagine how remote this is, there were signs that would say Even Furthur… Even Furthur… Even Furthur.

"So finally we got there, it was great, and I remember that they had this laser light show outside and everybody went out to watch the lasers. And what I realised was that right after the laser show Daft Punk were going to be on in the tent. I was like: 'Well, fuck a laser show.' So we waited inside but the tent had completely emptied. 'Da Funk' was out (on Soma) but they were not that big!"

**Caroline:** "'Da Funk' was released (on Virgin) in December 1996 and at that point they didn't have an agent in the UK. So I said: 'I can book them as part of the promo. I've been raving for years, and I've got friends who are promoters.' I wouldn't call it a tour, but we did some club gigs. In January 1997, I took them on the train from London to Leeds to Back To Basics to play (infamous Basics promoter) Dave Beer's birthday party. Goldie was the headliner on the flyer and then it said: 'also playing Daft Punk'. They DJed that night, and the reaction was just mind blowing. I remember at the end of the night Dave Beer finding a bunch of plastic flowers that had been part of the décor and he was like holding them up to Daft Punk in the booth with everyone cheering and it was just rapturous… and that moment will stick with me forever. Pure, full-on, crazy Basics vibes."

**Soulwax:** "At the height of French Touch, they were untouchable. It wasn't like there were all these other acts and Daft Punk were on the same level. It was like Daft Punk were Bob Marley and the rest were just reggae bands. Great reggae bands but they weren't Bob Marley."

**The Blessed Madonna:** "The Roulé releases were already huge in the Midwest scene. And then 'Da Funk' was included at the end of a really classic American Midwest mixtape by Terry Mullan: 'New School Fusion 2'. And 'Da Funk' was like a huge Midwest record. I mean people would stop their sets to play it. Because at that time things were very fast. Even your house DJ was playing well over 130 beats per minute. It was a very hyperactive kind of period in tempo, which I feel like we're kind of going back into now. 'Da Funk' was a good, 20 or 30 bpm slower than what you would normally hear and it had been the finale on this tape which just stops completely at the end. You hear the traffic sounds. I could still identify the traffic sample from 'Da Funk' anywhere, anytime."

**Pedro:** "Because it's 110 bpm, 'Da Funk' was slower than a club track which is 125 bpm. It's like what George Clinton and Funkadelic did: it was dirty, it was sexy and more Prince and George Clinton than techno. And I think that's the magic of 'Da Funk', to bring back this groove into the clubs. Certainly I saw that in Paris."

**Mylo:** "Without a doubt 'Da Funk' is the Daft Punk track I've played most as a DJ. It's one of a select number of bona fide classics that can save the gloomiest dancefloor."

**The Blessed Madonna:** "Looking back on 'Homework', 'Da Funk' is a perfect record. It still stands alone from everything else that came before and after it by anyone. It remains fresh – it still sounds fresh to me today."

**Soulwax:** 'Rollin' and Scratchin'' (on the B-side of 'Da Funk'] had the biggest effect on our musical consciousness. We're indie rockers, that's where we come from. We're a band and when we heard 'Rollin' and Scratchin'' it blew us away. It was the same impact as hearing My Bloody Valentine or when we heard Public Enemy: something that just went boom. We were like: 'Oh cool, this could be... this'."

**Erol:** "My favourite on 'Homework' is probably... I could easily say it was 'Da Funk' because of the memories attached to it, but it's also because musically it's weird. There's a lot of clashing dissonances in it. It sounds like a couple of people making a record in their bedroom but not really knowing what they're doing. That's what I love about it. I don't think you can intentionally write a track like that – and I find that a massive curiosity."

**Pedro:** "'Homework' was done in Thomas' bedroom in the heart of Montmartre in the north of Paris. Thomas' parents were living in Avenue Junot, which is a posh area in the 18th (arrondissement [area]). They had an amazing apartment on two floors. Thomas' room was on the first floor, and they had a guestroom and he took out the bed and did his own studio there. Very tiny, very small and also, no chairs. I have some photos, always with Guy-Manuel sitting on the floor and Thomas on his knees, with his ankle bouncing to the rhythm. I'm sure the reason he was on the floor is also that he could easily plug and unplug stuff. The studio was very small, very like a kid's room, but pretty well equipped for 1996, when all that equipment cost a lot. To have a sampler, it was like thousands of francs, so it was not accessible to everyone. Luckily, he was coming from a wealthy family, and got some equipment to experiment on directly from his father."

**Soulwax:** "'Homework' had a huge impact because it was one of the first times that a dancey thing that wasn't sort of cheeseball had an impact on the charts. Like most of the cool dance music was underground. And this had the album artwork, the videos: it was a pop record using underground techno and house. It kind of opened up the door to the idea that you can push the borders, you can have a pop or rock or punk sensibility but make electronic music. And around that time is when we bought a sampler and we started doing remixes."

**Mylo:** "I remember loving the 'Homework' sleeve design, the very stagey photo of the desk in the bedroom with all the ostentatiously displayed teenage stuff. I remember it as having numeric labels and a key describing each item, but I can see that I must have imagined this. The overall effect hits a note between dorky and cool."

**The Blessed Madonna:** "I think it was the first time for me that an album that was electronic music truly was an album. It really tried to tell a whole story. Even when you look at the art on the inside you can see all the influences in it. Like, there's a Ramones patch and then you listen to a song like 'Rock'n Roll' it sounds like the Ramones, it's got that Ramones clapping thing. It felt like cohesion, a real consistent point of view and you were entering their universe. Before that, for me as a listener, things had been very track-orientated. But you start this album and even the fake radio station, even that really appealed to me, all of that kind of world building shit."

**Soulwax:** "To this day I don't think it's been bettered. It's still an incredible album."

**Mylo:** "It was one of the first dance music albums I was aware of that really worked with that format; the CD. Not just a bunch of tracks but sequenced, structured as an album. Overall, I suppose, the entire premise of 'Homework' was an album made by a couple of young guys at home with limited equipment. It was encouraging to see that it could be done."

**Erol:** "The most important thing I learned from Daft Punk is never to be swayed by the feeling that I need expensive equipment to make music that sounds good. If you look at what those records were made on, the early records especially, they were made on very, very basic instruments. The big 3630 is the compressor that was known as the Daft Punk compressor and it cost £60 to buy. Shelling out £3000 on some showy tech, valve thing is not going to make your music sound magically better. If you research what they used, it was very ordinary equipment, but with a lot of innovative artists, it's about the desire to go that bit further to get the best out of something, to go beyond it with your ideas and your ambition in what you want to create."

**Mylo:** "I vividly remember listening to 'Homework' on a CD boombox outside the dorms in my first year at uni, with some medical students. The track playing is 'Around the World' and I am thinking this is perfect, these three or four parts coming in or dropping out in different permutations every eight bars, like a code of some kind, or a machine in motion. This was shortly after I had suffered my first episode of SSNHL – a form of irreparable hearing loss which was to eventually drive me into an early withdrawal from music production. So I was feeling quite gloomy, especially about music, but this album, in that moment was like magic to me."

**Caroline:** "In 1997, the main meeting of music minds in our scene was the Miami Winter Music Conference. All the DJs and the record companies in the dance world would congregate at the Fontainebleau Hotel. And I'd got the Masters At Work remixes of 'Around the World'. My job was to be there for a week to go and vibe on the records and I didn't even have an international mobile phone. With some of the records I was working, I'd have to run around all the clubs and try and track down the DJs and interrupt them, sometimes mid-set to press these records on them. That was how you got records to international DJs and that's where the buzz would come.

"I can remember thinking I might as well do this Daft Punk record first. So I called everybody before I got there and asked them to meet me at the back of the pool as I had some records for them. Specifically, this Kenlou (Kenny Gonzalez and Louie Vega – Masters At Work) remix of Daft Punk. And I went to the pool, and it was about 4 o'clock in the afternoon and I couldn't believe it. Every massive American DJ was there: Todd Terry, Armand Van Helden, obviously Masters At Work, Derrick Carter. There was a pre-approved list of who was allowed to have it. But they'd told their mates and everyone else had turned up. I'm supposed to be trying to encourage people to take the records and I was literally, I can see myself now, clutching onto my little vinyl bag going: 'No, no, no. I haven't got enough! I can't, I've only got five. I've only got five!'"

## HOMEWORK EQUIPMENT LIST

**Sequencers**
Alesis MMT-8
Apple Macintosh
+ Emagic MicroLogic

**Samplers**
Akai S01
E-Mu Emulator III
E-Mu SP-1200
Ensoniq ASR-10
Roland S-760

**Synthesizers**
Roland Juno-106
Roland MC-202
Roland MKS-80
Roland TB-303
Sequential Prophet-VS

**Drum Machines**
Linn LinnDrum
Roland TR-707
Roland TR-808
Roland TR-909

**Effects**
Alesis Microverb III
Alesis 3630 Compressor
Behringer Compressor
Behringer Parametric EQ
Ensoniq DP/4+
Lexicon Vortex
Lexicon JamMan
LA Audio Gate/Compressor
Waldorf MiniWorks 4-pole
Yamaha Digital Delay

**Mixers/Recorders**
Mackie MS1202
Mackie CR1604
Panasonic SV-3700

**Other**
Iomega Zip Drive

## PRODUCTION EXAMPLE

1.

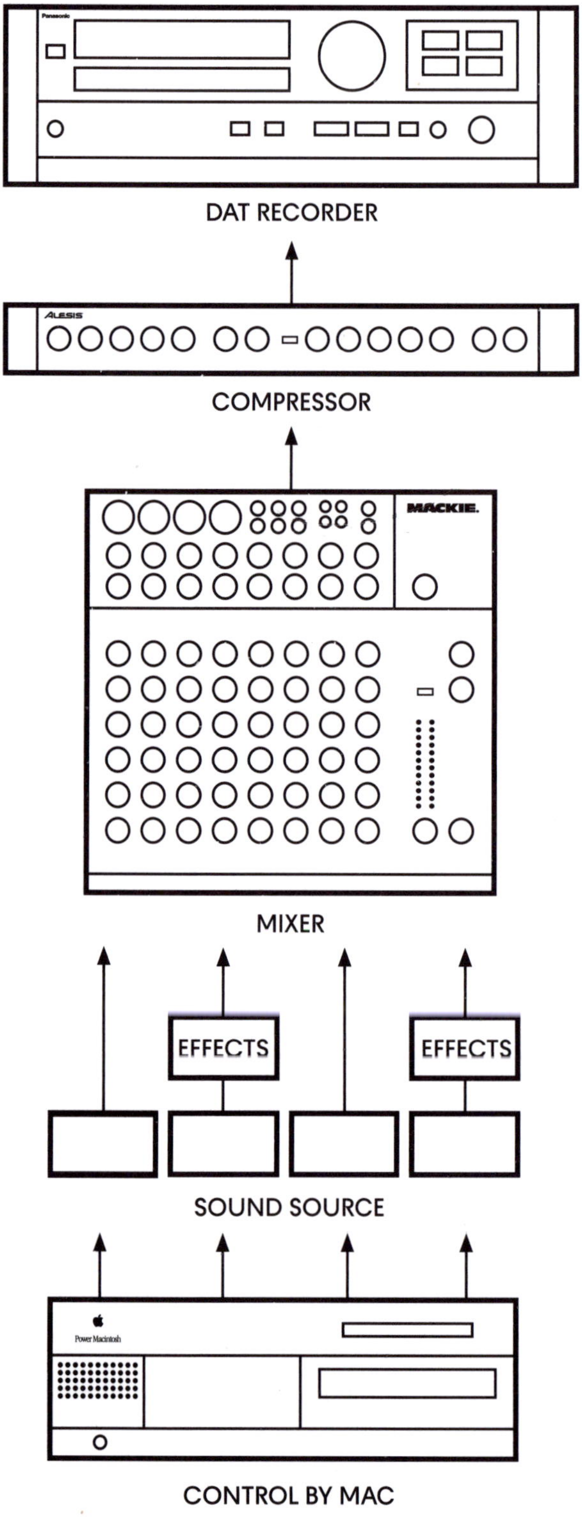

2.

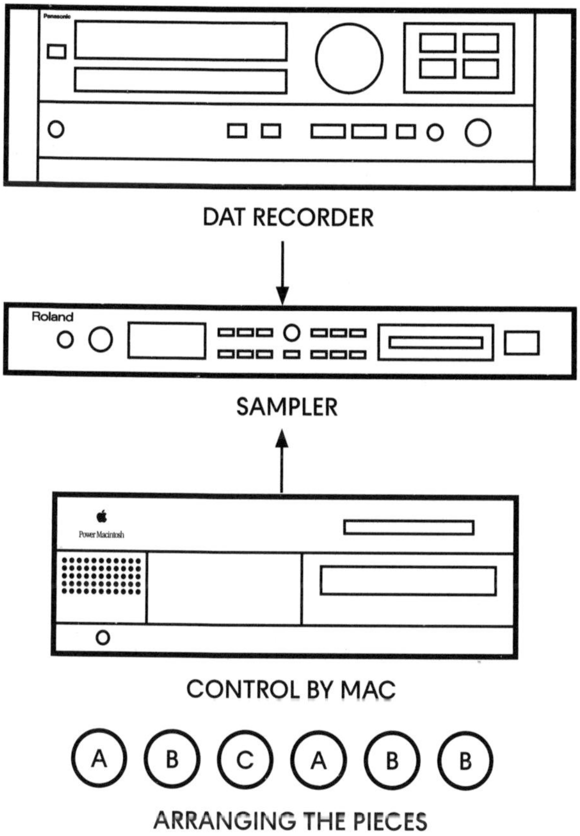


3.

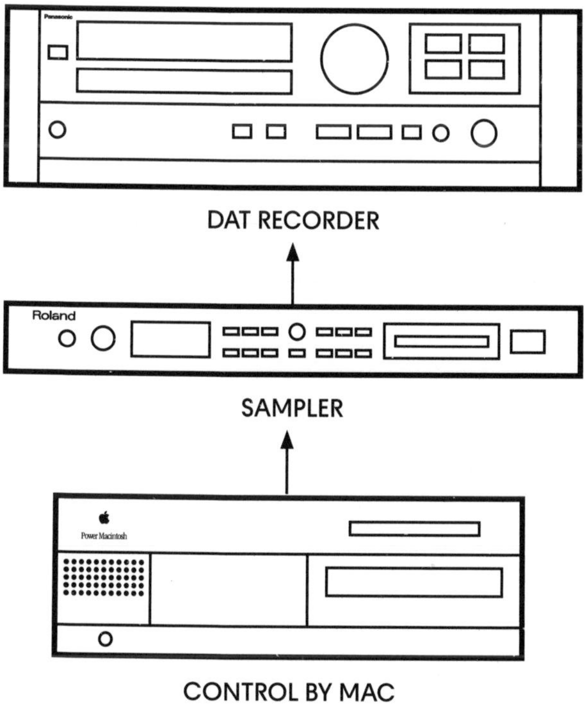


**The Blessed Madonna:** "The track on that album that I play the most is probably 'Indo Silver Club'. I have such a specific memory of Roy Davis Jr. dropping that in Nashville once and just seeing the way that the compression makes you feel almost like your ribs are going to break. It's a study in weaponised compression. It's a really astonishing record. I mean if you asked me next week, I would have a different one. Sometimes it's 'Burnin'', sometimes it's 'Rollin' & Scratchin'' which I literally played two weeks ago. It's a moving target."

**Joe Mount:** "When I was first trying to properly make music on my computer, I remember I basically took 'Around the World', and, with the track that I was trying to make, kind of copied the structure bar by bar. Everything they were doing, like with filters and building up and stuff like that, I literally used it as a template of how to make a club track. A banger. I mean, it didn't quite work! But the kind of cutting or editing, the little melodic refrains that they would have done using weird little sounds or samples, if you listen to the first Metronomy record you can definitely hear that influence.

"The 'Nights Out' album was mastered by Nilesh at the Exchange, who mastered both 'Homework' and 'Discovery' and who has sadly passed away now. I remember asking him how he got that 'throbbing' on the Daft Punk records and he said: 'That wasn't me, that was sidechain compression.' Which was almost a Daft Punk invention, and I used that for 'The English Riviera' album and very obviously (2011 single) 'The Bay'."

**Mylo:** "The production was an open book. And quite deliberately, self-consciously, so. There was nothing hidden. In a sense, then, the much-vaunted 'Daft Punk Compression' is quite literally – hear me out, here! – the least important aspect of their sound. 'Around the World' would be the same banger with very little channel or master-buss compression. It's the arrangement of parts that matters. It was as if they were jamming the 'dumb' and 'clever' buttons down at the same time, and this incongruity made me smile. I am reminded of the joke about how if you press the accelerator and the brake down at the same time, your car windscreen takes a screenshot."

**Soulwax:** 'Rollin' & Scratchin'' is so unique. It's a techno record but, in some ways, weirdly enough, it's pop music. I don't know how but it becomes instantly translatable to so many different situations on a visual and even cerebral level. It works in so many different ways. It's never something trying to be, it is exactly what it set out to do."

△

**Joe:** "When I was a teenager, I had a friend who lived in Reading, and he had MTV, and I didn't have anything like that where I was growing up. So much of my discovery of music in those days was through trips to this guy's house. And that's where I remember seeing the 'Da Funk' video for the first time: the dog video. Seeing it and just being like: 'This is crazy'. I was making music and I was playing in a band. I was getting into more electronic stuff. I realised there was this kind of world out there which I could be a part of."

**The Blessed Madonna:** "When 'Da Funk', and later 'Around the World' were on MTV that was very shocking to us. Because it felt like, wow, what the fuck is this? We had no idea that there could be anything like that, from our scene, on MTV, it was just incomprehensible, even though the ratings were huge it still felt like it was our secret."

**Pedro:** "Of course, at some point, when the album sales are more than one million, you're like, ok, well, that's becoming serious. But the guys weren't calling me asking: 'Oh, what are the sales today?' It was more about: 'What's next? What can we do with this? Ok, we sold one million: do we have enough money to make another video that costs Fr.1 million?' Those Daft Punk videos with Spike Jonze, Michel Gondry, Seb Janiak, Roman Coppola: it was their own money. Of course, Virgin were helping, but they were advancing and three weeks later they were getting the money back from the sales."

**Caroline:** "MTV was the only tool that was available in those days really to pass them over into the mainstream. But they weren't following anything that had gone before, they were creating their own vision and their own interpretation of who they were. When they got Spike Jonze to do the video for 'Da Funk', that was an underground dance track with a stop-you-in-your-tracks video. There weren't thousands and thousands of videos on YouTube back then: this was a stand-out."

**Pedro:** "Emmanuel de Buretel was the head of Virgin France, a very big French music mogul, still today. And he knew Spike. We knew him as a great skateboard photographer, and someone who'd done videos for the Beastie Boys and The Pharcyde, definitely one to catch. The funny thing is that Spike Jonze sent us a one-page fax with the idea: 'A guy, head of a dog, walking in New York: I hope you will like the idea.'"

**Caroline:** Then came 'Around the World': a soft, warm, accessible vocal track but still with that mind-bending production. And then the video came for that with Michel Gondry with the dancers; again it was a unique aesthetic, so different to anything we'd seen before."

**Mylo:** "I don't think my enthusiasm for Daft Punk needed any boosting at that time, but the videos probably boosted my envy of them. Not only were they cool but there was this multiplying effect of collaborating with these visual designers and filmmakers. Something I was later lucky enough to do, working with designer David 'Phantom' Ross and filmmaker Johnny Barrington. There is a now-famous clip where Michel Gondry explains his video for 'Around the World'. I remember loving it because it chimed quite precisely with my experience of listening to that track on the boombox in college."

**Pedro:** "I wasn't there, but Thomas and Guy-Man told me that Michel Gondry came to the meeting with a maquette. A miniature. He came in with a model of the ('Around the World' video) set and said: 'Ok, so the bass is the dancers here. The vocal is the robots.' And so on. He didn't write any pitch, he explained with the model and of course it was amazing. So this time I went to the shoot, outside of Paris. It's funny, the video looks easy, but you had to build everything. The lights in the back that were created by Michel's brother were something completely new: linking the video, the music and the lights at the same rhythm, and this was magic, the choreography was by very famous Spanish choreographer, (Blanca Li). And I think it was the perfect match again, you know after Spike and 'Da Funk', Michel Gondry and 'Around the World' – the song and the video fits perfectly."

**Pedro:** "It was the same for the 'Burnin'' video with (director) Seb Janiak that was shot in Chicago and cast a lot of DJs. DJ Sneak, Roger Sanchez, Derrick Carter, Roy Davis Jr., Paul Johnson – they were all there at the shoot. The Roman Coppola 'Revolution 909' video with the spaghetti recipe. They built something strong with those first videos. The videos are all classics."

△

**The Blessed Madonna:** "Every song on (Thomas Bangalter's) 'Trax On Da Rocks' on Roulé had been an enormous hit in the Midwest and they were played by everybody. The South Side Of Chicago, people who loved Dance Mania, everybody. It was an event when 'Homework' came out, it was like, sit down, put it on the CD player and listen to it. We understood them to be a part of house culture. Those people on 'Teachers' were the people that were playing Midwest raves at the time. That and the first thing they say is Paul Johnson. I mean my friend was dating Paul Johnson! It was crazy. I mean we knew those people and later on I would go to work with lots of those people in various ways. And it was just such a creative success. It just crystallised everything: they saw American dance music from the outside – and reflected it back to us."

**Erol:** "Whenever there are scenes that are thriving, somebody will kind of come through it all and will soak it all up and create something which will encapsulate what has been said already, but do it in a pretty powerful way, that may seem like it's... It's not more important than all those other artists who helped influence it or create it. It's just the way energy just keeps getting created, you know, it passes through until some people can make something of it."

**Soulwax:** "I think a lot of things that people projected onto us maybe I don't know ten, five years later, where they said that we were injecting some kind of rock or indie energy into dance music. It's definitely something we got from Daft Punk's 'Homework' for sure. In fact on our album 'Nite Versions' we did our version of 'Teachers', which was our homage to Daft Punk."

**Soulwax:** "I remember the first time we met Erol Alkan, the first time we played Trash, he opened up his record bag and we opened up ours and inside we both had 'Windowlicker' but also 'Rollin' and Scratchin''. And instantly we felt like we were like kindred spirits."

**The Blessed Madonna:** "'Homework' is the single number one thing that I consistently reference on a daily basis as a producer, and even literally today in the album that I'm writing right now for Warner Brothers. There is this one moment, there is an homage to 'Homework'. Just like one second. But if you know, you know."

**Pedro:** "It was definitely much later (than during 'Homework''s release), that I realised that it had *become something*. And I think also it's a good thing to sometimes wait. Rather than being in the middle (of the process) and saying: 'Ok, it's happening!' To instead keep it growing... and then later step back and then realise the achievement."

Left to right, back row: Dr. Dre, Jeff Mills, DJ Hell, Kenny 'Dope' Gonzalez, Brian Wilson, Ashley Beedle. Front row: Dave Clarke, Armando, Green Velvet, Luke Slater, 'Little' Louie Vega, DJ Sneak, Armand Van Helden, George Clinton

# A Positive Education

A who's who guide to Daft Punk's musical mentors. **Jim Butler** presents the 'Teachers'...

Upon its release in January 1997, Daft Punk's debut album, 'Homework', was met with universal acclaim. No wonder. The likes of 'Alive', 'Da Funk', 'Indo Silver Club' and 'Revolution 909' sound as fresh and vital today as they did over a quarter of a century ago.

For those looking to dig a little deeper, however, track nine was arguably the album's most important – certainly the most instructive – song on there. 'Teachers' was an unapologetic love letter-cum-clarion call to those musical artists who inspired Thomas and Guy-Man. Over half the artists cited – all read by Thomas in a weird shapeshifting robotic monotone voice backed with a helium accompaniment – hailed from Chicago and it was from that fertile musical hotbed that the duo came up with the idea for the track. (We'll be charitable and forgive the complete lack of female artists and blame it on the, you-know, 90s.)

Based upon Parris Mitchell's expletive-laden 'Ghetto Shout Out' featuring Waxmaster, 'Teachers' demonstrated that, at heart, Thomas and Guy-Man were two music fans in thrall to the sounds being teased out of the house (and techno) nation.

It's often said that those that can, do. And those that can't, teach. Well, Daft Punk certainly could, and did. But on 'Teachers' they also taught, by applauding their innovators and creating a cheat sheet for future generations to jump into with gusto.

Respect, in this case, was – and remains – a never-ending two-way street.

## PAUL JOHNSON

It's no coincidence that Paul Johnson is the first musician honoured in 'Teachers'. The sonic aesthetic laid down by the Chicago stalwart across both his productions and DJing would act as a de facto blueprint for Daft Punk. Johnson's signature style - looped disco; urgent, filtered vocal samples; relentless beats and an uncanny eye for a hook – was much admired by the duo. In a wheelchair from the age of 16 after a shooting accident, he never let his disability hinder, or define, him. His 1997 track, 'White Winds' was the second release on Guy-Man's Crydamoure imprint. In 1999, as if to pre-empt the great end of the century party, he scored his biggest hit in 'Get Get Down'. He died from complications with Covid-19 in 2021, aged just 50.

**CHECK OUT:**
**'SUMMER HEAT'**

## DJ FUNK

A pioneer of ghetto house (he coined the term in the early-90s), DJ Funk, known to his nearest as Charles F. Chambers, has been a mainstay on the Chicago music scene since the 90s. By adding a barely-veiled salaciousness to house music's four-to-the-floor rhythms – no wonder it was also known as booty house – Funk, alongside DJ Deeon, DJ Milton and DJ Slugo, more of whom later, would have twisted the ears of the young French neophytes.

**CHECK OUT:**
**'BOOTY HOUSE ANTHEMS'**

## DJ SNEAK

One of Chicago's famed second wave of house producers, Carlos Sosa, aka DJ Sneak, is a veritable dance music legend. The larger-than-life star was a clear influence on Daft Punk when the duo were starting out – 'Burnin'' owes a debt of gratitude to his 'Sneak's a Freak'. Sneak was a member of the loose DJ collective, Da Mongoloids (more a nice idea than a reality), he remixed 'Burnin'' to great effect and even supplied the lyrics for 'Digital Love'.

**CHECK OUT:**
**'YOU CAN'T HIDE FROM YOUR BUD'**

## DJ RUSH

Another Chicago house don, DJ Rush (Isaiah Major) cut his teeth DJing in the city's hallowed dance institutions Music Box, Warehouse and the Powerhouse, before turning his hand to producing (his first release coming out on the seminal Trax). He continues to DJ and produce to this day.

**CHECK OUT:**
**'HEAD RUSH'**

"I'm from the hood of Chicago, and we had to fight and struggle to get noticed amongst our peers, back in the day, when trying to make it on the scene. It was hard to get people to respect what you did and recognise your art, music and worth. After having your music ripped off, cheated and being billed on events that you had no knowledge of and [then] to come across an album from an artist on the other side of the world, giving you respect that you wished your own people should've done, I was happy to be included.

"It meant a lot to be noticed. For them to mention me I felt validated for doing something I love, because I am inspired from so many things and given the chance I always mention and acknowledge it. I will always remember Daft Punk and what they created and how they kept the scene exciting and fun."

## WAXMASTER

Waxmaster, or, as he was better known, Waxmaster Maurice is another from the Chicago old school, famed for his ghetto house productions on influential labels like Dance Mania. He was a notable influence on Chicago's juke and footwork movements. His frenetic cut 'Waxscratch Trax' was featured on Daft Punk's acclaimed 1997 Essential Mix.

**CHECK OUT:**
**'FREAK'**

## HYPERACTIVE

Chicago's DJ Hyperactive (Joseph Manumaleuna) was a vibrant and prolific presence in the city's musical story from the 90s onwards. His tougher, almost techno-like, take on house provided him with a distinctive sound. Indeed his relentless 1994 'Chicagoan' EP on Contact is up there with Jeff Mills for pummelling intensity.

**CHECK OUT:**
**'CHICAGO'**

## JAMMIN GERALD

Jammin Gerald's run of singles on Dance Mania in the 90s – all titles prefixed with Factory – were another take on ghetto house that, sound-wise, were a clear antecedent for Daft Punk's 'Homework'.

**CHECK OUT:**
**'ENERGY'**

## BRIAN WILSON

The Beach Boys' innovative, yet tortured, genius defined a sound for a generation thanks to masterpieces like 'Pet Sounds', 'Smile', 'Surf's Up' et al. The honeyed, sun-kissed musical melodies – what Wilson sometimes called "Teenage symphonies to God" – proved to be a towering influence on Thomas and Guy-Man's first band, Darlin', themselves named after a Beach Boys track from 'Wild Honey'.

**CHECK OUT:**
**'ALL I WANNA DO'**

## GEORGE CLINTON

The second bona fide musical deity to be mentioned outside of the environs of the Windy City needs little introduction. Clinton's extraordinary songwriting and production skills led to the emergence of a new style of music, P-Funk (coalesced around his two long-standing bands, Parliament and Funkadelic). The P-Funk Mothership used on the band's outlandish tours in the 70s and 80s would help define Daft Punk's feted Pyramid. Thomas and Guy-Man's edit of Scott Grooves' 'Mothership Reconnection' (itself a reworking of Clinton's 'Mothership Connection') was an immediate post-'Homework' highlight.

**CHECK OUT:**
**'GIVE UP THE FUNK (TEAR THE ROOF OFF THE SUCKER)'**

## LIL LOUIS

One of house music's totemic founding fathers, Lil Louis began DJing at the age of just 12 (hence his moniker – given to him by a police officer who raided a party the young Louis Burns was playing at in his hometown of Chicago). His iconoclastic productions reached an orgasmic apex, quite literally, with the release of 'French Kiss', a supreme slice of dance music that crossed over into the mainstream in 1989. It remains a thrilling listen to this day.

**CHECK OUT:**
**'FRENCH KISS'**

## ASHLEY BEEDLE

The first non-American featured on 'Teachers', Ashley Beedle is a British dance music God. Over the course of his 30-plus-year-career, he's joined the dots between disco, house, soul, reggae, ska, bluebeat, funk, gospel and more besides. His prolific 90s work in Black Science Orchestra, The Ballistic Brothers and X-Press 2, plus his remixes and re-edits, was a clear, formative influence on Daft Punk.

**CHECK OUT:**
**'MUZIK XPRESS'**

"I was doing a semi-regular show on Radio Nova [in the mid-90s]. Every couple of months I was going over there. And I bumped into Daft Punk at Radio Nova – this must have been around the time when they were starting to blow up on the back of the whole Soma deal. I was introduced to them and they were really, really shy. But they were very sweet. I didn't spend that long with them – maybe five minutes or so.

"I noticed their development and then all of a sudden I heard this tune, 'Teachers', and I was like: 'What? They just mentioned my fucking name! (Laughs)'. I think it might even have been Rocky or Diesel that pointed it out. I'm not quite sure. I was like: 'Damn, I've been thrown in with these guys.'

"But what blew me away more than anything was as much as I adored and respected a lot of the people that were mentioned on the record, it was the fact that they threw in Brian Wilson. I'm on the same fucking record as Brian Wilson! Do you know what I mean? That blew me away.

"In terms of the record, no ego intended, it's been a bit of a gold card. It's a great one for conversation. I could be having a meeting or be abroad or something and someone will go: 'He's on Daft Punk's 'Teachers'.' And all of a sudden the atmosphere changes. And they go: 'Oh, *right*. Ok.' And this reverence starts cropping up, it's really funny."

## NEIL LANDSTRUMM

A mixture of jackin' Chicago-flavoured grooves and stripped-back minimalism, the sounds Scottish producer Neil Landstrumm coaxed from his bank of musical machinery in the mid-90s (and released on labels like Tresor, Peacefrog and Ferox) resonated perfectly with Daft Punk when they were just starting out.

**CHECK OUT:**
**'TELEX'**

"That sound was very much what was happening in the Edinburgh clubs at that time. Twitch and Brainstorm who ran Pure had brought over a lot of these people – black producers from Detroit and Chicago. So we had an early ear to that sound. It was very stripped-down and raw. I remember coming across Daft Punk at the time. I was getting booked a lot in France around '96. Quite often we would be on the same bill together – we were very much on the same page.

"There was one time at a château in France when they requested to meet me. It was quite bizarre (laughs). I remember going to the top of the château with their very chic Parisian girlfriends and they didn't speak much English. But we smoked a joint and hung out. They told me they loved my records, particularly 'Inhabit the Machines' which they said was a big influence. I was just hanging out. It was all a bit too much. But I do remember they had really cool trainers and these beautiful French girlfriends.

"I think it's great what they went on to do. They had the common touch which is something that is very difficult to do. A lot of people dismiss pop music as throwaway, but to make good pop music that will last is really fucking difficult.

"I feel proud to be included with the other people to be honest. I feel proud to have at least made a dent in that sound from Scotland."

## KENNY DOPE

New York's first Teacher. Kenny 'Dope' Gonzalez is best known for his peerless recordings alongside 'Little' Louie Vega in Masters At Work, Nuyorican Soul and co. His pop savvy, best exemplified on his Bucketheads solo work, would not have gone unnoticed by Daft Punk.

**CHECK OUT:**
**THE BUCKETHEADS: 'THE BOMB!'**

## DJ HELL

A disciple of punk and new wave and bringing a touch of glamour – and sex – to a sometimes faceless and sterile dance scene, it doesn't take much to explain Helmut Josef Geier's appeal to Daft Punk. His 1992 debut track, the incendiary 'My Definition of House Music' took a cheeky sample from a David Byrne and Brian Eno theatrical production, and dressed it up with some funky motorik rhythms.

**CHECK OUT:**
**'MY DEFINITION OF HOUSE MUSIC'**

## LOUIE VEGA

MAW's other Master, 'Little' Louie Vega. With Kenny Dope, he gave house music a sophistication and musicality few other producers could muster. After being named in 'Teachers', Masters At Work repaid their students with a delicious set of Ricanstructed remixes of 'Around the World'.

**CHECK OUT:**
**'THE NERVOUS TRACK'**

## K-ALEXI

Keith Alexander Shelby is another Chicago pioneer who might not be as instantly recognisable as some on this list – a point that makes Daft Punk's homage to their inspirations even more crucial. The track has kept alive the names of some of those less-heralded innovators and originators whose contribution to house music might otherwise have been forgotten. K-Alexi's work on tracks such as Risque Ill's 'Essence of a Dream' highlight a true Chi-town jackin' genius.

**CHECK OUT:**
**'ESSENCE OF A DREAM'**

"We talked when they came into town – way before all that shit happened. They came into town and we talked about techniques and sampling and all that. So it was funny to be on a record called 'Teachers' because I really had shown them some techniques and things. Me and Paul (Johnson) would hang out with them.

"They didn't play much in Chicago back then. It was more like reconnaissance for them. Meeting people they knew about and liked. It was more hanging out. I was onstage with them when they played at the Winter Music Conference in Miami and I noted their showmanship. They opened their set with the theme tune from 'Miami Vice'. It was beautifully poetic. I love things like that. That shows preparation and preparation is what I'm about. Actually, it shows giving a damn, which is something which is lacking in the scene right now. But them dudes cared and that's why their career took off as it did.

"At the time I just thought it was cool [being mentioned on 'Teachers']. But as it went on, I look back on it now with a different perspective. I look back on it now and I'm like: 'Wow!' I had been mentioned before. But you don't think it's going to reach as many people as this did. Whenever I post that clip or people send it to me, I just crack up. Look at me! Little old me! It makes me proud. For sure. Because I've been doing this for a long time, and to have that certain validation was cool. And for them to show people that they had learned something from this group of people was good."

## DR. DRE

A member of the World Class Wreckin' Cru, the creative linchpin of N.W.A, a pioneer of G-Funk... Dr. Dre needs little introduction. Dre's quality control and self-assurance was no doubt appealing to young Thomas and Guy-Man.

**CHECK OUT:**
**'DEEP COVER'**

## DJ OMEGA

Arguably the least well-known producer on 'Teachers' – certainly on this side of the Atlantic – is DJ Omega (Willie Simpson). A fixture on Detroit's lurid and salacious ghettotech scene, he was originally hailed by Juan Atkins before hooking up with DJ Godfather.

**CHECK OUT:**
**'SHAKE THAT THANG'**

## GEMINI

During house music's second imperial wave in the 90s – an era crystallised in and propelled by Chicago – producers would have traded their favourite drum machine in exchange for a release on one of Relief, Cajual, Peacefrog or Planet E. Spencer Kincy – aka Gemini – was releasing 12-inches on all of them. A preternaturally talented producer and DJ, Gemini eventually faded from view in the new millennium, amid tales of bad deals and declining mental health. Daft Punk's citation means his reputation is permanently cast in stone.

**CHECK OUT:**
**'DEEP IN THE FLOWERS'**

## JEFF MILLS

While Daft Punk worshipped most notably at the altar of the Chicago groove, they weren't averse to Detroit's man-machine rhythms. Techno, as birthed by Jeff Mills, was a clear influence on tracks like 'Rollin & Scratchin'', 'Indo Silver Club' and 'Alive' and also upon Bangalter's early Roulé releases. The Wizard behind the early days of Underground Resistance before moving onto Axis, the Waveform Transmission series and his Purpose Maker releases was an obvious inspiration.

**CHECK OUT:**
**'PURPOSE MAKER' EP**

## DJ DEEON

A ghetto house innovator in an era riddled with forward-thinking producers, Deeon Boyd came through the ranks of South Side Chicago's fertile musical grounds. You can draw a line from his 'Southside DJ Shouts' to 'Teachers' by way of Parris Mitchell's 'Ghetto Shout Out!!' He told DJ magazine that Daft Punk's acknowledgement of him – and others like Milton and Slugo – helped gain the respect of his contemporaries. Has regrettably been beset by a number of illnesses in recent years.

**CHECK OUT:**
**'FREAK MODE'**

## DJ MILTON

Another Chicago pioneer to fall on hard times – DJ Milton was convicted of first-degree murder in the early-00s. Milton was fast friends with Deeon, and, eventually, one-time South Side Chicago rival Slugo. All three released classic ghetto house tracks on Dance Mania.

**CHECK OUT:**
**'TRAX-4-DAZE' EP**

## DJ SLUGO

The final point in the Deeon-Milton-Slugo ('DJs on the low' Bangalter intones on 'Teachers') ghetto house triangle – and quite possibly, the funniest and filthiest practitioner of a style of house music not known for restraint. "You gotta understand – me, Deeon, Milton, Waxmaster, Jammin Gerald, we come from ratchet lifestyles," he told blogger LeBron James (not that one) in 2019. Still DJing to this day.

**CHECK OUT:**
**'WHERE THE RATS'**

## GREEN VELVET

In a Chicago house scene quite often dominated by lovable tough nuts, Curtis Jones' flamboyant and playful persona would have shone as bright as the green mohawk across his head. Daft Punk certainly noticed. Whether producing under his Cajmere or Green Velvet monikers, this Chicago legend has always garnered attention.

**CHECK OUT:**
**'FLASH'**

## JOEY BELTRAM

One of dance music's first poster boys, Queens native Joey Beltram's incendiary, and both aptly-titled, cuts 'Energy Flash' and 'Mentasm' gave house and techno a thorough going over in the early-90s. So much so that writer Simon Reynolds described Beltram as having "revolutionised techno twice before the age of 21" in his book 'Generation Ecstasy'. Has released tracks on R&S, Warp, Tresor and Nu Groove.

**CHECK OUT:**
**'ENERGY FLASH'**

## DJ ESP

He might be one of the lesser-known names on Daft Punk's inspirational register, but DJ ESP – aka Woody McBride – played a pivotal role in Thomas and Guy-Man's ascent, certainly in America. As one of the Midwest co-promoters of 1996's infamous Even Furthur rave, ESP – who released brilliantly snarling and expansive acid techno under his own name and as ESP – booked Daft Punk for their first American show.

**CHECK OUT:**
**'PSYCHOPOCAPLYP' (BY FREDDIE FRESH & WOODY MCBRIDE)**

## ROY DAVIS JR.

A Chicago house music stalwart. From partying to Lil Louis and working with DJ Pierre, Armando and Marshall Jefferson, to pioneering a soulful take on house (that went on to form the basis for much of UK garage) with his classic cut 'Gabriel'. Released his frenetically funky take on French Touch, 'Rock Shock', on Roulé.

**CHECK OUT:**
**'GABRIEL'**

## BOO WILLIAMS

Willie Griffin was one of the best to come out of Chicago's second wave of house producers in the 90s, alongside the likes of Ron Trent (surprisingly absent from 'Teachers'), Glenn Underground, Derrick Carter, DJ Sneak, Gemini, Cajmere and co. Played alongside Daft Punk at their first show in the city, and 20 years later played a special Chicago Boiler Room 'Teachers' set with Paul Johnson, Mike Dearborn and more. Recorded on Cajual, Relief, Peacefrog, Djax-Up Beats and Ovum.

**CHECK OUT:**
**'A NEW BEGINNING'**

## DJ TONKA

Although Thomas and Guy-Man were only a few months younger than German artist Thomas-René Gerlach, when they started Daft Punk, Gerlach had already proved himself a prolific producer. Alongside his childhood pal Ian Pooley he had released a string of 12-inches as T'N'I and Space Cube, before venturing forth as DJ Tonka. His breezily ebullient 1995 track 'Feel' (on Force Inc.) has long been hailed as an explicit influence on 'Around the World', Tonka spent time in the studio with the pair the following year.

**CHECK OUT:**
**'FEEL'**

## DJ SKULL

Despite his foreboding name, DJ Skull is one of Chicago's most cherished underground DJs and producers. Without ever reaching the fame of some of his contemporaries mentioned here, Ron Maney has continued to preach his take on the Windy City sonic gospel. In truth, his harder, tougher aesthetic owes as much to techno as it does house – little wonder his productions found a home on Djax-Up Beats.

**CHECK OUT:**
**'STOMPING GROUNDS'**

## DJ PIERRE

The godfather of acid house. As one-third of pioneering Chicago trio Phuture, DJ Pierre (aka Nathaniel Pierre Jones), took his hometown sound and tweaked it via some extraordinary manipulation of the Roland 303. The group's signature 12-inch 'Acid Tracks' was hammered by Ron Hardy at the Music Box and eventually released on Trax Records (produced by Marshall Jefferson). Pierre went onto popularise the Wild Pitch-style of layering while DJing and producing. A true innovator.

**CHECK OUT:**
**'ACID TRACKS'**

## MIKE DEARBORN

Like DJ Skull, Mike Dearborn gave the lie to the assertion that Chicago in the 90s was purely about Jackin' house. Some of Dearborn's bone-crushing acid workouts were the equal of what was coming out of Europe at the time. Again, it was unsurprising that so many of Dearborn's releases at the time came out on Djax-Up Beats. Now a cop in his hometown, Dearborn remembers his brush with Daft Punk with affection.

**CHECK OUT:**
**'STRICTLY UNDERGROUND' EP**

"I wasn't aware I was mentioned until I bought the album. No-one told me. There had been other shout-out tracks where I'd been mentioned, but since this was such a big release it was definitely extra cool. I think my friends got a bigger kick out of it than I did because they would always walk up to me and say: 'Mike Dearborn in the house!' That was always fun. For me, what was a bigger thing was not that they had mentioned me, but so many people. They didn't blow up and then think fuck all the underground dudes. They gave respect and I thought that was pretty commendable. Sometimes Chicago forgets about certain people. So for someone like them, who made quality music, it's something to be proud of. It wasn't like they were some shit band. They put out good records.

"Just a week ago, some random guy, who's not in the scene, said: 'Hey man, I heard this record by that band Daft Punk and they mentioned your name.' He was really excited. I guess he had just heard it that week. The tracks acts as a primer for the younger generations? Yeah, I didn't even think about it from that perspective. That's absolutely right."

## TODD EDWARDS

Influenced by Todd Terry and Masters At Work, New Jersey's Todd Edwards went on to to popularise a sound as distinctive and singular as those his heroes had developed. His early cut-up, highly percussive releases on Nervous (particularly 'Guide My Soul') and i! Records laid down a blueprint for what would become speed and UK garage. Before the release of 'Homework', Daft Punk had been in touch to discuss a collaboration that never happened. Speaking to Ransom Note in 2017 he admitted he thought they weren't interested in his music. "And then I listened to 'Teachers' and I heard my name." Edwards went on to co-produce and sing the track 'Face to Face' on 'Discovery', repeating the trick on 'Fragments of Time' from 'Random Access Memories'.

**CHECK OUT:**
**'GUIDE MY SOUL' (RELEASED AS THE MESSENGER)**

## ROMANTHONY

Anthony Wayne Moore – Romanthony – might be best known for helping kick-start Daft Punk's second act when he sang on 'One More Time', but his haunting and infectious vocals had entranced clubland long before then. Releasing tracks on Azuli, 83 West Records and his own Black Male Records, his vocals were compared to Prince in some quarters. His collaborations with Daft Punk (he also sang on 'Discovery''s closing track, 'Too Long' and released 'Hold On' on Roulé) and a fruitful relationship with Glasgow Underground cemented his legacy. He tragically died from complications of kidney disease in 2013. He was just 45.

**CHECK OUT:**
**'HOLD ON'**

## CVO

Glenn Underground, or to give him the name Daft Punk used, Chicago's Very Own Glenn Underground (CVO), was

another integral member of Chicago's second coming of house. His USP was a deeper, more soulful, jazzy and reflective take on the four-four sound.
**CHECK OUT:**
**'C.V.O. TRANCE'**

## LUKE SLATER

Despite (or because of?) not hailing from 313 country, Luke Slater is one of the very best to ever do the techno thing. This figurative and literal distance from Detroit, gave Slater an edge as he emerged in the early-90s to become one of the UK's most notable proponents of rhythmical man-machine minimalism. His Planetary Assault Systems releases on Peacefrog still flick all the right switches today.
**CHECK OUT:**
**'PLANETARY FUNK VOL 1'**

## DERRICK CARTER

Cut Derrick Carter and he bleeds Chicago. This house music legend worked in the city's famous Gramophone Records store, assisted at Cajual, even going onto remix Chicago's post-rock icons Tortoise to memorable effect. But it's his relentlessly grinding and funky DJ sets and productions that would have warmed him to the two boys from Paris.
**CHECK OUT:**
**DERRICK CARTER VS SKYLA 'THE TRIP'**

## ROBERT HOOD

Techno godfather and one of the first recruits to join Underground Resistance, where his role was initially Minister of Information. Hood left the collective at the same time as Jeff Mills in 1992, working with him on Axis, before going on to great success as a solo producer, label boss (M-Plant) and DJ. His uncompromising and seditious aesthetic no doubt appealed to Thomas and Guy-Man.
**CHECK OUT:**
**'MINIMAL NATION'**

## PARRIS MITCHELL

A key figure in the early days of Dance Mania and the wider Chicago scene, Victor Parris Mitchell released records under the aliases Victor Romeo, Pleasure Inc and as part of The Dance Kings. But it was as the Parris Mitchell Project he released his most important track in the Daft Punk story. His 'Ghetto Shout Out', featuring Waxmaster, was the basis for 'Teachers'. It also took pride of place on Daft Punk's acclaimed 1997 BBC Essential Mix. Thomas and Guy-Man sent a gold disc of 'Teachers' to Mitchell and Waxmaster by way of thanks.
**CHECK OUT:**
**'GHETTO SHOUT OUT'**

## DAVE CLARKE

The Baron of Techno (hat tip, John Peel). Dave Clarke's uncompromising productions – particularly his 'Red' series of releases – and his evangelical passion for techno fascinated Daft Punk. Particularly Thomas.
**CHECK OUT:**
**'RED 2'**

"Thomas would sometimes come to my gigs at The Rex and chat. Thomas and I, at that time, with his Roulé tracks, were a lot more syncopated in how we were and how we approached music. I knew his passion for a lot of different music. Especially Chicago house and – to use that delightful English journalistic term for up-and-coming things, nascent – the nascent English techno scene that started around the early-to-mid-90s. They were fans of that.

"They explained to me – whenever I say they, assume it's Thomas because that's who I spoke to – that they did a reverse drum loop because they liked my reverse edits. That's when it says, 'Dave Clarke in the house', it goes backwards because it's a homage to that. I have to say that everyone they mentioned… it shows a deep knowledge. You have to remember this is pre-internet as well, or pre-usable internet, and it shows a deep knowledge and a love for the music.

"I wear it as a badge of pride. To this day, people still talk to me about it. There's a couple of things that get behest upon you when you have a long career and sometimes they last. I still feel the same way about John Peel, with what he called me. And with this track, it still lives on with people and actually I think for those that are newer to the music – those that maybe started getting into it in 2010 to 2020 – it gives them pointers in finding out how the music got to where it got to. Some real underground producers are in there who made tracks that you would really have had to dig for. Which shows their passion. I'm a cynical fucker, but this, I see it as truly from the heart. I don't see it as them trying to get themselves into something because they proved they didn't need that in the first place.

"Weirdly enough, I indirectly gave Thomas, and therefore Daft Punk, some sort of production tips. There was a compressor I was using called the Alessi 3630. I can remember it really clearly. I was at The Rex and Thomas was sitting at the back talking and he was asking how I got that pumping sound. And I told him about the Alessi 3630 compressor, and I believe they used it afterwards.

"I think the last time I saw Thomas would have been '97, maybe '98. Apparently he follows me on Facebook, but you never know who anyone is these days."

## ARMAND VAN HELDEN

Armand Van Helden's influence upon Daft Punk is obvious. Here was a prolific and singular talent who, whether via his own productions on such stellar labels as Strictly Rhythm, AV8, Nervous or Henry Street Music or his spellbinding remixes of Tori Amos (helping invent speed garage in the process), The Bucketheads and CJ Bolland took house music on a variety of colourful journeys. Alongside the likes of Daft Punk, Roger Sanchez, Todd Terry, DJ Sneak and more, Van Helden was a member of Da Mongoloids collective. He also remixed 'Da Funk' to stunning effect.

**CHECK OUT:**
**'WITCH DOKTOR'**

## ARMANDO

Every scene or city needs a facilitator. Armando Gallop was Chicago's enabler. According to those who knew him – and we're talking a who's who of Chicago talent – Armando helped join the dots between the city's first house wave in the 80s and its 90s crescendo. Ron Hardy, Paul Johnson, Mike Dearborn and DJ Deeon all say he helped get their respective careers off the ground. His DJ sets were legendary and his use of a 303 was unparalleled. His death from leukaemia in 1996 robbed Chicago – and the world – of a musical maestro and, even worse, an all-round loveable guy.

**CHECK OUT:**
**'LAND OF CONFUSION'**

## SURGEON

A true sonic scientist, Tony Child melded the kind of experimental soundscapes favoured by Faust, Coil, Can and co to the raw sounds coming out of Chicago and Detroit. He released tracks on key labels such as Tresor and Soma. His long-standing club night, House of God in Birmingham remains one of the key techno nights in the UK.

**CHECK OUT:**
**'MUGGERSCUM OUT'**

"Being mentioned was a mixture of flattery and bemusement, if I recall. I knew about them from the Soma releases – 'Da Funk' in particular. I remember at House of God their track 'Rollin' and Scratchin'' was played a lot.

"I'm fairly sure that I haven't met either of them – I could be wrong. I guess it was happening at that time with music. I did a release on Soma. It's a great list of names so I was very flattered and bemused to be included in that.

"At that time my music was making a lot of noise. I assume they liked it! I definitely relate to their love of that jackin' Chicago, raw, house kind of stuff. My guess is that they heard a bit of that in what I was doing and they connected with that. I think there was a mutual appreciation of that raw Chicago sound.

"People still mention it occasionally – when they split up for instance. In a way my name is hidden in there. They pronounce my name in a really bizarre way. I think some people don't realise they're saying Surgeon. They think they're saying 'Ser-gi-on' or something like that. It's hidden in a way."

# DAFT PUNK GET BUGGED OUT!

Before the masks, six Grammy wins and the Pyramid, there was a time when Daft Punk were as fêted for their incredible DJ performances as their music. Some of their most euphoric and celebrated appearances came at Jockey Slut's sister club, Bugged Out!. **John Burgess** remembers those halcyon nights...

I don't have any photographic evidence that Daft Punk played at Bugged Out!, but they did, four times (five if you count their record box as an appearance). The only device I remember using in the 90s was a disposable 'fun camera'. I had one on me when they DJed at Nation in Liverpool in 1998; I managed to get a shot of the back of Green Velvet's head while he was watching them play ('Camera's ready prepare to flash…') but not one of Thomas and Guy-Manuel. It wasn't that they were being famously camera shy or wearing masks, no one bothered to take photos back then and it seemed especially boring to take snaps of people playing records. But despite the lack of visual evidence I still clearly remember what happened over 20 years ago.

## BUGGED OUT! AT SANKEYS SOAP, MANCHESTER: 1995, 1997

Jockey Slut had been the first to interview Daft Punk in 1994. We loved their most techno track – 'Alive' – and the quantum leap they took artistically with 'Da Funk' the following year. Although 'Da Funk' didn't get played as often as you'd expect at Bugged Out! – as it was so slow – everyone knew it was a genius lone wolf prowling around a forest of 130bpm techno tracks.

We didn't book many live acts in the first year of Bugged Out! (which started in November 1994), but The Advent and Secret Knowledge had performed and Sankeys had a stage at the end of the rectangular room begging for more artists to tread its boards.

Despite their small arsenal of tracks Daft Punk were to visit the UK to play live for their Glaswegian label Soma one weekend in October 1995 and we agreed to take them on the Friday night. It was a fiver in and they were supported by label boss Stuart McMillan who shared our appetite for the afterparties, though the two young Parisians did not align with their Glaswegian boss' hedonist bent. They turned up with their studio kit and were super shy. Pedro Winter, a relatively new friend of theirs, did most of the talking.

"Guy-Man was very much in his own world," Winter remembers. "Thomas was more easy to speak with but I was definitely the shield. This is always how I took my job, you know, I tried to protect them."

In an age before laptops, they brought over some impressive studio devices as Winter recalls: "There were no computers on stage. We were putting the equipment into towels, into suitcases, so it was completely freestyle and not well organised."

We watched the show side stage, a simple set up – two blokes behind studio gear laid out on tables – and I remember the gnarly 'Rollin' & Scratchin'' being the highlight that night, it particularly suited where Bugged Out! was that year. Pedro also remembers they played 'Short Circuit' which they didn't release until the 'Discovery' album.

The next time they played for us at Sankeys was in January 1997 the week after 'Homework' had been released. Their approach then was similar to what Richie Hawtin was doing with his dex and fx and 909 tours, or Jeff Mills, who was regularly adding drum machines to complement the vinyl. It was a glorified DJ set which they termed 'The Daft Mix'. Since the album their arsenal of tunes was vastly extended and they had some major bombs to drop including other artists like Paul Johnson and Armand Van Helden.

Pedro: "I loved it when they were doing back-to-back, you can feel Thomas definitely playing more disco, Guy-Man was harder. The Daft Mix was their DJ skills but in a new way with samplers and a drum machine. It was still exciting for people to see hardware on stage."

Later that year, in November, they played to twice as many people at Manchester Academy. I met the duo backstage and they gave me a big box of plastic 'robber' masks and asked if I'd hand them out to the crowd. They were to wear a mask from the box on stage themselves and wanted to blur the lines between themselves and the audience. Wish I'd kept one now, but then I didn't take any photos of that event either.

### BUGGED OUT!'S 4TH BIRTHDAY AT NATION, LIVERPOOL: 1998

Pedro Winter was now Daft Punk's manager and had become known as the 'No' man. They didn't have a DJ agent so we – and everyone else – would call his office landline, or fax him, to ask if Daft Punk would come and DJ at our club nights. By 1998, the answer was always 'no'. It was the year following the hot fuss of 'Homework' and Thomas hitting big with two of the songs of the summer – 'Music Sounds Better With You' and his Jane Fonda-sampling bootleg 'Gym Tonic'. Both were a far cry from 'Rollin' & Scratchin'' but at least one was still a masterpiece of French Touch.

Bugged Out! had moved to the huge Nation in Liverpool when Sankeys closed abruptly in 1998. Nation was a multi-room barn that held nearly 3,500. We'd filled it on our first night in September with The Chemical Brothers DJing but our fourth birthday fell in November and we were keen for Daft Punk to play, or even Thomas to come and add some stardust to the night. But Pedro said no. So we proceeded with a line-up that would still fill a huge room today: Green Velvet, Harvey and Surgeon.

Then a week before the event Pedro called our office and asked if we would still like Thomas for the event as he fancied playing his new Roulé material live to what he knew would be the right audience. We said yes to the No Man. The thing is – and this is unbelievable to think now, when artists have agents that broker huge fees, 5 star hotels and idiosyncratic riders – we told Pedro, quite honestly, that we had spent all our budget. He came back to us later that day and said Thomas wasn't doing it for the money, but could we cover a train fare and hotel. Yes, of course we could. Hey, we'd even throw a hot meal in for him.

Then the following day Pedro called again: "Guy-Man is feeling a bit left out and wants to come and join in. Are you OK if he comes too and you can bill this as Thomas Bangalter – live and Daft Punk DJs?" We agreed to cover another train fare and hotel room and it was confirmed.

Back in 1998 there was no widely-used internet so the only way we could get this incredible news out, with days to go, was to send someone out to fly poster the city adding A4 sheets bearing the news to our existing posters. To say 'Thanks' to the chaps we asked the (4 star) hotel if we could be let into their rooms before they arrived and we laid a recently-released Beach Boys 'Pet Sounds' CD box set on each of their pillows (Brian Wilson being one of their 'Teachers' and inspiration for their first band name Darlin'). They joined us for dinner, Thomas bashful when we told him we had named him our No.2 artist of the year in the upcoming issue of Jockey Slut, one place behind Norman Cook.

What I remember from the sets: Thomas played for about 20 minutes concluding with a mix of 'Music Sounds Better With You' and Madonna's 'Holiday'. Madonna would later incorporate this 'mash up' into her own live set – under the guidance of musical director Stuart Price – on her Drowned World tour. Then Daft Punk began their set with a nod to the occasion with Stevie Wonder's 'Happy Birthday'. It was quite a moment. And at least I got a photo of the back of Green Velvet's head to mark the occasion.

Pedro: "It's important to share these stories because people think everything was controlled and organised by an agent. But the relationship was really unique and special and they know they owe you a lot at the beginning and the good thing with Daft Punk is they have a big heart."

### BUGGED OUT! AT AMNESIA, IBIZA: 1999

We often shot ourselves in the foot financially in the 90s by being a bit ahead of the curve with bookings and events. One painful example was our season in Ibiza in 1999. We had been offered the Saturdays at Amnesia and being green about the island we had no idea this night of the week should be given a wide berth – it's the changeover day for most young holidaymakers. We also booked a lot of techno acts that were regulars at our night in Liverpool – but they were not seen as typically Ibizan at the time. Muzik magazine even printed: "Techno in Ibiza? Who cares."

Obviously people did care with Sven Väth's Cocoon soon becoming one of the island's 00s success stories while we lost a fortune. The club always looked packed but we found out later we were entertaining a lot of hospitality workers who were let in for free, the Saturday being their night off.

We had Daft Punk booked to play the terrace on the night Jeff Mills was in the main arena and we were en route to a restaurant we'd booked for the DJs prior to the night when Pedro Winter called. Thomas and Guy-Man had left the villa they'd all been staying in for the week and departed the island. It turns out Romanthony was in Europe and this was the only chance they had to go and record what would become 'One More Time' with him.

We still gathered at the restaurant, Jeff Mills, his French DJ friend Frederick, Jeff's manager and Pedro. Talk soon turned to the fact that Thomas and Guy-Man had left their record boxes behind at the villa for Pedro to bring back to Paris. So Daft Punk's records were still on the island and there were two French men sat before me who could both DJ.

Fast forward a few hours and Pedro and Frederick are playing on the terrace of Amnesia. I don't think anyone in the crowd would've got the memo it was not the genuine article, there was no social media to announce the news widely. So if you thought you saw Daft Punk play at Amnesia in 1999 I'm afraid you didn't, though you would've heard their records played by two French men.

Pedro: "It went well, I have a good memory of it. No one threw tomatoes."

## BUGGED OUT! AT FABRIC, LONDON: 1999

For their non-appearance in Ibiza we were surprised that Pedro contacted us to offer us a replacement gig. "Oh yes, I remember, it was to apologise," Pedro recalls. "Very Daft Punk."

Similar to Liverpool the previous year, they just asked for their travel to be settled and hotel (though this time they chose the swanky Metropolitan, the famed celeb hangout Liam Gallagher or All Saints would frequent or fall out of).

The hastily-made, last-minute notice to announce Daft Punk for Bugged Out's 4th birthday bash

It was one of the first-ever nights at fabric and they were excited to see this much lauded new venue. It was a historic night for those that attended, one person in particular was inspired: Erol Alkan spent the whole night on the dancefloor and then never missed one of our parties, until he started playing for us on the other side of the decks.

This was to be Daft Punk's final show for us. We came close to having Thomas at one of our parties again in 2002, when we moved our residency to The End. We'd booked Together to DJ – Thomas and DJ Falcon – who had released 'Together' and 'So Much Love To Give' on Roulé. But sadly Thomas cancelled the week of the show with an ear infection that would become problematic and hasten the end of his DJing career.

We tried again for our 15th birthday in 2009 and received a respectful email reply from him, thanking us for our support in the early years but stating that he had hung up his headphones for good.

“I WOULD LOVE TO WORK WITH DAFT PUNK... [I’M] JUST WAITING FOR THEM TO RETURN MY CALL.”

Madonna/Ask Madonna Almost Anything (Reddit)/2013

# Roulé-in' The Airwaves

Thomas Bangalter's side project became the definitive imprint of the French Touch scene. **Ben Cardew** charts the label's progress and gives his verdict on every Roulé release...

Thomas Bangalter's Roulé was, in its eight-year burst of activity, a buy-on-sight label. You didn't need to know the artist involved; you didn't need to hear the record first; Roulé's distinctive gold record sleeve was a guarantee of quality, like the purple Warp Records design before it. And Roulé never - or *almost* never - disappointed, with only the label's final release, Bangalter's 'Outrage', dipping below its usual gargantuan quality.

For dance music scholars, Roulé offers a kind of alternative history to Daft Punk's trajectory. Bangalter's production was at the beating heart of Roulé, at a time when Daft Punk was making the leap into the major leagues. Bangalter released four solo 12-inches and one solo album through Roulé.

The label's biggest release – Stardust's 'Music Sounds Better With You' – saw the talkative half of Daft Punk hook up with Alan Braxe and Benjamin Diamond; Together, who released two records on Roulé, comprised Bangalter and DJ Falcon; and Bangalter also provided remixes for Alan Braxe and Roy Davis Jr. on two early Roulé releases.

On the three Roulé records where Bangalter didn't have a hand in the actual production – The Buffalo Bunch's 'Buffalo Club', Romanthony's 'Hold On' and DJ Falcon's 'Hello My Name Is DJ Falcon' – you can still sense his A&R sensibilities, Bangalter's love for house music that moves the soul and tickles the feet shining through.

It is no surprise, then, that a lot of the music on Roulé sounds like Daft Punk, particularly on Bangalter's first release, 'Trax on Da Rocks'. What is more surprising, perhaps, are the alternative routes and occasional blind alleys that Roulé allowed Bangalter to explore, from the gnarled breakbeats on 'What To Do' to the extreme minimalism of Together's 'So Much Love to Give'. These are paths Daft Punk could have gone down if they chose to. Now that Daft Punk are no more, these excursions are more important than ever.

ROULÉ 301

## THOMAS BANGALTER 'TRAX ON DA ROCKS' [1995]

Thomas Bangalter's debut 12-inch ranks alongside his finest work, both solo and in Daft Punk, with five tracks of jaw-dropping quality and breadth. The songs on 'Trax On Da Rocks' kicked off Roulé in an electric, eclectic fashion, running from the 'Homework'-adjacent funk of 'On Da Rocks' – a kind of cocktail hour 'Da Funk' – to the vicious, elastic and somehow very European techno of 'Ventura'. But it is 'What To Do', the EP's most unusual moment, that gets the most traction these days, the track's stuttering, breaks-and-bounce house a portal into another world far from Daft Punk, where drum'n'bass meets the Chicago house thump of DJ Deeon.

ROULÉ 302

## THOMAS BANGALTER 'SPINAL SCRATCH' [1996]

For all of the label's undoubted quality, you can see Roulé as a way for Thomas Bangalter to let off steam, away from the major label expectations of the Daft Punk day job. 'Spinal Scratch' is perfect in this regard, with the track marking one of the most ludicrous, yet inspired, moments in Bangalter's career, as he kicks, mauls and manhandles a couple of (pretty much unrecognisable) samples from George Benson's 'The World Is a Ghetto' around in the mix, until they beg for forgiveness, interspersed with the kind of overblown, rough-cut scratching noises that could have come from a children's toy. It's dumb, delightful, outlandish and pretty much perfect. The B-side, meanwhile, serves up pure beats.

ROULÉ 303

## ALAN BRAXE 'VERTIGO' [1997]

Roulé was a family affair: Alan Braxe, (who met Daft Punk on the Paris rave scene in the early-90s) was the first external artist to release music on the label; and his cousin, DJ Falcon, would both record solo for Roulé and form Together with Thomas Bangalter. 'Vertigo', Braxe's debut single, is a brilliantly modulated, constantly shifting take on the French Touch sound, with drums that twitch and shift like a sprinter's leg muscles. Bangalter's 'Virgo Edit', on the B-side, pared the song down to an unsettling intensity that absolutely destroyed dancefloors. Some entrepreneurial bootlegger then strapped Bangalter's edit to the Beastie Boys' 'Intergalactic' and dancefloors went off *even further*.

ROULÉ 304

## ROY DAVIS JR. 'ROCK SHOCK' [1998]

Roy Davis Jr. is a Chicago house hero, who Daft Punk paid homage to on 'Homework's' 'Teachers'. But bizarrely, on the original mix of 'Rock Shock', he turned in what sounds like his own, not entirely satisfactory, take on the French house sound, with guitar licks, filters and laconic groove. Bangalter's 'Start-Stop' remix on the B-side rescues the day, however – its weird drum machine echoes and fitful rhythms showcasing one of the most unique brains in house music. It's a nightmare to mix – and yet DJs still flocked to it, such was the song's quality.

ROULÉ 305

## STARDUST 'MUSIC SOUNDS BETTER WITH YOU' [1998]

For its fifth release, Roulé casually dropped a one-sided 12-inch that would almost immediately be recognised as a house music classic, going on to top the charts around Europe on its major label re-release. 'Music Sounds Better With You', the only song ever released by Stardust (aka Thomas Bangalter, Alan Braxe and singer Benjamin Diamond), was effortlessly profound in its ode to the simple pleasure of enjoying music with friends, its six-line vocal and guitar loop (taken from Chaka Khan's 'Fate') tapping into eternal truths and fundamental joys. The group were offered $3m to make an album; they turned it down; and so 'Music Sounds Better With You' lives on in singular perfection.

ROULÉ 305RMX

## STARDUST 'MUSIC SOUNDS BETTER WITH YOU' [REMIXES] [1998]

... Or not *quite* singular: Roulé also released a 12-inch of 'Music Sounds Better With You' remixes, courtesy of Chateau Flight, Bibi and Dim (aka Dimitri From Paris) and DJ Sneak, who turned in two versions. 'Music Sounds Better With You', of all tunes, really didn't *need* remixing, although DJ Sneak's remix and dub are satisfactorily intense, shaking down the 'Fate' loop like a school bully after your lunch money.

ROULÉ 306

## THOMAS BANGALTER 'TRAX ON DA ROCKS VOL. 2' [1998]

After the brilliance of Volume I, 'Trax On Da Rocks Vol. 2' had a lot to live up to and Bangalter's third solo record wasn't *quite* there. 'Trax On Da Rocks Vol. 2' is a strong release but the five tracks don't add that much to the idiosyncratic vision of house music that Bangalter so brilliantly expressed on Volume 1. That said, 'Colossus' lives up to its name, building a gargantuan wall of house-d up noise, while 'Extra Dry' would lead Daft Punk down fascinating new paths, when Slum Village sampled it on 'Raise It Up', the first examples of the US hip hop community paying heed to the French house sound.

SCRATCHÉ 701

## THE BUFFALO BUNCH 'BUFFALO CLUB' [1998]

The Buffalo Bunch's basic, but hugely exciting, disco house mélange was perhaps better suited to Guy-Manuel De Homem Christo's Crydamoure label (for whom they also recorded) than Roulé's more experimental turf – and not just because Play Paul, one half of The Buffalo Bunch, was Guy-Man's brother. But that is to take nothing away from 'Buffalo Club', the only release on Roulé sub label Scratché (as in, Roulé and Scratché), whose lolloping bass line, tightly-coiled disco drums and nagging, addictive sample combine for a nigh-on irresistible groove, that proved very popular in Paris clubs.

ROULÉ 307

## ROMANTHONY 'HOLD ON' [1999]

Daft Punk had long expressed their love for Romanthony, aka American house genius Anthony Wayne Moore, eventually meeting him at the 1996 Winter Music Conference. Romanthony would famously contribute vocals to 'One More Time' and 'Too Long' on 'Discovery', Daft Punk's second album. But before that, Roulé re-released Romanthony's 'Hold On', a gospel house masterpiece of emotional resistance, first released in 1994 on Romanthony's Black Male Records. The full-on vocal and R&B influences make 'Hold On' something of an outlier in the Roulé catalogue, but it is a particularly gorgeous, silk-wrapped sore thumb among the label's more forthright moments.

ROULÉ 308

## DJ FALCON 'HELLO MY NAME IS DJ FALCON' [1999]

DJ Falcon, aka Stéphane Quême, is an important name in Daft Punk history, contributing production to 'Contact' on 'Random Access Memories' and teaming up with Thomas as Together. First, though, was his solo debut on Roulé, four tracks of perfectly realised filter disco that were as utterly seductive as they were unoriginal (with the exception of the brilliantly diverting mobile phone mic drop on 'Honeymoon'). 'Hello My Name Is DJ Falcon' sounds *precisely* like what people expect of French house music from the 90s. But it is arguable whether anyone has ever done the filter disco sound with more perfect craft and ineffable nous than Falcon.

TOGETHER

## TOGETHER 'TOGETHER' [2000]

The two records by Together – Thomas Bangalter and DJ Falcon – offer a fascinating vision of minimalism in house music. That this baton was never really taken up may be a tribute to how astoundingly well Together nailed the sound in their brief recording career. 'Together', their debut single, is an absolute classic in this regard, bringing together two perfect samples (from Slave's electro funk anthem 'Because of You'), a model synth bass line and very little else, in seven minutes of gloriously uplifting house music that ranks among Bangalter's very best work. Daft Punk would later use 'Together' as part of the encore on their Alive 2007 tour.

TOGETHER 2

## TOGETHER 'SO MUCH LOVE TO GIVE' [2002]

'So Much Love To Give', which followed 'Together', is breathtaking in its audacity, taking minimalism to extreme and ultimately exhilarating/infuriating new heights. Over close to 11 minutes, one brief sample – two bars taken from The Real Thing's 'Love's Such a Wonderful Thing' – loops around again and again and AGAIN as Bangalter and Falcon play around with their drum machines and filters. It is simultaneously entirely stupid and brilliantly clever, like a Ramones' B-side remade by Andy Warhol or Robert Hood's minimalist electronic vision played out in glorious jumbotron Day-Glo. Naturally, it became massive.

ROULÉ LP 01

## THOMAS BANGALTER 'IRREVERSIBLE' OST [2002]

Roulé's only album release was the soundtrack to Gaspar Noé's controversial film 'Irréversible', which pairs a number of previously released Bangalter tracks with nine new solo songs, Gustav Mahler's 'Symphony N° 9 In D Major – Adagio', Etienne Daho's 'Mon Manège A Moi' and Beethoven's 'Symphony N° 7 In A Major Op. 92'. Musically, the older Bangalter tracks are the highlights, while the vortex-dark new songs work best in the context of the film, their sparse, foreboding drones reflecting the malevolent atmosphere. You could see the album as a cousin to Daft Punk's 'Tron: Legacy' soundtrack, were the second 'Tron' film to take place entirely within a world of corrupted computer disks and degraded digital filth.

ROULÉ 309

## THOMAS BANGALTER 'OUTRAGE' [2003]

Roulé bowed out in 2003 with 'Outrage', three tracks taken from the 'Irréversible' soundtrack. 'Night Beats' and 'Paris by Night' are essentially the same song, a combination of a disinclined disco beat and spiky synth riff, while 'Outrage' is a barbarous techno number that slowly succumbs to a steel bath of distortion. The labours of 'Outrage' confirm the rather unfortunate fact that Roulé came in with its best record and bowed out with its worst. And yet, for all that, it's still a pretty great record, all brooding rage and headache intensity.

# A Cry For Survival

Crydamoure, Guy-Manuel de Homem-Christo's label, alongside Eric Chédeville, only released a handful of 12-inches. But each one was beautifully-rendered filtered house. And that, says **Ben Cardew**, was more than enough...

Crydamoure and Roulé, the record labels set up by Daft Punk's Guy-Manuel de Homem-Christo and Thomas Bangalter in the 1990s as an outlet for their increasingly voracious activity, were like two estranged brothers: they may have come from the same stock – in this case house music – but their characters were very different indeed. Roulé, Bangalter's label, was experimental, sometimes harsh, packed with ideas and rather unfocused; Crydamoure, which De Homem-Christo founded with Eric Chédeville, was sunny, laidback and a heap of fun, its catalogue laser-focused on the sweet sound of filter disco.

In this way, the two labels reflected the characters of their owners: Bangalter was the permanently curious musical genius, always open to new ideas; De Homem-Christo was the group's ears, with an unfailing talent for picking exactly the right sound or musical moment. Bangalter is the kind of person you would take out to an experimental dance piece; De Homem-Christo would know all the best nightclubs in town.

Crydamoure grew out of the ashes of Pumpking Records, the label that Parisian producer Eric Chédeville founded with Médéric Nébinger (who later found French Touch fame as Funky Derrick)

Eric Chédeville in the Crydamoure studio

in the early 1990s. Chédeville, an old-school Paris raver, first met a teenage Thomas Bangalter through Nebinger, whose mother was friends with Thomas' mum. A few years later, when Daft Punk had started in earnest, Bangalter and De Homem-Christo went to the Pumpking studios – a party spot as much as a place of business – in the Paris suburb of Nanterre with their first DAT tape, which they wanted to test out on a crowd.

A friendship developed between Chédeville and De Homem-Christo and, as Pumpking fell apart in 1996, Guy-Man asked Chédeville to form a new label with him. "The only goal we had was to do the music we liked, without having to ask people to release it," Chédeville explains. At the time, Daft Punk had yet to release their debut album. But they were the toast of the Parisian dance music scene and Guy-Man could have launched a label with pretty much anyone. You get the feeling that he chose Chédeville – at least in part – because of those Pumpking parties. As Chédeville describes it, Crydamoure was equal parts social club and label, with the Crydamoure studio in Neuilly becoming a hive of activity, both professional and more relaxed.

Chédeville says he initially suggested cri-cri d'amour as a name for their fledgling label – in the popular French sitcom 'Hélène et les Garçons', Christian Roquier, one of the lead characters, was known as 'cri-cri d'amour' – only for Guy-Man to suggest the rather more poetic Crydamoure (cri d'amour means cry of love in English). Guy-Man also designed the very elegant Crydamoure logo, which looks like a medieval coat of arms crossed with a desert hallucination.

The idea of the label, according to Chédeville, was to do something more than just music. "Every Christmas we did big parties in Paris and we asked for people to come with presents for children," he says. "We wanted to do some humanist things with the music. Not just the music."

Guy-Man and Chédeville also started to work together musically as Le Knight Club and it was this group that would launch Crydamoure in 1997 with the brilliant two-track 12-inch 'Santa Claus'/'Holiday on Ice', a record that managed to utterly nail the Crydamoure party aesthetic at first try. 'Holiday on Ice' saunters along like 'Around the World' on slightly wobbly crutches, with something admirably silly and yet utterly irresistible in its lolloping funk pace, while 'Santa Claus' has the swinging beats, disco samples and filter effects that Daft Punk fans would recognise from 'Musique'. There's nothing particularly complicated about the two tracks. But – as many of the French Touch latecomers would soon discover – sounding this louche and laidback is *much* more difficult than you might imagine, a tribute to Chédeville's production nous and Guy-Man's particular musical focus.

Chédeville hasn't spoken to Guy-Man in years. But he is still clearly in awe of his erstwhile musical partner, who he says has one of the best pairs of musical ears he has ever encountered. When Guy-Man says something is right, Chédeville explains, you know it is right. But until you find exactly the right mix, Guy-Man isn't happy. "Guy-Man can stay three, four, five hours to make the perfect rhythm on a drum machine," he says. "I have never seen anyone spend so much time."

'Santa Claus' and 'Holiday on Ice' have the feel of the best night out you could possibly imagine, the fabled adventure where there was no queue at the club door, the DJ was entirely on point and the night bus took you straight back to your home. These two songs – and the work of Crydamoure more generally – are the sound of a good time itself, fun made musically manifest, a result that was not entirely coincidental.

"At the beginning it was funny because we had a nice studio in Neuilly, just beside Paris," Chédeville explains. "And we put the studio in a really, really small room, around seven square metres. We had a big room. And in this big room, we had parties. So we spent a lot of time partying. And when we came back to the studio, Guy-Man was doing lots of rhythms with the SP1200 (sampler). And we were sampling also, lots of samples, Guy-Man was playing some guitar… and we had some bass and we used also lots of guitar pedals." Other key pieces of gear, in what was a fairly basic set up, included the Ensoniq ASR10 sampling keyboard and the Roland S760 sampler.

For 'Santa Claus', Chédeville explains, Guy-Man created a rhythm and they used an inverse sample. But then they hit a creative block. "It stayed like that for a long time, a few months," Chédeville says. "We felt like something was missing but we didn't know what. Every day, we were listening to the loops. And we said: 'Ah it's a nice loop; something is missing but it is a nice loop.' During a few months, every day we listened to the loops and one day Thomas [Bangalter] came to the studio, he listened to the loops and he made the bass [line] with the Minimoog and the record was finished." (That 'Santa Claus' is, effectively, the work of Daft Punk plus Chédeville, seems obvious when you know it: 'Santa Claus' could easily have slotted onto 'Homework', right after 'Phoenix', or perhaps in-between 'Burnin'' and 'Indo Silver Club'.)

Making Le Knight Club records was fun, Chédeville says. But it was also hard work, thanks in part to Guy-Man's perfectionism. "Guy-Man always wanted to listen to the structure [of the song] from the beginning," he says. "So, when you have to check a break, when it's at five minutes, you know, you have to listen from the beginning to see if the break is cool… That is a very serious part. But globally it was fun."

Le Knight Club would go on to release eight 12-inches on Crydamoure between 1997 and 2002, their music never straying too far from the beautifully-rendered filter house of their debut. This was a time of startling innovation for Daft Punk, who went from the Chicago house/Detroit techno stylings of their 1997 debut album 'Homework' to the glisteningly futuristic disco metal sound of 'Discovery', which was released in 2001 and is generally acclaimed as one of the most innovative records of the last 20 years. Roulé, too, had a series of dazzling releases that topped

"We put the studio in a really, really small room. We had a big room. And in this big room we had parties. So we spent a lot of time partying."

the global charts (Stardust's 'Music Sounds Better With You') and perfected the minimal house style (Together's 'So Much Love to Give').

Crydamoure neither topped the charts nor particularly pushed the envelope. But, according to Chédeville, it was never really meant to. They made "the music we wanted to hear", he says, and that meant brilliantly realised house music, designed for the clubs. The genius in Le Knight Club came not from doing something different; but from doing the same thing, over and over, without ever losing interest. They were like the Ramones to Daft Punk's The Clash, a band focused to the point of obsession on one sound. The songs on Le Knight Club's final 12-inch on Crydamoure, a three-track EP, 'Soul Bells'/'Palm Beat'/'Tropicall', could have fit very snugly onto their first. And that suited fans just fine.

To put it another way, Daft Punk represented the experimental cocktail that might change your palate forever or make you grimace with disgust, while Le Knight Club were the ever reliable gin and tonic. There is something incredibly honest in Le Knight Club's work and this may be the reason it has aged so well. Le Knight Club may have taken their filter disco cues from DJ Sneak, Todd Terry and Daft Punk themselves. But once they got started, they managed to entirely own this sound. Le Knight Club, essentially, were the sound of late-90s/early-2000s Paris, even as Daft Punk's own work took them further from the dancefloor.

The same can be said for Crydamoure's output as a whole. On the one hand, the label was notable for the way it introduced DJ Sneak to the Daft Punk world, with 'Intergalactik Disko', Crydamoure's fourth release, featuring a DJ Sneak remix of Le Knight Club on its B-side, some three years before Sneak appeared on Daft Punk's 'Discovery', where he wrote the lyrics to and co-produced 'Digital Love'. Crydamoure also released a record ['White Winds'] by Paul Johnson, one of Daft Punk's Teachers and another influential Chicago producer. But by and large the label focused on a tight-knit group of French producers who worked together in various configurations.

The Buffalo Bunch (the only group to record for both Roulé and Crydamoure) comprised Play Paul, aka Guy-Man's brother Paul, and Romain Séo, who also recorded as Raw Man and We In Music. Both would release solo records on Crydamoure. Chédeville recorded as Crydamoure, releasing a joint 12-inch with Raw Man; Archigram (aka Julien Mallart and Nicolas Trichet) released three records on Crydamoure; Deelat (aka David Girier-Dufournier) released one 12-inch for the label, as did The Eternals and Sedat The Turkish Avenger. Crydajam, meanwhile, was an amorphous group that seemed to be home to pretty much all of the artists on the label in one form or another. And that, pretty much, was that, the label's output based around the work of a dozen people.

"We were not looking around. We were doing what we wanted to do," says Chédeville. "We were just out doing the sound we wanted to hear. We wanted to see the girls dancing."

He compares Crydamoure to 'a band', in the sense of a group of friends rather than a musical collaboration. "I came from the music industry, I was there when I was really young." Chédeville explains. "So I always listened to every tape I received, because I have this kind of respect, you know, for people. But in reality, we never signed a tape that I received... Everything that we signed came from people we know."

You can hear this closeness in Crydamoure's music. Their bands weren't interchangeable, exactly: The Buffalo Bunch had the best bass lines, for example, and The Eternals a winning sense of humour, responsible for one of the most hilarious songs in house music: 'Wrath of Zeus', in which the titular god gets annoyed by a couple who decide to leave a nightclub and sentences them to spend their eternal life "in a never-ending dance on this floor". But the Crydamoure acts certainly shared a sound, based around the satisfyingly limited palette of house beats, funk bass lines and filter effects.

Crydamoure acts took their music seriously. But there was something endearingly goofy about the label's output at times, too. Archigram's 'Doggystyle', for example, managed to transform The Stooges' proto-punk classic 'I Wanna Be Your Dog' into a bumping dancefloor number, a move simultaneously audacious and rather sweet, as if nothing could escape from Crydamoure's filter vortex.

And if Crydamoure never had a hit to rival Stardust's 'Music Sounds Better With You', then it came close to commercial fame, apparently passing up the opportunity to sign Modjo's club anthem 'Lady' on the basis that it was too pop. "Romain Tranchart [half of Modjo, with vocalist Yann Destagnol] is a really good friend of ours," says Chédeville. "He's still a good friend. I saw him two days ago, you know? But it ['Lady'] was too much pop for us."

Tranchart came to Crydamoure with 'Lady'. "And we listened to the music. We said: 'Oh, it's a really good track, we love the track, but the voice is too commercial for us so we can't release it.' You have to understand that at this time we are really: 'Fucking money, fucking system, fucking everything', you know?"

The contrast between this rather nihilist attitude and the major label system in which Daft Punk were operating must have been stark. Daft Punk may have imposed their own rules on the music industry, signing a contract with Virgin Records that gave them large amounts of freedom over their music and their image. But they were a huge commercial act, nonetheless, one that had far outgrown the Parisian party scene that Crydamoure was soundtracking.

Chédeville claims that Guy-Man was, at the time, maybe "more in love" with Crydamoure than with Daft Punk. (Without asking Guy-Man about this, it is impossible to tell if this is actually true. So for the moment we should take it as an anecdote.) "Daft Punk started with 'Da Funk' and 'Homework'. It was very good but after that it started to become commercial, you know?" says Chédeville.

"Crydamoure, it was really cool at the studio… with a really, really good vibe," Chédeville adds. "Thomas also has a good vibe. But Thomas is a really serious guy. He thinks about business, he thinks about strategy, he thinks about everything, you know? He really is a genius. Crydamoure was more comfortable. We have no strategy. We don't know what we are going to do in one month, we were just living."

'Waves 2', released in 2003, would be Crydamoure's last commercial release and it proved a fitting tribute to the label, with 15 of its greatest hits mixed into 70 minutes of pure French Touch delight that remains perfect for dancing, socialising or just wandering energetically around town, looking at the lights as the sun slowly sets.

Most of the Crydamoure bands would go on to release music on other labels. But it never quite felt the same, separated from their disco band of brothers. De Homem-Christo and Chédeville, meanwhile, went on to remix Daft Punk's 'Technologic' as Le Knight Club, also producing a handful of remixes for other artists. And if their musical collaboration slowed as Crydamoure itself faded, then there was time for one fairly spectacular encore, with Chédeville and Daft Punk sharing songwriting credits on The Weeknd's 2016 hit 'I Feel It Coming', which has more than 1.3 billion Spotify plays.

The track came about, according to Chédeville, after Guy-Man returned to Paris from the US in 2013 and the two friends decided to make music again. "At this period, he came every day to my studio in Paris," he relates. "I was living near Paris, in the top of a tower, on the 41st floor. It was really amazing place. And Guy-Man came every day."

'I Feel It Coming' is not the only music that emerged from this time. In 2015 'The Fight', a new song by Le Knight Club, surfaced online, apparently taken from the Algerian film 'Les Portes du Soleil: Algérie pour Toujours' (known as 'Gates of the Sun: Algeria Forever' in English). The song, a moody synth number that weighs in at around two minutes, was apparently intended to soundtrack a fight sequence with Mike Tyson, although it ended up in a nightclub scene in the finished film.

The chances of a full-on Crydamoure/Le Knight Club revival, however, appear to be nil. At the time of writing, Guy-Man has yet to make his first post-Daft Punk move and Chédeville says he hasn't talked to his former musical partner in years, although he remains philosophical about the label's legacy.

"The music corresponds to a time, when the time changes, the music is not the same," he says. "It is a philosophical reflection. It's not about the quality of the music. I could say the same about the Rolling Stones, the Beatles or Earth, Wind And Fire. The music was really cool, it was really amazing in '95, in 2000, in 2004. But now it is finished. This isn't bad, what I am saying. It's not negative."

Crydamoure's music – like Roulé's – is not to be found on streaming services or download stores. And the 12-inch records go for high – if not eye-watering – prices. But you can find Crydamoure's music easily enough online. Chédeville says people who are interested in Le Knight Club should start off with 'Boogie Shell', from 1999, or 2002's 'Rhumba', a twisting, turning, funk number that also kicks off 'Waves 2'.

Wherever your starting point, though, you will be unlikely to turn back: Crydamoure's output is one of the most convincingly finite of any record label. A party on vinyl where the drinks are always cold and the house never less than funky.

As Daft Punk became the crème de la crème of dance music with their 1997 debut album 'Homework', a particularly Gallic take on house music was winning over dancefloors and DJs around the world. **Kate Hutchinson** looks back upon the music that came to be known as French Touch, discovering what, exactly, it was, and how it came to take over the world...

# The French Touch Revolution

At the start of the 90s, a revolution was stirring in France, and it was coming from the rave. House and techno had reached Paris, igniting the country's predilection for four-to-the-floor beats and all-night excess in forests and dilapidated chateaus on the outskirts of the city.

The DJs, musicians and recording engineers inspired by the jackin' music of Chicago, Detroit and New York emanating from the makeshift sound systems soon retreated to their studios. There they began to construct their own takes on these era-defining sounds. But not before splicing them with home-grown influences: disco, machine funk, space-age synths, hip hop production and a sense of humour. A certain je ne sais quoi if you like. And out of this maelstrom came the scene that waved a flag for Gallic dance. It was called French Touch.

Until that point, French music was regarded by the rest of Europe with a smirk, if at all. Germany had krautrock, then minimal techno; the UK did acieed, which they'd pinched and adapted from Chicago via the Spanish Balearics; the Italians were demons with disco. So, although France also had "a huge disco culture" on its home turf, according to French Touch pioneer Étienne de Crécy, with names like Cerrone, Patrick Juvet and Patrick Hernandez – and the odd synth pioneer like Jean-Michel Jarre – they were not regarded as great musical innovators.

"A few nerds knew about Serge Gainsbourg and a few of the 60s things (like yé-yé)," says the DJ and musician Ivan Smagghe, "but French Touch was the first time that French music got on the map massively."

In the short sharp shock between 1994 and 1998, French Touch signalled a huge cultural shift. When police started clamping down on illegal raves and house started to dominate over techno, dance music moved into Paris clubs and a party scene blossomed with flagship nights like Respect.

Artists and their aliases like Philippe Zdar and Hubert Boombass as Cassius, Zdar and de Crécy as Motorbass and de Crécy as Super Discount, as well as Alan Braxe, Alex Gopher and DJ Falcon, jostled for chart space and became internationally known. French Touch became shorthand for the frantic, disco-loopy, sample-heavy style of house music so popular in this period, as well as being a bit of a byword for anything Daft Punk released. But like any scene that crystallises into a sound, the evolution to revolution is never clear-cut.

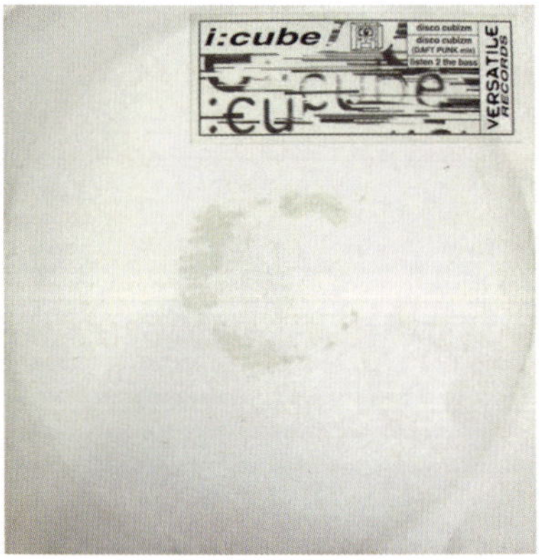

> "French Touch wasn't electronic. It wasn't filter disco. That's what it became. It was hip hop... techno... jazz, prog-rock - all these things were in the milieu of Paris."

In the beginning, French Touch was more about a fresh confidence, a catch-all term for a wide variety of electronic styles that were bubbling up from the dancefloor at the same time. During this period, there was a proliferation of producers and musicians who were mingling at a small number of record shops in the creative Bastille district, having fun with the filter settings and swapping musical ideas.

Buoyed by the excitement of house music, "suddenly there was a conglomerate of people from different backgrounds, releasing records sold in independent shops that were located all in the same area," says Smagghe, who was then working at one of them, Rough Trade.

Stylistically, these artists did not exactly sound alike. St Germain's 1995 album 'Boulevard' was hailed by the UK music press and was a gateway for the French Touch movement and yet it melded hip hop and reggae with jazz and deep house. I:Cube, another leading producer of the time, was also big on jazz – check out his 1996 track 'Disco Cubizm', which Daft Punk famously remixed. Drum'n'bass was big in Paris around this time, too. And the compilations on the French Touch-affiliated label Source in the mid-90s, featuring the likes of La Funk Mob, Motorbass and Air, were like the French take on the UK's Mo'Wax label, where trip hop met house and jungle.

Martin James, the British journalist who is often credited with making the scene's title stick, and who was one of 'Boulevard''s early champions, says: "This is really important. French Touch wasn't electronic. It wasn't filter disco. That's what it *became*. It was hip hop. It was techno. It was jazz, prog-rock – all these things were in the milieu of Paris."

The artists of French Touch were bound by location and, more than anything it seems, by attitude. "We had no teachers," says de Crécy of France's lack of house music heritage. "We were looking to the US and the UK." Specifically towards producers like Louie Vega, Todd Edwards and Larry Heard. However, to a degree, they had to make it up for themselves, redrawing the rulebook in their own manner – without over thinking it.

Zdar was a key instigator of the new house wave: he'd been making hip hop as part of the early-90s duo La Funk Mob and formed

Vulture
ALAN BRAXE
&
FRED FALKE
presents
"RUNNING"
Side A
33⅓ rpm
1. Intro
All tracks produced by
Alan Braxe & Fred Falke
for Vulture
3 539932 101976
℗ & © 2000 Vulture
VULT 001

STARDUST
"MUSIC SOUNDS BETTER WITH YOU"

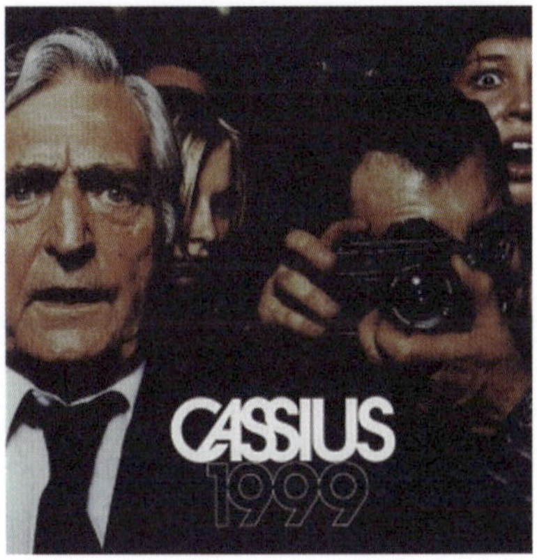


Motorbass with de Crécy in 1992, after going to their first rave together. A year before Daft Punk released their first single, Motorbass were making tracks that marked out Paris's unique musical mix. Their 1996 album 'Pansoul', with its loop-da-loop funk samples, squelchy basslines and almost gleefully deranged scratching, had an effervescent energy that would come to define the French dance music that came after.

But the "quintessential" French Touch track, says de Crécy, was actually another release from 1996: Cheek's 'Venus (Sunshine People)'. Three artists, among the lesser-known names associated with French Touch, masterminded the single. It was produced by DJ Gilb'r, with the B-side remixed by DJ Gregory and I:Cube – and came out on Versatile Records. Listening to it now, it unmistakably laid the template for the style of French Touch that's more closely aligned with 'filtered house' or 'filter disco': a catchy vocal sample lifted from a funk or disco record; a sunny guitar riff or bassline, looped and submerged like a rhythmic rollercoaster, coming in and out of view through the clouds; a hypnotic beat; and flagrant use of filtering that give the effect of tripping under a spaceship. Understandably, says James, "it blew up in the clubs."

Alan Braxe – whose dreamy 2000 track 'Intro' with Fred Falke is another one of the definitive French Touch singles – says that looking back, what unites them all could be as simple as a piece of musical equipment.

"At the time I didn't care, but retrospectively I think there is something distinct about the French sound," says the producer, pulling out his SP-1200, a drum machine and sampler combined, from a cupboard from his Toulouse studio. It was this machine – which was favoured among classic hip hop beat-makers of the 80s and 90s – that was also used by Paris's small circle of house producers and generated French Touch's "very raw and yet sophisticated" template. "It was the perfect balance," he adds.

The reliance on fiddling with the high and low filter pass dial, meanwhile, owes a lot to the style developed by the Chicago house pioneers, especially second-waver DJ Sneak.

"When you're working with samples in house music, you have one problem," says Braxe. "Repetition. Filtering gives you the option to fade or shadow the sample and build intensity. It's the same technique DJs are using when they are playing in clubs, they're playing with EQ and cutting the bass. It's a very old technique, it's just blending sounds together and making waves of emotion with the two."

It's a blend that took off massively in part for two reasons: the UK press and Daft Punk. James, then a critic at British magazine Muzik and who has written a book about the movement, 'French Connection', says he took the French Touch phrase from the Parisian promotions company who sent him music and he began using it in his increasing coverage of the scene.

Others claim that it came from a slogan, 'We give a French touch to house', that was printed on the back of bomber jackets by the FNAC record label in the early 90s. Either way, the Eurostar opened in 1994, says James, which meant that French DJs could cross the Channel cheaply and easily, and take their releases with them, and UK fans could head to Paris and sample the home-grown nightlife. Respect, which was weekly at queer club Le Queen for over 1,000 partygoers and hosted DJ sets from the French Touch glitterati, was soon being talked about outside of France as a must-attend party and its resident DJs started touring around the world.

It was Daft Punk, however, who blew the hinges off. The widespread success of 'Homework' in 1997 – as well as the numerous producers they'd asked to remix their singles – focused the global spotlight on Parisian talent (as well as referencing those aforementioned teachers in a track of the same name).

Though, in interviews, Thomas Bangalter and Guy-Manuel de Homem-Christo would never claim to be part of the movement; they had come a little after. Indeed, so the legend goes, track down a copy of Daft Punk's 'Da Funk' – released on Scottish label Soma in 1995 – and in the middle of the credits you'll see the sentence: "Music respects to Motorbass".

"'Pansoul' drove that idea. And Daft Punk picked up on that," says James of their musical formula. "In earlier days, they were the kids watching the French Touch people. Pedro (Winter, who had run the Hype parties at Folies Pigalle and was an important player in Parisian nightlife) was a key figure and managed them, and that was their buy-in into the scene. But they weren't the linchpins, by any stretch of imagination."

Clearly, though, Daft Punk's own Midas Touch was inescapably influential. "They were always an overpowering force in the background," says Smagghe, "but at the same time, not at the core of the everyday French Touch."

Bangalter's Roulé label especially – an outlet for his experimentation and playfulness outside of Daft Punk – helped define French Touch as it flipped into filter house. Roulé released much of DJ Falcon's work, as well as French Touch's pièce de résistance, 'Music Sounds Better With You', one of the definitive club anthems of the last century. Written by Bangalter, Braxe and vocalist Benjamin Diamond under the name Stardust, with a riff that samples Chaka Khan's 'Fate', it was "made in one day, so simple," says Braxe, and yet it was "the best track made in this style," says de Crécy. In a way, it was as if Bangalter was royally showing off.

As, seemingly, was Zdar, who tragically died in 2019, two days before the release of Cassius'

Étienne de Crécy in the tiny studio where he made the first Super Discount album in 1996

"French Touch became France's Britpop. Daft Punk could have been France's Oasis. They didn't want to align themselves with the nationalism of French Touch."

fifth and final album. As 1998 morphed into the final year of the 20th Century, Cassius released their debut studio longplayer. Called '1999', with tongue placed firmly in cheek, its lead single 'Cassius 1999' punctured the US Dance and UK chart top 10s.

But every trend reaches its event horizon and by the dawn of the new millennium, says James, filtered house had become too formulated.

"Every producer started doing this sound. And it wasn't French Touch, it was the filtered disco that was now called French Touch."

It led to tracks like Phats and Small's awful Stardust parody 'Turn Around', as well as Modjo's 'Lady (Hear Me Tonight)' in 2000, and 2001's saccharine, Minnie Riperton-sampling '2 People' by Jean Jacques Smoothie, who wasn't from France at all but a musician from Gloucester using a French-sounding name.

"At the start of the millennium, French Touch became a caricature," says de Crécy. "It wasn't surprising anymore." Electronic music began to fade out, guitar bands swaggered in. "There were really great rock bands like The Strokes and The White Stripes," he continues. "French Touch was thought of as music for the VIP room in clubs. That was a bad period for us."

And you know an underground sound is over when Madonna channels it on an album, as she did with French Touch on 2000's 'Music', produced in part by Frenchman and Daft Punk influence Mirwais. Sensing the end from the wings, Daft Punk released 'Discovery' in 2001, the album that introduced the robots and robo-soul sound.

"That album was the end of French Touch," says James. "They moved away from it the day they put those masks on. French Touch became France's Britpop. Daft Punk could have been France's Oasis. But they didn't want to align themselves with the nationalism of French Touch. It was all about internationalism. It's not about them being mysterious – it's them not wanting to be seen as from a particular city, or place. They made a conscious decision to put masks on and... change their identity and become internationalised."

Smagghe ponders this for a moment. "Were Daft Punk even French after a while?" he says. "They were just themselves."

It's notable that the scene's core stars never made it to the Hollywood heights of Daft Punk. But collectively they put Gallic club culture on the map forever. In the end, French Touch's legacy is vast: Daft Punk's manager, Pedro Winter, started Ed Banger, with its maximalist stadium electro sound led by Grammy-winning duo Justice, while Gildas Loaëc, who'd worked on Roulé, co-founded the Kitsuné Maison label which defined indie discos in the mid-2000s. Phoenix's, (featuring Laurent Brancowitz who was in Darlin' with Thomas and Guy-Man) early singles were distinctly in the French Touch mould and they went on to become a huge festival act. Today, you can hear echoes of filtered house in music by the cutting edge of DJ/producers, from I. JORDAN to Julio Bashmore, all harnessing French Touch's playful vitality.

"We were just having fun," says Braxe of those heady days. "Sometimes, we didn't know what we were doing. Years later, you are in a studio with a lot of equipment, and you start to make things as they should be. And suddenly what you're doing is very bad because you're thinking about it too much."

You can hear that carefree, uncalculated freedom in the music. "This is probably the main point about what happened in French Touch," Braxe adds. "Let's take a sampler and just do it. Don't care. Just do it."

# BANGALTER'S GOLDEN YEAR

**Ben Cardew** demonstrates how everything Thomas Bangalter touched in 1998 turned to gold...

In 1998, Daft Punk only released one piece of music, a galactically funky remix of Scott Grooves' P-Funk house banger 'Mothership Reconnection', making it their quietest year since 1994. And yet, if we can consider this a fallow period for the duo, for Thomas Bangalter it was one of the most miraculous periods of relative inactivity in dance music history. A year that gave birth to two world-straddling hits, an ingeniously strange remix for a Chicago hero and a solo record that paved the way for Daft Punk's entry into the world of hip hop.

Stardust's 'Music Sounds Better With You' and Bob Sinclar's 'Gym Tonic' – the two massive hits – stole the headlines in 1998, the former an eternal house classic that topped the charts globally, the latter a more controversial release that had its own chart success when covered by Spacedust as 'Gym and Tonic'.

But the year for Bangalter started with more underground concerns, in the form of Roy Davis Jr.'s 'Rock Shock', which was released on Bangalter's Roulé label towards the start of the year.

Davis Jr.'s original is a fairly straight-up piece of filter house that Bangalter signed after hearing the Chicago producer play it on white label in Paris. On the B-side, however, Bangalter's devious Start-Stop Mix plays merry hell with the mellow house groove of 'Rock Shock', starting off with a deliberately stuttering beat that makes even the most competent DJ sound like a blazing amateur, before lurching into a funkily bizarre groove that sounds like little else in the world of house.

It was the next Roulé release, however, that would break 1998 open. Stardust's 'Music Sounds Better With You', released on Roulé in July 1998 as a one-sided 12-inch and later re-released by Virgin, is the perfect example of the casual genius of Thomas Bangalter's annus mirabilis. A song knocked up by Bangalter, Alan Braxe and singer Benjamin Diamond in a Paris rehearsal studio when they realised they didn't have enough material for a forthcoming Braxe gig.

The inspiration for the song came from a loop taken from Chaka Khan's 'Fate', with an evocative two-chord melody rent in two by a cosmic guitar flash. Around this, Diamond added lyrics about the beauty of music and togetherness, uniting listeners with the eternal idea that music sounds better with you, while inviting each and every one of us to ponder who that "you" might be.

The trio played the song at Braxe's Paris gig, with Bangalter on keyboards and Braxe on SP1200 sampler, then spent a week in the studio moulding their demo into the gem they knew lay beneath. This was a process of constant reduction, getting rid of superfluous vocal lines and musical flourishes until there remained just loop, drums, filters and a six-line vocal, each element entirely perfect in its own way. Immortality beckoned.

The story of 'Gym Tonic' is rather more complicated, even if the song itself is refreshingly simple. Bangalter claimed in a 1998 interview with Muzik magazine that it took two hours to make, winding a distinctly impertinent loop from Motown Sounds' 1978 disco song 'Bad Mouthin'' around a Jane Fonda workout, to make a dancefloor disco aerobic banger. In retrospect, adding a workout vocal to house beats seems so brilliantly obvious, it's a miracle no one had thought of it before. But that, perhaps, is where genius resides…

What happened next is more opaque. According to various reports, Bangalter gave the track to Sinclar to feature on his new album, in return for Sinclar's remix of Stardust, with the one proviso that 'Gym Tonic' was not to be released as a single. When the song went out on promo copies of Sinclar's 'Paradise' album, DJs went mad and Yellow, Sinclar's label, released 'Gym Tonic' on a promo 12-inch, as Bangalter continued to vet its single release.

Into this void stepped Spacedust, a conveniently named British duo who released 'Gym and Tonic', a song, shall we say, inspired by 'Gym Tonic', with Bangalter's Jane Fonda sample re-recorded. The song went to the top of the UK charts in October 1998 – one step higher than 'Music Sounds Better With You' – and was also a hit in Belgium, Iceland, Ireland and New Zealand. For many house fans, this piggybacking left a bad taste in the mouth, and it is perhaps for this reason that you won't hear 'Gym Tonic' in clubs today, while 'Music Sounds Better With You' remains a perennial, up there with dance music's most iconic records.

Wrangling aside, though, 'Gym Tonic' is a brilliant example of Bangalter's tongue-in-cheek sense of humour and sense of the ridiculous, which you can see right through to Daft Punk's alien-bating 'Contact', with 'Gym Tonic' also showing Bangalter's innate understanding of the dancefloor.

Bangalter ended this most triumphant year with a solo release, 'Trax On Da Rocks Vol. 2', for Roulé. The five-track EP was home to the 'Da Funk'-at-a-cocktail-party shuffle of 'Club Soda'; the towering 'Colossus' – a title that, if anything, undersells the song's Herculean intensity – the abrasive 'Turbo' and the distinctly cute 'Shuffle'. However, the EP's most important track – if not necessarily the best – was 'Extra Dry', a grainy tech thumper that had the unlikely side effect of introducing French house to US hip hop when J Dilla sampled it on Slum Village's 'Raise It Up', slowing the frantic pulse of Bangalter's original down to a nonchalant stroll.

Rather than get the legal hump, Daft Punk suggested that Slum Village remix their own 'Aerodynamic', with the track surfacing via the band's Daft Club online site and on a 12-inch of hip hop remixes. Thus began a rather beautiful relationship between Daft Punk and US hip hop that would end with Kanye West sampling 'Harder, Better, Faster, Stronger' on a US number one hit.

Would this have happened without 'Extra Dry'? Quite possibly. But making a track that attracted the ears of one of hip hop's most venerated producers was a sign of Daft Punk's surprisingly universal appeal, not to mention a beautiful extra to Bangalter's miraculous year.

Nor was that quite it, either. Throughout 1998 'Discovery' was slowly edging into life, while Roulé had one more record up its sleeve, coming in the shape of The Buffalo Bunch's rolling funk monster 'Buffalo Club' (released via one-off Roulé sub label Scratché), with the title track becoming an underground hit in Paris' clubs.

Bangalter would not exactly go quietly after 1998 was out. 1999 was largely taken up with recording 'Discovery' while 2000 saw him debut the devastating minimalism of his Together project with DJ Falcon. And yet, for Bangalter, few years would resonate with the aura of undeniable casual genius like 1998, when musical inspiration seemed to fall off the young Parisian like autumn leaves in a high wind. It wasn't just the exceptional music Bangalter released in 1998; it was the way he did it, without great hue and cry, looking like he was barely breaking a sweat. That's not the case, of course: Bangalter has always been a hard worker and if 'Gym Tonic' only took a couple of hours to produce that's because of the back-breaking toil he had put into learning his art. But looking this casual takes a remarkable talent and Bangalter's 1998 was proof of this.

"I believe in luck," he told Muzik, in an interview to mark 'Music Sounds Better With You' being named its song of 1998. "It's a lot of luck and a lot of work also. We wake up every morning and think we're kind of lucky. If people like our music, it's just something I can't explain."

In 1998 the luck was all ours.

## HE'S COME A LONG WAY, BABY!

**At the end of 1998, Jockey Slut placed Thomas Bangalter second in its 50 Main Players of the Year (behind Fatboy Slim). Here's what he had to say:**

"It was good to get back in the studio after a year of touring and promotion of the Daft Punk album, and to do different projects like Stardust. There was not really any promotion planned with Stardust, we just came down to the Miami (Winter Music Conference) with a few copies. I'm always surprised when a small DAT out of the studio becomes big.

"Miami was fun, we played (Jan Hammer's) 'Miami Vice' theme at the Maxi party and everybody was acting it out, putting themselves into a little movie.

"'Gym Tonic' was a disappointment. That's another track I did in my studio but the whole thing went really wrong. What did I think of 'Gym and Tonic' (rip-off track by Spacedust)? I'm not in a position to comment on that... yet! But I don't approve!

"This year has been really big for Roulé. It was great to see this other personal thing, other than Daft Punk, become big, successful and respected. It was pleasing to do both: an independent label and then have the experience with Daft Punk on a major."

"WE'RE LUCKY TH
ON THE PLANET. T
GET BACK ON THE
BROUGHT THEM H
AND LEAVE US. BU
GRACIOUS, THEY'
THEY CHOSE TO S

Y HANG OUT
EY COULD JUST
SPACESHIP THAT
ERE AND GO,
T THEY'RE
E NICE ROBOTS.
AY."

Featuring bad reviews, disgruntled purists, songs that inspired a generation of producers and a massive vat of macaroni and cheese, the story behind Daft Punk's second album, 'Discovery' is as colourful as the music contained therein...

By Duncan Dick

# HARDER BETTER FASTER STRONGER

## The Cast

### Ben Cardew
Author of 'Daft Punk's Discovery'

### Erol Alkan
DJ, super producer for the likes of Duran Duran, Ride and Mystery Jets, one half of Beyond The Wizards Sleeve, founder and resident of Trash (1997-2007)

### Joe Mount
Founder and creative force behind Metronomy

### Kevin McKay
DJ and label boss at Glasgow Underground

### Myles MacInnes
Aka Mylo, DJ and producer behind 2004's smash hit album 'Destroy Rock & Roll'

### Pedro Winter
Daft Punk manager and DJ/producer under the name Busy P

### Soulwax
Musicians, producers, DJs and remixers David and Stephen Dewaele. Also known as 2manydjs

### The Blessed Madonna
Kentucky-by-way-of-Chicago DJ legend and producer

**Pedro Winter:** "During the process of 'Discovery', I was seeing them every day. They were next door. And through the whole process, I can remember Thomas and Guy-Manuel coming to the office. 'Oh, we are working on this. We are doing this. Oh yeah, look, we have the solo violin, guitar, do you like it?' 'Yes, of course I like it.'"

**Pedro:** "It was super collaborative. I wouldn't want it another way because I was contacting all of the collaborators. I was calling Sneak, I brought Todd (Edwards) to Paris. I arranged for Thomas and Guy-Man to go to New Jersey to Todd Edwards' parents' house at the time. It was really collaborative, very respectful, even though Daft Punk were already in the Champions League compared to Todd Edwards or Romanthony or Sneak, who had stuck to the underground house scene. Of course, we knew them because we knew this music, but the mainstream audience didn't know who the fuck Todd Edwards was."

**Kevin McKay:** "I put out a single for Romanthony – 'Do You Think You Can Love Me' – on Glasgow Underground in the early part of 1998. And then we just kept on. He didn't release on many other labels after that. We did a few 12-inches and then he had a solo album that he'd been working on, the follow up to 'Romanworld'. When he sent me 'Bring U Up' I was like: 'What do I have to do to get this album? I'll do whatever it takes.' I was totally sold. I think it cost me $20,000 or $25,000. So then we started working together on his solo stuff and then at some point in 1999 he told me he was speaking to Daft Punk because they wanted to do 'Hold On'."

**Kevin:** "A lot of people don't realise 'Hold On' originally came out on Black Male (Romanthony's label), but it sounded rubbish because Roman had this thing where he made things sound crap in the mastering process. I've got no idea why! I would hear recordings that he'd taken off his 8-track and they would be way better than the Black Male version. All Thomas did was re-press 'Hold On' with proper mastering, but it sounded amazing and everyone loved it. That began a relationship between those two. Thomas just knew how to get the best out of Roman."

**Pedro:** "In 2001, Todd Edwards was famous for his production and cut-up samples, and they were asking him to sing. Sneak was famous for his clever beats and stuff, and they are asking him to write the lyrics of 'Digital Love'. And Romanthony, it's funny to ask like a Prince-level singer [to do a vocal] then change his voice."

**Kevin:** "Romanthony was very particular about who he would work with. I remember he turned down Masters At Work, who wanted to remix 'Bring U Up'. I couldn't get him to understand why it was a good idea! I was forever going: 'It's a marketing thing. Putting those two names together will create hype and you need hype.' He was like: 'I can make music like Masters At Work. It's all about the music, I don't care about hype.' Daft Punk had Romanthony over to Paris and basically treated him like royalty: Thomas had a lovely home studio; he had an analogue studio; he had a digital studio. So he had the best of both worlds. Roman was very impressed with him."

**Pedro:** "I heard 'One More Time' in bits because we flew Romanthony to Paris later. So I heard it without the vocal, without the autotune. The autotune: I need to be totally frank. At the beginning when I heard it, I was like, wow, okay, it's very Cher! Cher was first [with 'Believe']."

**Soulwax:** "Before the record came out, we got given 'One More Time' by a guy from Virgin in Belgium. He knew that we'd be into it. We played it at a party that night and people were looking at us like: 'What are you playing?' But we really wanted to challenge people, so that was perfect. That party was right at the beginning of 2manydjs starting to play all over the world. And 'One More Time' was in our record bag right up until the day we started using CDJs. The 12-inch is still here in our studio, all scratched and fucked up."

**Ben Cardew:** "What I remember most is the reaction to 'One More Time'. I remember people really not being happy about it. Like, it's cheesy and it's got a vocal effect that Cher had just done. And it was this big, big pop tune. There were lots and lots of people who didn't like it. I remember people being quite confused with 'One More Time' and it was basically the same with 'Discovery'."

**Kevin:** "I think Thomas is obviously a fantastic songwriter, but he's a very different songwriter from Roman, who wrote absolutely classic house songs. And I think 'One More Time' is one of them. I'm not sure if it's Romanthony's best, but if Romanthony had had a producer like Thomas he would have made loads more big records like that."

**Pedro:** "The hardcore fans of Romanthony, I think they were disappointed. I think they were like: 'Whoa, where is the 'Ministry of Love'?' But I think it's again the genius of Daft Punk to get the best out of the artist they love."

**Kevin:** "The thing is Roman didn't have any fame from 'One More Time'. It didn't help sell his other records, as he wasn't credited as a feature on the track. It's not like Duane Harden and Armand Van Helden [on 'U Don't Know Me']. The video is like animé. There's not a Romanthony character in the video, he's completely and utterly anonymous. He's only mentioned on the credits, and you've got to be a music nerd like us to be kind of checking the credits. Now everyone knows Romanthony is the voice of 'One More Time', but at the time, and even 10 years later, I was still trying to get people interested. I was like: 'He's the vocalist from 'One More Time'' and people were like: 'You're kidding?'."

**Pedro:** "I remember we played 'One More Time' for the first time at Queen [the renowned Parisian club] during a party and people went crazy. But it was, I think, very ambitious and courageous for them to come back in 2000 with this. It wasn't low-tech, or Chicago house. And of course, some people hated it. It took time for them to digest it, understand, and of course, on the album there were some other songs that would connect the dots."

**Kevin:** "Romanthony brought them their biggest hit. But also, if you think about it, it was a huge leap for many Daft Punk fans to go from 'Homework', with all its super-cool DJ records – the coolest album ever, you can't get cooler than that – to 'Discovery''s soft rock disco. 'One More Time' was a bona fide club record, with a house legend on it. It was the bridge between the two."

△

**Pedro:** "'Discovery' was definitely a more ambitious and collective thing because of course we had to include the Japanese people that were working on the animation. The animation and the music were being written at the same time. I remember, Thomas gave us – and I think I still have it – like a scenario of what will become the animation. They wrote a story and printed us each two or three pages. It wasn't like a big book. 'Ok, I don't want it online. This is yours, keep it safe.' Later Thomas was flying to Tokyo every month for a year. It was insane, the work."

**Soulwax:** "I remember 'Discovery' had come out and we were on a beach in Portugal and Erol rang us because it was getting bad reviews. And he said: 'People are insane'. We were like: 'This record is unbelievable, amazing, and it's getting mediocre or snarky reviews?'"

**Pedro:** "The ambition was to go somewhere else. It's a modern pop album – in fact, I don't think they cut the influences from the Chicago house or the techno scene, but they wanted to link again with their childhood memories. The music from the 80s, the music from the radio and you can hear it, of course. You can hear it in there."

**Pedro:** "They took the bad reviews very badly. Yes, of course. Because the feedback at the beginning was either 'that's phenomenal' or 'Ok, you've turned your back on the underground scene'. But Daft Punk, I know them, they never change. When they did 'Discovery', they were the same people as when they did 'Homework', with the same passion. So they were sad that people could believe they turned their back on them or were going for the money, or whatever it was. As if Daft Punk had to prove they were doing it for the love of art!"

**Erol Alkan:** "The first time I met Daft Punk, or to be more precise, Thomas, was possibly the first time I DJed in Paris, in 2001. I remember there was this big hall and Thomas Bangalter was DJing there and 2manydjs or the Flying Dewaele Brothers, as they were known then, were going to play after them. I was in this backroom with The Rapture playing live – Paul Epworth doing sound for them that night as well. Miss Kittin was downstairs. It was interesting, actually, because I was hearing these murmurs of like Paris being quite anti-Daft Punk off the back of the success of 'Discovery'. It being like a sell-out or something. Or there were some purists who were kind of implying that. And obviously, me being a big fan of that record, I couldn't understand it. But then again, I didn't live in Paris, I wasn't experiencing the club culture there. You'd kind of hear it in a few conversations here or there, this slightly, anti-Daft Punk thing."

**Pedro:** "We love Supertramp, Genesis, all those 80s sounds that sometimes can be a bit too cheesy. We grew up with Frankie Goes to Hollywood, Culture Club, Depeche Mode or The Cure. People are always making fun of the 80s music, the girls and stuff, but the 80s popular artists were innovative with drum machines and samplers in their music, and in a way this is I think what Daft Punk tried to do with 'Discovery'."

**Ben:** "I think it did put some people off, particularly the more serious techno fans they had. You know, some people wouldn't accept pop vocals and they didn't like people pretending to be robots. It's like: 'If you're not from Detroit and your record isn't made up of filthy hard loops then we're not listening.' I remember at the time, techno was really, really dominated by Ben Sims-type loops and post-Jeff Mills imitators basically. It certainly wasn't people doing big pop records."

"You can't look at 'Discovery' and not draw a direct line between that and people like DFA... A generation of people who had been in indie bands wanted to make dance music."

**The Blessed Madonna:** "I struggled with 'Discovery' in the beginning. I feel like 'Homework' was about an obsession with American underground house and techno and also just house and techno in general: the ultimate fandom record. And 'Discovery' was that, but for American pop music. And at that time I was too cool for pop music. I did not want an homage to 10cc. I didn't want those things. I wanted Stardust or I wanted 'Homework 2.0' and I think they gave us something that was ultimately more sophisticated than that. And it went over my head in the beginning."

**Kevin:** "As a kind of house snob at the time I remember being sort of: 'I don't get it.' And then I later learned in my 30s that not getting it doesn't mean that you don't like it; not getting it means you need to spend a bit more time with it. I think there's a joy in 'Discovery' that is not in 'Homework'. 'Homework', doesn't have those absolutely teeth-clenching, fist-pumpingly joyous tracks such as 'One More Time' and 'Digital Love'."

**The Blessed Madonna:** "You can't look at 'Discovery' and not draw a direct line between

that and people like DFA. I mean explicitly, there was a whole generation of people who had been in indie bands that wanted to make dance music and for them that was a really freeing thing. But not for those of us who loved dance music and hated bands, which I did at the time. I mean you have to understand I was in my freshman year of college and so cool. I liked Jeff Mills, the last thing I wanted to hear was a guitar. To hear a guitar you know it felt like: 'Urgh.' Like treason. And then of course I loved it. And then it became like an opening point for me for lots of stuff: 'Harder, Better, Faster, Stronger' is the reason I figured out who Edwin Birdsong (pioneering funk and disco keyboard player) was. And I started to see things like that. And I really warmed up to even the ballads like 'Something About Us'. I love 'Face To Face'. So it took time for me to open up to it."

△

**Ben:** "I was living in Madrid at the time and it had just come out. I bought it the week it came out. I bought the CD, took it home, I put it on and remember thinking 'One More Time' was all good and then 'Aerodynamic' comes on it's like: 'What the hell is this? What is that guitar solo? Why are they playing guitar? What's this like classical thing?' And the first kind of two times I said: 'I think I like it, but I don't know.' And then it clicked. But I love that. That's what I look for in music. Like listening to My Bloody Valentine or something. You're like: 'Eh? What?' But then it works."

**Soulwax:** "'(You Gotta) Fight For Your Right (To Party!)' by the Beastie Boys is seen now as this masterpiece, but it got horrible reviews. I guess whenever somebody makes a completely different thing it's hard for people sometimes to get their heads around it. And I guess with 'Discovery', they could've made 'Homework 2', but they didn't. That was the brilliant thing about it."

**Mylo:** "'Discovery''s release coincided with when I took a break from a philosophy PhD program at UCLA (Los Angeles) and moved back to Glasgow, with the vague idea of making a pop record. This album, along with the Röyksopp ('Melody A.M.') and The Avalanches ('Since I Left You') albums, definitely got the most plays in the kitchen of our flat around that time. It was a big influence on 'Destroy Rock & Roll' in terms of pushing sample-based work into really quite kitsch territory and getting away with it - or at least hoping to."

**Joe Mount:** "What I personally realised when I was listening to their music during that period was that there was this subculture of bedroom producers, these people who were making massive records and they were doing it in really inventive, and sort of low-key ways. I think it's like: 'Ok, well, these are my people.' All around the world, there were people who were feeling that same way, you know? It inspired a generation of beat makers and bedroom producers."

**The Blessed Madonna:** "As a producer I would have once said that 'Homework' was the most influential on me, but now I would say 'Discovery', which completely shocks me. Now that I'm making an album, I understand that desire to record live with people like Todd Edwards, Sneak or Romanthony. All of these people that became a part of the larger Daft crew. Saying: 'Ok, making an album is like a wide process and we're going to write with a whole bunch of people and try to bring these ideas into a kind of cohesive collaborative thing and build this whole universe.'

"It's one thing to say you're going to make something that is influenced by Todd Edwards, it's another thing to have Todd come sit in a room with you and show you how he chops samples. That ended up being for me a real guiding principle and today, as I sit in the studio, that is how I work now. Making music doesn't have to be some kind of solitary thing where we're all satellites with dark windowless rooms floating out in space. I would much rather work and be influenced in a really transparent way. By the people that I hold to be the very greatest."

**Kevin:** "I think people love 'Discovery' so much because it's not 'cool'. It's very honest and I think that's fantastic. A lot of dance artists write cool records and not everyone is cool all the time. If you look at the list of people that Daft Punk have worked with, they all have that, but I think their honesty about music involved a lot more pop than Romanthony's honesty about music. Romanthony's honesty about music is like Stevie Wonder and Prince and minor keys and 'The Wanderer' and 'Life's Tough' and that kind of honesty. Whereas Guy-Man and Thomas' honesty is obviously very different: it comes from a happier place."

**Mylo:** "'Superheroes' is an absolute banger and the most overlooked track on Discovery. I guess I never played it out as a DJ because it's fast – 140+ bpm – but the best track on the album is 'Voyager'. It's pure nonchalant French house."

**Ben:** "'Digital Love' has got an amazing tune, just genuinely brilliant. It could have been a global number one pop tune, plus it's weird as hell, with all the experimental bits. It's just astounding. I mean, I love so many songs on that album, but I had to think about this when I was doing the book, and I know my favourite."

**Joe:** "I love 'Veridis Quo'. I probably want that track played at my funeral. Even though I only realised the name of the track was a pun on 'very disco' the other day (after all these years!) when my French girlfriend said it."

**Pedro:** "Of course, I love 'Harder, Better, Faster, Stronger'. But 'Short Circuit' is one of my all-time favourites of Daft Punk, and, in fact, it was part of the live show way back in 1995. I remember it very well because it was the moment on the live show when it's Guy-Man, as the lead artist. Everything's coming out from his SP100. So I'll choose 'Harder, Better, Faster, Stronger' as my favourite on 'Discovery'. But 'Short Circuit' is definitely also a special one for me."

**Erol:** "'Discovery' definitely fell into place at Trash quite easily. I remember the first person to play something from 'Discovery', was, fittingly, Jacques Lu Cont (Stuart Price, aka Les Rythmes Digitales). I'd been trying to get Stuart to DJ at Trash for ages and eventually he gave in and we set a date. He came down with Junior Sanchez - I remember Liam O'Hare (general manager) at The End being quite taken aback because, you know, if you were to book those two on a Friday or Saturday night, you'd pay a fair penny. And I remember Stuart having 'One More Time' on vinyl. That night he played the Todd Edwards mix of Phoenix's 'If I Ever Feel Better', and he played 'One More Time'. Everyone was like: 'Oh, it's going to be Daft Punk!' And yeah, it fitted really well.

"Bear in mind, this was just when electroclash was coming into focus a bit more at Trash. Later, 'Harder, Better...', and 'Aerodynamic' would take the roof off. But I think those Daft Punk singles from 'Discovery' – they felt like pop singles more than electronic singles. They'd kind of taken on the same life as if we were to play, you know, a Destiny's Child record, which we did, you know? It was kind of in that league, more so than playing a record on International Deejay Gigolos or something like that. Daft Punk at that point, within the lens of Trash, were a fully-formed pop act."

**Ben:** "'Discovery' was always a classic, but I think we (the world) all needed to catch up, if that makes sense? Autotune becoming a lot more popular suddenly meant it wasn't the 'Cher sound' anymore, it was everywhere in pop music. And other people started using soft rock references and other people started using this big DayGlo sound. And perceptions started to change. I loved 'Discovery' right from the start, I always did, but even working in journalism when people were talking about the best albums of the 2000s, it wasn't on many of those lists."

**Pedro:** "The good thing with Daft Punk is that they are the most patient people on planet Earth. So maybe at the beginning they were sad, you know, the feedback was not like super positive, but a few months after people realised, that the music... the music called them. And then the 'Interstellar 5555' animation came out and then people realised: 'Oh, that's the soundtrack of the animation.' Musically it makes sense: they wrote a

musical for an animation by a legend, Leiji Matsumoto. We sold three or four million copies of 'Discovery' at the time."

△

**Mylo:** "I think the biggest force towards 'Discovery''s rehabilitation as a classic were the phenomenal live shows from 2006 onwards. Particularly in the US where it coincided with, or rekindled, a mainstream interest in electronic music. There was honestly very little interest in dance music in the US in the early 2000s."

**Erol:** "Every time I've met Thomas he always makes you feel like he's pleased to see you. It was like that, you know. He was very polite and courteous and warm and that was the first time I'd met him. I was really taken aback a little bit. I thought he was super lovely. That was the first time I met him and then we used to – remember iChat? He was one of my iChat buddies. I remember just before the big Coachella show, the Pyramid, he kindly gave me a little bit of insight as to how expansive the tour was. He just seemed really excited."

**Mylo:** "I was in the tent for what I'm fairly certain was their first big live show [at Coachella in 2006]. It was of course brilliant, and really exciting to feel the excitement it generated in the crowd. It is also a weird memory for me because it occurred shortly after I suffered the second bout of SSNHL (sudden sensorineural hearing loss), and I remember standing there at the edge of the tent thinking that I might be finished."

**The Blessed Madonna:** "Radek from (Chicago label) Dust Traxx had met Daft Punk in 1996 at the same Even Furthur rave I had been at as a teenager. But when he would talk about how tight he was with the two of them, I just thought there's no way that this is actually true. So, one day in 2007, I'm working in the Dust Traxx office, the Thursday before Lollapalooza weekend and Radek called me from the house we shared (I lived in the basement) and he said I need you to get home immediately and start cooking, we're going to have a barbecue in the backyard. So I run home, thinking: 'Great, I'd much rather be making potato salad and macaroni and cheese, than sitting in the office doing nothing.'

"So I came home and about two or three hours later the Daft Punk tour bus pulls up in front of our house in this residential area of north-western Chicago. Daft Punk, Falcon and their crew, and Pedro Winter and their security, they literally walk into my house and it was one of the most shocking things that has ever happened to me in my entire life. I had made these massive vats of macaroni and cheese and mashed potatoes and Radek was making beer can chicken, like real American backyard food. And they all just piled into my backyard.

"There was maybe 30 people and a few Chicago people and everybody just sat in like lawn chairs in the backyard. Just Daft Punk and a bunch of French people eating American barbecue food. And then afterwards they took us out and it was so funny because at that time especially, nobody really knew what they looked like. Watching Chicago girls trying to figure out which French guy to hit on. And totally failing because Thomas and Guy were very quiet, lovely, unassuming. The club kind of illegally opened for us after closing time at 1am. And that was the beginning of this incredibly long weekend. They also took us all to Lollapalooza from the party. We had all access wristbands and I was able to watch the show from basically inside the Pyramid. They were so generous and in so many ways it changed everything for me, just in terms of thinking of what was possible. It was a big moment."

**Joe:** "We [Metronomy] actually played a gig with them when they played at Hyde Park, at the Wireless festival in 2007. We were playing quite a bit further down the bill, obviously. I feel like now, especially, to have been able to share a stage with Daft Punk, for them to be on a line-up which includes us, it's one of those times where you think: this makes the younger me very happy. It was one of the most incredible days of our lives."

> "There was maybe 30 people and a few Chicago people... just sat in lawn chairs in the backyard. Just Daft Punk and a bunch of French people eating American barbecue food."

**Soulwax:** "When we met and we were asking questions of Thomas and Guy-Man it wasn't necessarily about the music, it was more about like how do they get those crazy ideas, how do they come to fruition? And also hearing about the ideas that didn't happen. They inspired everyone to push things further."

**Erol:** "I remember Pedro contacted me asking if I would play before them at Global Gathering. Of course I was like: 'Yeah, of course. Sure.' And after the show, I was backstage, obviously they were mind-blowing live. After I went backstage, Thomas said: 'Would you like to see inside the Pyramid?' Yes! Inside was pretty simple, from what I remember. There were two touchscreens, two tower computers, I think there was like some Ableton controllers, maybe, or something. And then a Moog either side. I think they were Voyager. But to me, whatever they did in there or didn't do in there, I wasn't fussed about. I mean, for me, I always kind of viewed it as being this art installation that you can dance at. Not just for its sheer scale or how colourful or engaging it was visually, but also musically, culturally and historically. There were so many memories attached to those records for me.

"Hearing them played back in a slightly – in a way that's constructed like a DJ set, which at that point was perfectly put together in respect of that sound, which was happening around 2006 where it was like a hook every four bars or something, there was nothing techno about it. It was techno in sound, house in sound, but its intention was pop. Its intention was to really just elevate. It was amazing to hear it constructed in such a way where all it wanted to do was just entertain people and lift people. 10,000, 20,000, 30,000, 40,000, 50,000, 60,000 or however many people facing this gigantic pyramid, celebrating a couple of robots and kind of pedalling through almost 20 years of electronic music. It was quite something."

△

**The Blessed Madonna:** "They say don't meet your heroes; but I found that to be the opposite [with Daft Punk]. And I have to say they have not, as far as I know, changed in any respect. Even recently I was working on something and one of the potential collaborators was Thomas. I fully did not even expect a response – much less one that was as generous and warm and detailed and, frankly, long as the email he sent. It was like a personal message: 'Dearest Marea, would love to be a part of this but I'm really wrapped up in this thing... I have every confidence that you will do this and bring the same level of beauty to this that you have showed in this and so on.' It was so nice that I had it printed on a canvas and it's in the wall of my dressing room."

**Ben:** "I wrote a whole book about 'Discovery' because it's not just brilliant: it's interesting and innovative. 'Homework' is brilliant, but I could maybe write 5,000 words on it, whereas Discovery I wrote a long book about and could have written a lot more. I called it 'an album that predicted the future'. I think that's kind of fair enough because you do see so much music and so many other things that come from 'Discovery' these days. And I think Daft Punk are slightly misunderstood. I think that the image we have of them as demi-gods basically, is seen in retrospect. It's after the 'Alive 2007' tour did really well and after 'Random Access Memories' did really well. And people kind of forget that you know people didn't like 'Discovery' at the time, they didn't like 'Human After All.' I like reminding people that maybe it wasn't as straightforward as it seemed."

**The Blessed Madonna:** "'One More Time' was such a huge record. And that really felt for me, looking back, maybe like a bit of the birth of EDM, the genesis of the moment that EDM becomes a thing. But the fact that they did it right and so many other people did it wrong, is not down to them. It's not their fault that Steve Aoki decided to throw cake later. That's not their responsibility. I mean they are brilliant, thoughtful, decent, sophisticated, creators of dance music who succeeded by being incredibly good. The fact that they were imitated a thousand times by lesser mortals is both understandable and forgivable."

**Kevin:** "At some point shortly after 'One More Time' came out, Roman just stopped making records for Glasgow Underground. He told me his publisher had phoned him and told him he had like a lot of money coming for him. Roman, Guy-Man and Thomas had a three-way split on the writing. And a number two in the UK, number one in the US, in the CD era, you're kind of set-up for quite a good while, and Roman didn't have a head for figures. But he knew himself. He told me that, he said: 'If you send me that amount of money, I'll end up killing myself.' Not by suicide but like in a rock star-style fashion. And so he was like: 'Can you put me on, like a monthly?' And so he had $10,000 a month wired to his account every month. So from then he would make music and I would meet him and we would hang out in Miami and he would play me tunes and he would be talking about putting records out. But he just didn't need to. I would phone up his house and sometimes all sorts of people would be answering the phone. There was obviously a party going on in the background. He enjoyed partying."

---

# THE MAN BEHIND THE MASKS

**Tony Gardner** tells Sean Griffiths how he helped the robots rock...

Animatronic and prosthetics specialist Tony Gardner has one of the most impressive CVs in Hollywood. He's worked on everything from the Child's Play 'Chucky' films and Danny Boyle's '127 Hours' to 'Zombieland' and the 'Jackass' franchise in his 30-plus-year career. But when Spike Jonze introduced him to a French electronic duo he knew little about in the early-2000s, he stumbled upon the most iconic project of his career.

"I first met Daft Punk through Spike Jonze. At the time, I was working on the prosthetics for 'Shallow Hal' so it must have been around 2000. Thomas and Guy-Man were trying to figure out how to create these personas and they wanted to do something specific rather than just grabbing a mask from the shelf for every concert and winging it. They had all these great ideas regarding LED displays and were talking to Spike about it and Spike said: 'Well, I have no idea what you're talking about but I know someone who might help figure it out.'

"At the time, the only thing I really knew about Daft Punk was the 'Around the World' video. I loved that because it worked in the way my brain thinks. The way the visuals work with the music and everything just pieces together is just incredible.

"They came to the studios at Alterian Inc. (Gardner's LA-based company) and my first impression of them was that they were really nice and super polite, but the more I spoke with them, I realised I really liked them as people and I really enjoyed the music they were making too.

"I was explaining to them all the different films and projects we'd worked on, and they were like excited kids looking at all of this stuff in the workshop. It was definitely a new experience for them, and I remember they were excited about the prospect of getting casts of their heads made.

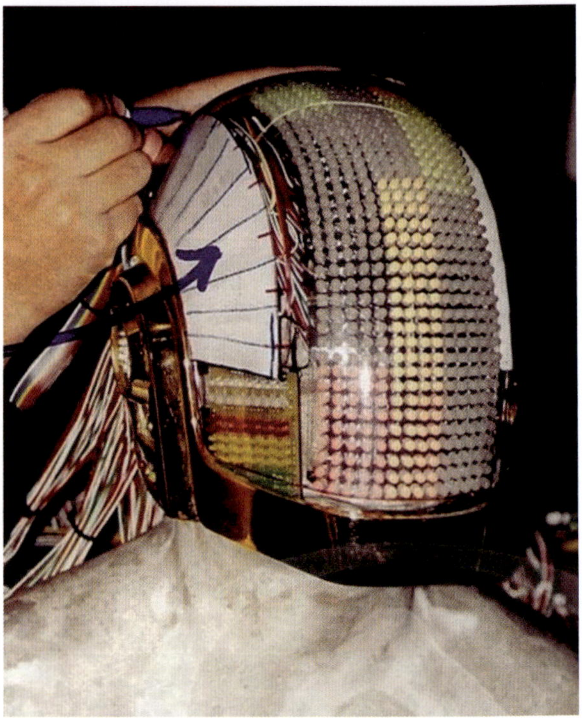

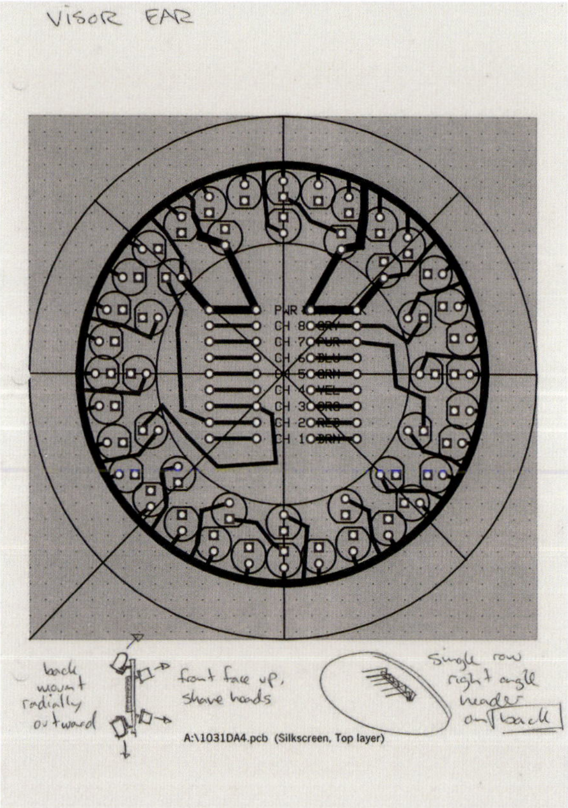
VISOR EAR
PWR
CH 8 GRY
CH 7 PUR
CH 6 BLU
CH 5 GRN
CH 4 YEL
CH 3 ORG
CH 2 RED
CH 1 BRN
back mount radially outward
front face up, shave heads
single row right angle header on back
A:\1031DA4.pcb (Silkscreen, Top layer)

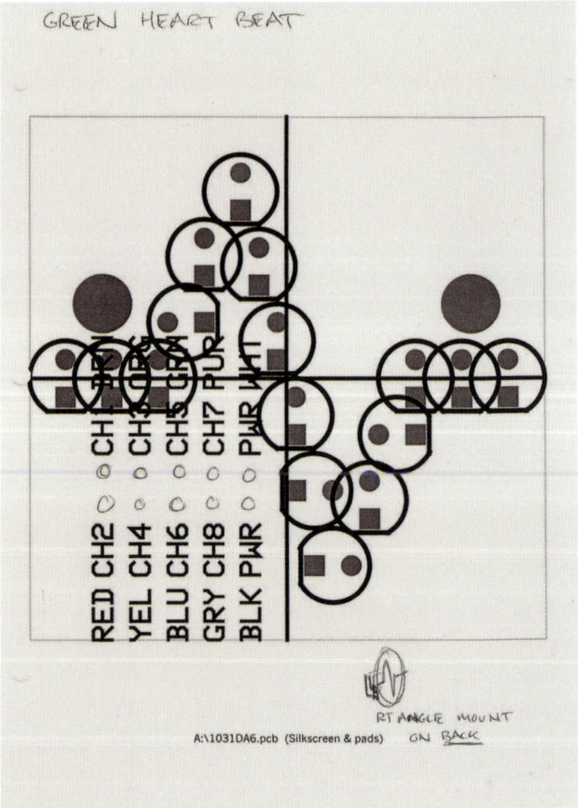
GREEN HEART BEAT
CH1 BRN
CH3 ORG
CH5 GRN
CH7 PUR
PWR WHT
RED CH2
YEL CH4
BLU CH6
GRY CH8
BLK PWR
RT ANGLE MOUNT ON BACK
A:\1031DA6.pcb (Silkscreen & pads)

> "Their initial ideas for the helmets was that they'd have hair, so they definitely changed a bit over time."

"My very first professional job had been working on Michael Jackson's 'Thriller' video and that was the thing that gave me the impetus to drop out of school and take this stuff seriously. I worked with a guy called Rick Baker and built the background zombies. So working with Daft Punk, it felt like coming full circle back to music after working in film and TV for so long.

"The first time they came to the studio, they brought Alex (Courtès) and Martin (Fougerol), who made music videos together and had worked with Daft Punk on these sketches of anime robots which were the starting point for everything. The other big influence Thomas brought with him was the film 'The Day the Earth Stood Still' which had a robot in it called Gort. It's funny because so many of our influences were the same. I'd been fascinated by that film since I was a kid. The other one was George Lucas' first film 'THX 1138' – that was a really big influence on all of us. There were police officers in that film who wore all black and motorcycle helmets and were very streamlined.

"The second day, we all got around a big table to work out what we needed to do. They'd come with such strong visual ideas that the design came together quite quickly, but there's always challenges when you go from 2D to 3D. We made casts of their heads using water-based clay, so we knew straight away where they'd need to see and breathe out of, and we could build the elements around that. We knew they were going to have to wear the helmets for long periods of time which was a challenge, as a lot of prosthetics we make are used for filming and worn for short periods of time. We'd made quite a few outfits for characters at theme parks before, where people are going to have to walk around in them all day but nothing where people are going to be performing in front of thousands of people while wearing the outfit.

"Originally, Guy-Man's helmet was going to be gold and their initial ideas for the helmets was that they'd have hair, so they definitely changed a bit over time. If you look closely, the prototype version of Thomas' helmet has him smiling while a few years later it has a straight mouth.

"One of the big challenges was all of the electronics that needed to fit in the outfit and helmets. At that point, an LED light was massive and if it was going to change colour, it needed three wires coming out of it. There's a weight issue with that if someone's wearing it all but figuring out all of that technical stuff was what was attractive about the project to me. It was a real challenge. We built these kind of robot backpacks, which fitted all of the electronics in. Another big challenge was making sure the front of the helmets weren't reflective, so if they were having their picture taken, you couldn't see the reflection of the photographer for instance. We had to put a visor inside which helped solve this. The outfits had a ribbed neck and figuring out how to make gloves which still gave a sense of touch for using controls on-stage took a while. Eventually we settled on making them out of spandex.

"We needed the helmets to have linear readouts on the screen and for Thomas to be able to type stuff that would come up on his helmet somewhere. Guy-Man's had pre-set images that you could press a button and they would come up. This was so far out of our wheelhouse we had to get a guy in who designed jumbotron screens for sports arenas. Nowadays that's quite a commonplace thing and you see that technology on a lot of billboards but at the time it was still fairly new and quite a big deal.

"Once we'd worked out the mechanics of the technology, we had to make sure the guys could see and breathe in these outfits and walk and talk. We realised they were going to use these in low-light scenarios, so we had to make the helmets easy to see through in the dark and while using consoles and pushing dials and knobs on stage.

"From start to finish the process took about four months and was more stressful than a lot of stuff I'd done before. Previous projects had all been familiar territory, but this was a completely new arena to me and the team at Alterian.

"The helmets are made from fibreglass. We made the prototype helmets and after that we made one each for performances and a set of back-up helmets in case anything went wrong with them. So there aren't many of them. Then a few years later we worked on 'Electroma' and had to build a whole town of robots which was challenging in its own way. We did adults' size, kids' size, there was even a little baby Guy-Man in a stroller so we had to make a teeny tiny helmet for that. They were exact duplicates, but luckily those didn't have to be built to such a high spec as the originals. These weighed almost nothing and we told the guys we could potentially rework their helmets to make them lighter but they actually preferred the originals as they felt more substantial.

"Working on the Daft Punk helmets ranks as one of the highlights of my career. I look at career highlights [in terms of] what was the most enjoyable project to work on and who were the most enjoyable people to work with and this is really up there. It's a pleasure working with people who are so passionate about what they do and are really creative and collaborative. And the helmets have really taken on a life of their own which is incredible.

"We worked on a bunch of stuff together afterwards including the video for 'The Prime Time of Your Life' with the girl peeling her skin off. We did a couple of animatronic things for them over the years for museums and even tried talking them into doing a big art show which is something I think they'd really enjoy.

"If you look closely at that footage, Guy-Man is walking off into the sunrise which is a new day. So who knows what the future might bring?"

"I went to see their show in the LA Sports Arena in 2007 as an audience member and it was amazing to see what we'd created in context. I went backstage after to speak to the guys but wanted to be removed from it all before and just take it in the same as anyone else. My daughter actually found our ticket stubs the other day.

"When they announced their split, I felt excited for them in a way as it gives them a chance to flex their creative muscles and not have to deal with any of the weight and responsibility of the Daft Punk name. As artists that's got to feel good for them so more power to them for creating some space for themselves. And I loved that they used the 'Electroma' footage to announce it. They're always mysterious about everything and if you look closely at that footage, Guy-Man is walking off into the sunrise which is a new day. So who knows what the future might bring?"

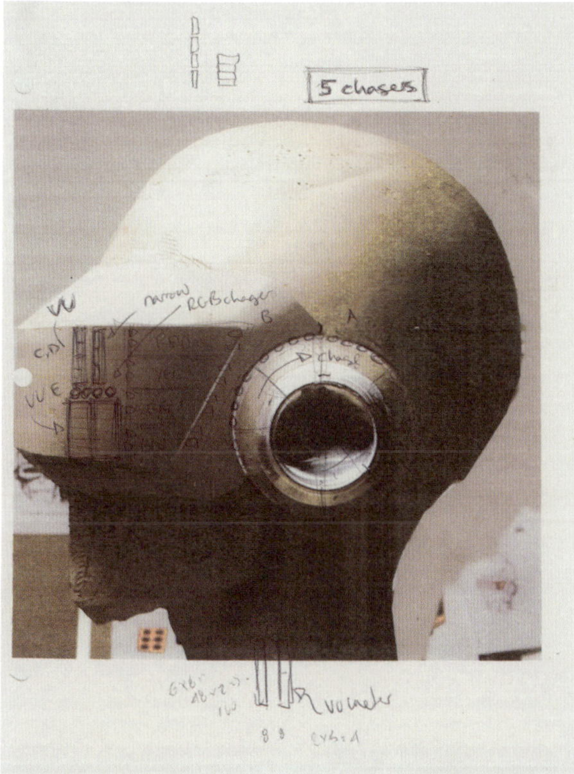
5 chases
narrow
RGB chaser
D chase
VU meter

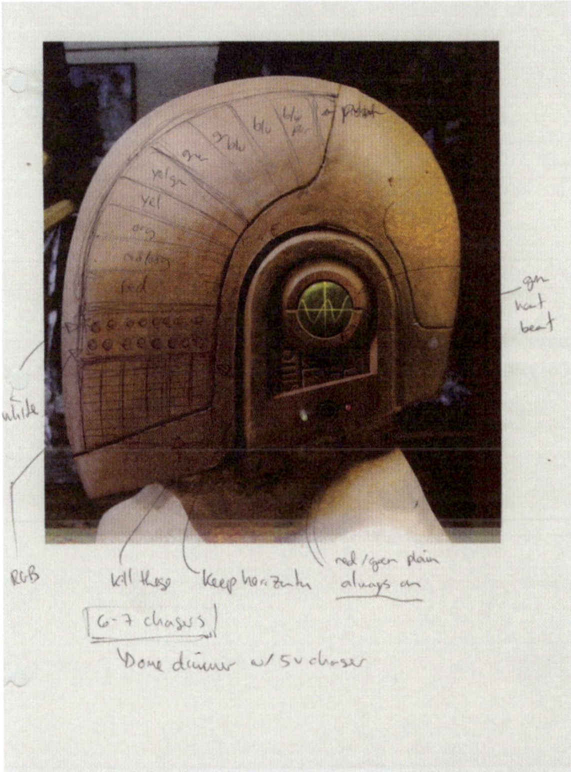
grn
heart
beat
white
RGB
kill these
Keep horizontal
red/grn plain
always on
6-7 chases
Done dimmer w/ 5v chaser

Dead Kennedys

Some news just in: Daft Punk have been injured in a horrible accident and have metamorphosed into robots. So they claim. **Paul Mardles** tracks them down to their Paris lair and finds a pair of apologists for the early-80s. "We just want to be kids again," they insist...

# METAL GURUS

While these days France enjoys a new-found reputation as the breeding ground for much that's cutting-edge and cool, its equivalent of The Brits, the NRJ awards, is as staid and artistically redundant as its black tie-only clause implies. Last night's backslapping, runny-nosed soiree saw Ricky Martin perform his trademark pooch-on-heat routine, the man who penned Whitney Houston's 'I Will Always Love You', David Foster, walk away with a lifetime achievement gong and archaic vocal troupe Les Dix Commandments (nope, us neither) laughably acclaimed as Best French Group. It's that kind of bash.

Today, 12 hours after last night's most determined reveller glanced at his watch in disbelief and turned the bedroom light out, the group who gave French music back its self-respect are sitting in a small meeting room in central Paris, apparently impervious to the aforesaid function. Where other acts would try to mask their obvious disappointment by tossing bitchy bons mots off in the direction of their peers, Thomas Bangalter and Guy-Manuel de Homem-Christo occupy a universe that's very much their own and as such would rather play with the latter's dog Goliath than fret about the arbitrary nature of awards. It could be an everyday scene were it not for one small thing: Thomas and Guy-Man clearly aren't like other people. For starters, they're not human. They are robots. So they claim.

"It's not a concept; it's an accident," says Thomas, impatiently. "There was an explosion at the studio which we could do nothing about, and we turned into robots. When was it? Oh," he continues, waving his right arm dismissively, "1999. September '99. Our faces got all fucked up, but it was very convenient. Because now that we're robots we don't need to wear masks. Robots are much funkier than masks."

Suddenly Goliath, hitherto peripheral, jumps onto his master's lap and begins to lick his face. He is sporting a black sock on his back left paw. Even Daft Punk's pets, it seem, have to be different.

Let's go back, way back. It's 1994. Jockey Slut's founders Paul Benney and John Burgess receive a record in the post from Scottish label Soma, the press release to which reads simply 'French Teen Techno'. The single, 'The New Wave'/'Alive', is good enough – especially the latter cut, a spiralling, grandiose track – but other factors prove more seductive than the sound.

For one, the record boasts an accompanying photograph which depicts two gawky-looking young Parisians staring defiantly at the photographer. One, tall and thin, has a pudding bowl-like haircut and the steely gaze of one who's studied iconography; while the other, flaunting what looks like a Shoreditch mullet, is shorter, fuller-faced and slightly effeminate, his right hand clasping a Gauloises to his lips just so. Benney and Burgess like the duo's insolence but, most importantly, they love their name: Daft Punk.

Nicked from a disparaging review in Melody Maker which described a single by their previous outfit Darlin' (a group of indie chancers whose ranks included Phoenix's Laurent 'Branco' Brancowitz) as the product of 'a bunch of daft punks', it suggested they weren't just musically adept but, unusually in ones so young, media literate.

"We were fed up with people going on about how faceless dance music was," remembers Benney. "We didn't think it was true. And here was this nice little package – two interesting looking, punky French kids who made electronic music and took their name from something out of Melody Maker."

Keen to afford the pair a wider audience, Benney rang up Soma who supplied him with their number, resulting in a 20-minute phone interview. The feature, the first ever Daft Punk article, ran in the May/June issue, a good three years before 'Homework''s acidic disco onslaught transformed 1997 into Daft Punk's year, altered the way in which their homeland was perceived and presented Madonna with the blueprint for 'Music'. In it Thomas, then 19 to Guy-Man's worldly 20, namechecked (Andrew) Weatherall, Luke Slater and Richie Hawtin, highlighted the debt they owed to Slam's Stuart McMillan ("We weren't even thinking of having 'The New Wave' released on Soma; we just wanted Stuart to hear our music. But he liked it, we did some more tracks

HX-9 :HY=H

and here we are") and was clearly flattered to be granted a platform.

"He couldn't believe that someone was showing an interest," reckons Benney.

Two years later, in 1996, convinced that the Frenchmen were destined to be huge having been impressed by a cluster of remixes and the grinding, muscular dynamics of 'Da Funk', Benney and Burgess chose to launch their first colour issue with a cover feature on Thomas and Guy-Man. Burgess travelled with the pair from Nottingham to London where they did the interview in a cramped hotel room which Guy-Man and Thomas were sharing with a friend.

"It was quite awkward," recounts Burgess. "Guy-Man was really sullen and kept on talking in French to his mate, who was staying on this rubbish little camp bed." If anything, however, the photo shoot was worse, with Guy-Man again reluctant to participate. Scarred, the camera-shy couple would later adopt masks, referring to it as the biggest mistake of their career.

But if Daft Punk circa 1996 were a trifle touchy they were at least, if nothing else, still accessible. Now in order to hear their new LP 'Discovery' ("Can you interpret it as 'disco very'?" teases Thomas. "Well, it's called 'Discovery' because everyone should discover it for themselves") you have to drop in on their London PR's office where you listen to it once, twice if you are lucky, contemplate taping it, make copious notes and leave. Now Daft Punk's influence on the zeitgeist is such that you share their precious time not just with NME but English Vogue, a Polish mag and a French journal for children which, according to the man from Virgin's Paris office, is aimed at "really young kids who're still learning to draw".

Now, lest we forget, Daft Punk have been reborn as robots, though they look deceptively, suspiciously human shorn as they are today of their metallic heads. Now, right this minute, they are sprawled across two sofas, a grape and apple-filled fruit bowl just within their reach. Guy-Man, the apotheosis of the adultlescent skate kid in his baggy jeans and unremarkable brown T-shirt, his centre-parted collar-length hair as lank as he is quiet, is staring absent-mindedly into

## "There was an explosion at the studio which we could do nothing about, and we turned into robots. When was it? September 1999. Our faces got all fucked up."

the middle distance while his louder colleague flicks through last month's Jockey Slut. Eventually he finds the page for which he's long been searching: 'Have You Ever Ridden A Horse?' with Romanthony.

"He's a Teacher," he gushes of the 'One More Time' singer who also graces 'Discovery''s final track, 'Too Long'. "Like Cajmere, he's shown that you can be minimal but also have soul and emotion as well as love and depth."

If Romanthony is indeed a Teacher, Thomas is by far the brightest pupil in the class. Decked out in a black sweatshirt and shiny combat trousers, he is the restless, edgy punk to Guy-Man's placid hippy, his inquisitive eyes betraying a fierce intelligence. Aged 25, he comes across as someone who's far older, thanks in no small part perhaps to his five-day worth of stubble. He also boasts the brusqueness of a grumpy OAP.

"What?" he'll growl to posers that he doesn't like the sound of then slump across the sofa, his head resting on one elbow, perusing his itinerary for an item of interest. Dislikes: queries which concern their metamorphosis from mask-wearing mavericks into fully-fledged robots, the love it/loathe it war of words that 'One More Time' provoked ("Some people loved it, some people

JOCKEY SLUT 2001 PAUL MARDLES

# "Electronic music, for us, is about innovation, inventing new things, trying to release the music in new ways. The word 'underground' doesn't mean anything anymore."

hated it. It's not a problem"), and the fact that they're not playing any British festivals ("There's too much stuff going on, that's all. That doesn't mean we're not interested"). Likes: open-ended questions which allow Bangalter to advertise the pleasure they derive from taking risks.

"Electronic music, for us, is about innovation, inventing new things, trying to release the music in new ways," he says, seemingly as comfortable in English as in French. "The word 'underground' doesn't mean anything anymore so it's really important to ask questions all the time.

"We're doing things to have fun and to prove to ourselves that we are free to do what we want to do. It's the essence of what we do. It's about waking up in the morning, having fun, making videos, making music or making no video. Just being really free. And if this freedom is transmitted and encourages people to be free too then it might be more important than the actual music. We were influenced by people who showed that there are no rules. And the most pleasing thing for us would be to influence people in a way that would ensure they'd create new rules themselves without following previous ones."

No rules indeed. If 'Discovery' possesses anything as po-faced as a message, it is this: ignore what's cool and be true to yourself. Allegedly informed by Aphex Twin's 'Windowlicker' and the flawless production sheen of hip hop's Jay-Z, it is, as second album law dictates, operatic, sprawling, huge, portentous and excessive. It is also, more importantly, a masterpiece. A masterpiece that bravely goes where few have dared to tread – the big-haired, rolled-up-jacket-sleeves early-80s – digging up the era's most embarrassing blunders and casually transforming them into A Good Idea by placing them in a fluorescent state-of-the-art context.

Some reference points: Buggles' 'Video Killed the Radio Star', stadium disco, shoulder pads, Rick James, Vangelis, spandex trousers, two-step, Andrew Lloyd-Webber, Van Halen, Rick Wakeman, 'War of the Worlds'... And that's just on first listen. You could go on and on.

"But it's not a retro album," argues Thomas, clasping a cushion to his chest like an insecure small child.

Suddenly Guy-Man, who thus far has been all but mute ("I think he said three words to me," laughs the journalist whose interview precedes Jockey Slut's), decides the time has come when he must contradict his pal.

"It's a nostalgic thing, I think," he says. "We were really young in the early-80s, like six and seven, so I think it's us touching on the sounds that we heard then."

"Yes," butts in Thomas, "it has a lot to do with our childhood and our state of mind back then when we were listening to rock, soul, disco, funk and electro. But we weren't asking ourselves back then if it was hype or not, if it was good or bad taste. We just loved those sounds. And that's really what we wanted to recreate – just being children again."

Certainly, as grandiose as 'Discovery' often is, it feels like the work of two impetuous, gifted schoolboys who've been given their older brother's dodgy record box, a sampler and as much free studio time as they require. 'Aerodynamic' – DJ Sneak directs his first rock opera – is so multi-layered and pregnant with ideas that it makes 'Bohemian Rhapsody' sound shallow and one-paced; 'Veridis Quo' is Air go techno in the 18th century; and 'Harder, Better, Faster, Stronger''s spittle-flecked electro, is Stephen Hawking freestyling at a party thrown by Prince. 'Work it! Make it! Play it! Do it! Power!', goes the 'chorus', evoking a gym instructor who has read too much Nietzsche.

And while 'Discovery' is rarely less than jubilant, the exquisite, melancholy 'Something About Us' ('I love you more than anyone in my life/I want you more than anyone in my life') suggests that beneath the robot masks and media-friendly concepts, Daft Punk are less mentalists than sentimentalists.

Its breathtaking scope owes a good deal to the fact that Daft Punk and Virgin have a special relationship. Ergo 'One More Time', their first single in four years (discounting Bangalter's 'Together' with DJ Falcon and Stardust's ubiquitous 'Music Sounds Better With You'), was released without a promo video. Further, Daft Punk are allowed to A&R themselves. Which begs the question how they guard against releasing rubbish? To whom do they play their new stuff?

Is there no one that they trust?

"What?" barks Thomas. "What? Who do we trust? Who do we trust? What do you mean?"

If no one else hears your work-in-progress, how do you know if what you've done is any good?

"The only people who heard our album were us," he says. "Our audience is ourselves. We don't know or care about other people's expectations. We just wanted to surprise ourselves. We don't control people's tastes. We don't *want* to control people's tastes."

On 'Homework', you will recall, there is a track called 'Teachers' ('Brian Wilson, George Clinton, Lil Louis, Ashley Beedle...') wherein the pair salute those acts who pointed the way forward and imbued them with the necessary urge to create. One wonders who, if today they re-made said record, Daft Punk would namecheck in their current frame of mind.

"We made 'Teachers' when we were 19/20 so I don't know now," says Guy-Man. "That was mainly about the roots of Chicago house because that was what we were listening to at that time. The list now wouldn't just include house or black music. Every time we pick up a pile of CDs or whatever there's always something. We have the chance to be open-minded about listening to whatever, knowing that..."

He asks Thomas for the English word he is looking for. Thomas, who is studying the press pack for Daft Club (a credit card-like invention which allows fans to download exclusive Daft Punk tracks), shrugs his shoulders listlessly. He doesn't know. Or care.

Guy: "... So, er... yes."

Thomas, it seems safe to say, has had enough. Later, walking past the room where they are ensconced, Jockey Slut catches some of their next interview. "But I thought you two were robots now," asks the Polish journo in a manner that suggests he is trying to raise a laugh.

"What?" comes the reply. A pause. Again: "What?" The dog barks. There's a nervous cough. And then it all goes quiet.

*Originally published in Jockey Slut, March 2001*

# QUESTIONS FROM THE 'TEACHERS'

### How many albums do you intend to release under the name Daft Punk?
*CAJMERE*

**Thomas:** "The same number that he intends to release under the name Green Velvet."
**Guy-Man:** "Many people think that we have all these masterplans, that we plan every strategy, but it's not like that at all. There's no plan regarding the number of albums we're going to put out. We really don't know."

### Any chance of a Daft Punk/ X-Press 2 soundclash?
*ASHLEY BEEDLE*

**Thomas:** "'London X-Press' and 'Muzik X-Press' were the biggest English house records along with Dave Clarke's singles, so we're big, big fans. Right now we're pretty booked up, but why not? We never say never. The cool thing right now is everybody doing their own thing – Ashley's doing his and we're doing ours – but one day it might be a good idea to unite. But if he wants to help us out, he should give us a ring."

### Who's your favourite French football player?
*DJ HELL*

**Thomas:** "I don't know. The French football team is an excellent one, as it showed at the European Championship and World Cup, so it would be really hard to pick one. Football is really all about teamwork."
**Guy-Man:** "If you look at it like 'Discovery', though, with all those 80s flavours then I would say (Michel) Platini."

### Do chimpanzees speak chimpaneez?
*DERRICK CARTER*

**Thomas:** "The answer is in 'Being John Malkovich'. There's a very interesting question about the way chimpanzees speak. It's a great, great film. I advise him to see it."

### Would you consider giving one of your teachers (me) a remix?
*DAVE CLARKE*

**Thomas:** "Yes, yes, yes, yes. We've met Dave Clarke a couple of times, and he was definitely the English house producer who influenced us the most. To me, 'Red One, 'Red Two' and 'Red Three' were the best English techno records. I'd say to him, would you consider helping us out with Daft Club 'cause I know he's really into new media and I'm sure that would really turn him on? So we can definitely work out something. Working on the second album was quite a lonely process, but now we're open to collaborations and working on different things."

### Your new LP is called 'Discovery'. Is ELO's Jeff Lynne an influence?
*LUKE SLATER*

**Thomas:** "We know some tracks by ELO, but we don't know about the 'Discovery' album."

# Daft Punk Were Playing At My House

Daft Punk were a pivotal act in **James Murphy**'s conversion to dance music. He recalls their impact on the early days of LCD Soundsystem and wonders why they didn't give him a wide berth...

"I first heard them at the DFA office, most likely from Marcus Lambkin (Shit Robot) or Tim (Goldsworthy). I think it was 'Teachers'. I never know what other people like and I'm always wrong. I always pick the song that's not the hit. 'Teachers' I was crazy about. It is quite like 'Losing My Edge' yes, it's a list of things.

"It took me a minute to get stuff because it wasn't my world and I didn't understand being in a room listening to dance music. I was puzzled and intrigued by it. I was surprised how blunt and dumb it was. I really loved all of 'Homework' and didn't really have track preferences until going out and hearing them. It was utilitarian, it wasn't hi-fi so it was quite punk which I liked. I wasn't a producer so sampling wasn't something I'd thought of since Deee-Lite, it wasn't part of my world. It was more of a curiosity to me. 'What the fuck is this?' Like when I heard The Fall. 'Why would someone leave the studio and think it's done?' Things I really like and mean something to me are like that. Things that grab me immediately aren't the things that stay with me.

"I didn't like rock-crossed dance music as it was done, the reason we did DFA-style stuff was I didn't like the dance music that rock kids liked. I liked 'Higher States of Consciousness' and 'Strings of Life', the early Warp bleep stuff and things like that. The DFA parties were '99/2000 so 'Homework' was our record. What I was gravitating towards was that it was clever, it was fun and it functioned.

"Why did I mention them in 'Losing My Edge'? Because I thought it was funny. It's all improvised, it wasn't written, it's a take from an improvisational performance. They were on my mind. It was a way of explaining a weird sentiment of a character of a DJ who is resentful of other people playing their records. They were emblematic of something people were proud of playing before other people. It wouldn't have worked if they weren't already pretty big.

lcd soundsystem
lcd soundsystem
lcd soundsystem
lcd soundsystem

# "I was there. I was the first guy playing Daft Punk to the rock kids. I played it at CBGB. Everybody thought I was crazy."

LCD Soundsystem: 'Losing My Edge'

'Daft Punk Is Playing at My House' came from me finding out they used to be in an indie band and got their name from a negative review in an English music paper. I was working with Tim and Marcus and David Holmes and discovering all this music that I'd missed because I was doing this other thing and I didn't go to raves like them or do ecstasy. I was thinking about what I did do during those same years was play punk shows in people's basements, play house shows. I would drive around and meet all these kids who were in bands and you'd show up at a house you'd heard about and some other band from the West Coast may show up and be kind of booked and they'd pass a hat around for money.

"I thought it would be really funny if someone who had been a punk house promoter had gotten into dance music and was obsessed about getting Daft Punk to play in their shared squat. They'd raise the money to meet the guarantee but nothing else, there'd be a cobbled together PA. Like everyone's practise PAs piled up. I liked the idea of an evangelical punk kid saving up their money to book Daft Punk. They'd have to show up in the bus, they'd be puzzled as to how it got booked and they'd show up next to the washing machine and do their show. I desperately wanted them in the video. I was going to find a good punk house and set up a show in a basement. They were being quite polite and said: 'Er, I don't think we have the time.' Ok, could we borrow your helmets?

I met Thomas after our Bataclan show in Paris (in 2003). He was very nice, very sweet, very polite. If I was him I'd have been: 'Why are you singing about my band?' It was brief, and I have great social anxiety, but I think we embarrassingly talked about the song. My memory is seeing lights and his face and the sound of my ears ringing. 'Don't worry I'm not a super fan trying to freak you out,' but how do I say that without insulting you and saying I'm not a fan? I've since become friends with them and met them millions of times over the years. It's easier because the band has gone on to do lots of other things, we're not just a band about Daft Punk, but in the beginning if I was them I'd be: 'We'll give this band a wide berth until we find out what they're about.'"

*James Murphy was in conversation with John Burgess*

"THEY SAID: 'NILE,
WE'D LIKE TO CO
APARTMENT AND
DEMOS FOR YOU.
MY APARTMENT A
THE CONCEPT OF
ME. THEY WANT T
AS IF THE INTERNE
AND I KNEW WHA

Nile Rodgers/Fender.com/2022

WE'RE IN TOWN.
E TO YOUR
LAY SOME
THEY COME TO
ID THEY EXPLAIN
THE ALBUM TO
DO A RECORD
NEVER EXISTED.
T THAT MEANT."

# FROM 'DA FUNK' TO 'EDEN'

## EXPLORING DAFT PUNK'S CINEMATIC LEGACY

Wading through an eccentric cast of melting cyborgs, sadistic record label bosses, and sad, human-sized dogs, **Thomas Hobbs** looks back at Daft Punk's cinematic portfolio, exploring the music videos, scores, and films that make up their impressive – and singular – legacy...

Sitting somewhere between euphoria and melancholy, Daft Punk's music opened electronica up to society's outsiders, prompting millions to consider the duality of technology and man while stuck in the middle of a sweaty dancefloor. But Daft Punk's contributions to cinema also deserve some credit, with the French duo consistently using the medium to boldly explore themes including identity, friendship, addiction, and isolation.

"We don't make films for others!" Guy-Manuel de Homem-Christo told Filmmaker magazine back in 2006. At the time he was promoting the duo's directorial debut, 'Daft Punk's Electroma', a surrealist midnight movie about two robots having an existential crisis in the desert. "We're not looking desperately for success or to make people like what we do. We want to make things the most honest and best way for us, which I think makes people like it even more."

In the same interview, his creative partner Thomas Bangalter added: "Filmmaking is usually very coded with a pre-formatted alphabet. We're trying to get our limits outside of that (with 'Electroma'), through maybe using some old language that you don't feel in theatres right now."

### KEEPING IT FUNKY

Released in 1995, the once-heard, never-forgotten 'Da Funk' was some introduction to Daft Punk – the sparkly, but inward-looking G-Funk present bringing something truly original to dance music. The track's neon-lit music video, which was directed by Spike Jonze (a veteran of music videos for the likes of Beastie Boys, Sonic Youth, Björk and R.E.M.), showed the duo were just as committed to leaving a mark visually.

Following a depressed dude, Charles, in a shrivelled-up dog costume hobbling through Los Angeles, it could be read a thousand different ways, with fans unable to agree whether it was an exploration of urbanism and displacement in the big city or just a straight-forward tale of a big socially awkward dog with a boombox.

"We shot it over three nights on the Lower East Side, when it was freezing cold, and we had a lot of drunks and hecklers to contend with," said Jonze in a DVD commentary. "Tony Maxwell who played Charles was like a silent movie actor from a different era."

The filmmaker, who went on to direct the celebrated feature films 'Being John Malkovich', 'Adaptation', 'Where the Wild Things Are' and 'Her', says the drunken hecklers only added to Maxwell's isolation and role as the outsider.

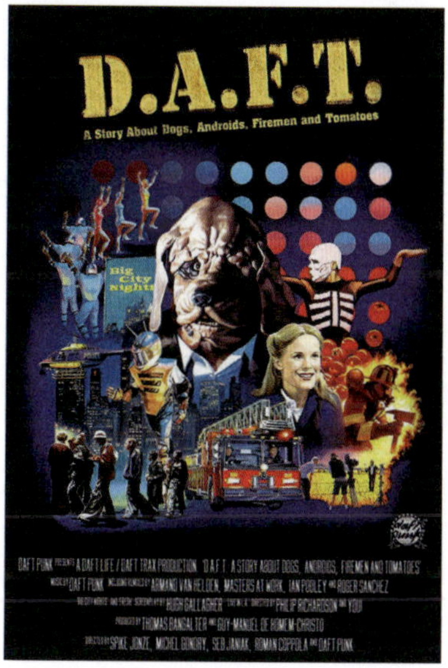


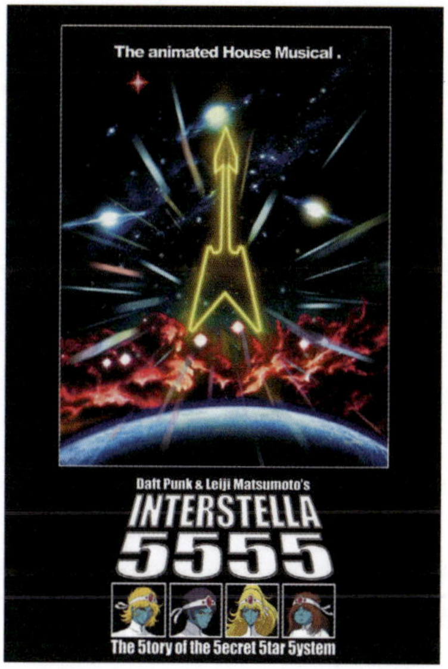


The fact the video's minimalism prompted so many different theories showed an awareness among Bangalter and Homem-Christo that experimenting with traditional story structure could give their on-screen productions a poetic edge, as fans formed their own interpretations and feverishly searched the background of videos for Easter Eggs with hidden meanings. This was a pop act beginning to create their own cinematic universe, where weirdos were at the epicentre, decades before it became commonplace like in today's Marvel-obsessed internet era.

## GLOBE-TROTTING ROBOTS

Just two years later Daft Punk put out the joyous music video for 'Around the World', which was directed by Michel Gondry (another auteur with impeccable music video taste having helmed promos for Björk, Massive Attack, Neneh Cherry and The Rolling Stones before going on to make 'Eternal Sunshine of the Spotless Mind') at the peak of his powers. With synchronised dancing by skeletons, ancient mummies and robots, who each move in time with a different layer of the music, this kaleidoscopic 1997 video captured the carefree optimism of the 90s.

But the reason it ranks among Daft Punk's greatest cinematic achievements is its simplicity, as the video makes the case for the healing powers of dance. The robots were also perhaps a nod to the future, where sci-fi would become a more integral part of the duo's act.

In fact, by 2005, the robot costumes were far more sophisticated and flamboyant, with that year's self-directed 'Robot Rock' video featuring the pair as androids playing double guitars and drums in a grainy, psychedelic studio, which was as sleazy as it was colourful. While their previous music videos (forming an excellent 2000 DVD collection 'D.A.F.T.: A story about Dogs, Androids, Firemen and Tomatoes') played around with narrative structure, 'Robot Rock' created an influential, 70s-aping, lo-fi aesthetic; the grounding for later videos like 'Get Lucky' and 'Instant Crush'. Much like 'Around the World', this music video freed pop stars to do spectacle on a tight budget.

## INTERSTELLAR TRAVELLERS

A bit like 'Fantasia' for someone gurning in awe at a house rave, Daft Punk's journey into animé – 2003's 'Interstellar 5555: The 5tory of the 5ecret 5tar 5ystem' – was a triumph. The duo combined with co-directors Kazuhisa Takenouchi ('Dragon Ball Z'), Leiji Matsumoto ('Harlock: Space Pirate'), Hirotoshi Rissen ('One Piece: The Movie'), and Daisuke Nishio ('3x3 Eyes') to produce a syrupy escapism that somehow never turned sickly.

These directors were recruited due to the duo's deep love of Japanese animation and a

childhood spent prioritising 'Captain Harlock' and 'Dragon Ball Z' binges over going outside and playing sports with the other kids.

Following the intergalactic rock band Crescendolls as they move through the galaxy playing different venues, 'Interstellar 5555' results in a surprisingly romantic meditation on the exploitation that fuels the music business. The group are imprisoned inside a cock-shaped spaceship (Jeff Bezos must have been a fan), where vampirical record executive The Earl de Darkwood – who is like a mix of Phil Spector and Sonic's arch nemesis Dr. Robotnik – uses the members to boost his profits. The dark capitalist soul of the music industry results in few happy endings, and this makes 'Interstellar 5555''s optimism feel genuinely refreshing.

The turbo-charged narrative suggests the band were fighting their own battle around being turned into a manufactured product – it was tellingly released at a moment where 2001 album 'Discovery' ('Interstellar 5555''s sonic companion) was about to send Daft Punk's pop credentials into the stratosphere. The influence of a Japanese manga like 'Space Pirate Captain Harlock' is obvious, as are the nods to 'Star Wars' and the stargate sequence in Kubrick's '2001: A Space Odyssey'.

Yet this short film shines so bright because it suggests a hopeful future, where artists can take control of their destiny and music can prompt togetherness that cuts through class or race. At a time where things are becoming increasingly tribal, watching 'Interstellar 5555' feels more and more like an act of self-care, and its influence can be reflected in hip hop via artists like Kanye West and Lil Uzi Vert, who channelled 'Interstellar 5555' in the creative direction for bold cartoonish records like 'Graduation' and 'Eternal Atake'.

## DRIFTING THROUGH THE DESERT

Not featuring any Daft Punk music (it instead relied on gentle introspective cuts from the likes of Curtis Mayfield, Linda Perhacs, and Jackson C. Frank), and built around a plot where little happens beyond two robots walking through sand while pondering existence, the duo went full arthouse with the self-directed 'Daft Punk's Electroma' back in 2006. It may have alienated the casual fans, but 'Electroma' became a cult classic thanks to popular, smoked-out midnight cinema screenings and a timeless plot that reckons robots will one day grapple with depression just like their human creators do.

'Electroma' has a surrealist leaning, channelling Spanish filmmaker Luis Buñuel's love of flipping social norms as well as the mysterious small towns at the heart of David Lynch's oddities. The 72-minute film follows two robots who put on rubber masks to try and appear more human, but

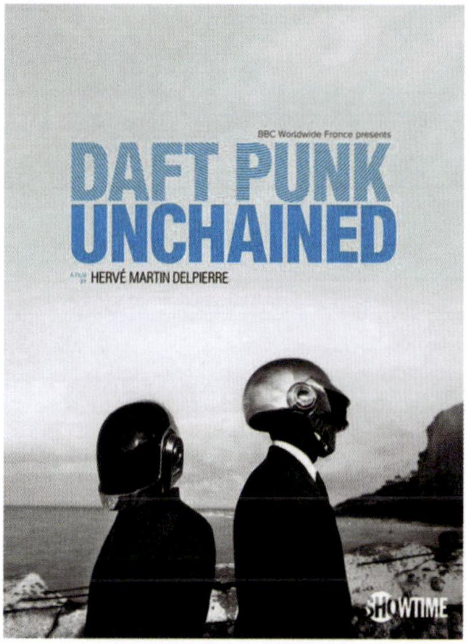


the uniforms quickly melt in the heat. The juxtaposition between a barren landscape and sentient machines able to self-destruct at will is fascinating, with the picture succeeding in making its robot leads appear like sad cowboys.

It's a restrained film that showed another side to Daft Punk as filmmakers, sacrificing the flashiness for stillness. And today, at a time when artificial intelligence is becoming more autonomous and self-aware, the film offers a prescient warning that forcing robots to emulate humans may ultimately result in disaster.

## HOLLYWOOD COMPOSERS

'Tron: Legacy', a sequel to the 80s Disney classic, explores the increasing ubiquity of human beings and the video game landscapes they like to get lost in. When Daft Punk were announced as the 2010 film's composers, many expected infectious 'One More Time'-style jams to play out as characters raced motorbikes through a glitzy Atari algorithm. Yet the film showed an incredible level of calmness from the duo.

It might have disappointed some, but there's something impressive about the way Daft Punk combine classical violins with heart-thumping bass without ever trying to supersede the visuals. If Homem-Christo or Bangalter move more seriously into scoring Hollywood films in the future, 'Tron: Legacy' suggests they'll do less flamboyant things that don't sit directly in the shadow of Daft Punk and know when to hold back.

But perhaps the most affecting use of Daft Punk's music in a film can be found within 2014's 'Eden'. Directed by Mia Hansen-Love, the film documents the rise of electronic and house music in Paris in the 1990s. Fictional DJ Paul rises through the ranks at the same time as Daft Punk, with the film hilariously showing the latter being refused entry to nightclubs for not being famous enough. An early performance of 'Da Funk' will make your hair stand on end, while the use of 'Veridis Quo', a Greek tragedy in synth pop form, perfectly aligns with Paul's descent into addiction and self-parody.

Daft Punk licensed their music for 'Eden' at the lowest possible fee ($3700), clearly impressed with an honest story that dared to show the fragile human beings left behind after all the parties had ended. Although the group is defined by its futurism, 'Eden' highlights Thomas and Guy-Man's human core, and the featured Daft Punk songs prove the French duo's songs can soundtrack just about any emotion. It also demonstrated electronic music doesn't just have to be the source of jubilation in movies, but can also prompt moments of self-reflection that offer a raw insight into the human condition; a message that aligns with Daft Punk's own cinematic journey.

# Human Behaviour

Daft Punk's third album, 'Human After All', was subject to a barrage of hostile reviews upon its release. **Jim Butler** looks back on the perceived first mis-step of the band's career and asks whether, 18 years on, it's really as bad as we were led to believe?

True genius, it's often said, is flawed. From the birth of Greek mythology, via the writings of Shakespeare and right up to the modern day we can't help worshipping at the altar of tragic heroes. Recent real-life modern variants would be Amy Winehouse and Diego Maradona – George Best, Elvis Presley and Marilyn Monroe before them. Their genius – so the argument goes – is amplified and made more relatable because of their very vivid imperfections.

It's an idea that is never far from the surface when analysing Daft Punk's third album, 2005's 'Human After All'. This was the album – knocked off in six weeks apparently – that rather than drowning in a sea of critical hosannas was panned beyond belief. Made without synthesisers, relying instead upon two guitars, two drum machines, one vocoder and a solitary 8-track machine, it's an abrasive, angry, almost nihilistic record – the polar opposite to what came before. And yet, despite the robotic conceits Daft Punk had embraced, it's the one album that exposes Thomas Bangalter and Guy-Manuel de Homem-Christo as not sui generis, but, instead, mortal - the title serving as a great, big flashing neon clue for starters. So when placed in the context of their career, it's the release that reveals and reinforces their brilliance.

In 2005, however, this wasn't the case. The album was predominantly met with derision and disappointment among contemporary reviews. Pitchfork, then at the beginning of its online authority, awarded it a damning 4.9 (out of 10), lamenting that: "It's Daft Punk going

through the motions and, for the first time in their career, sounding like cynics." American dance music magazine Urb called it "completely disappointing" and New York's influential Village Voice stated it was "determinedly monochromatic aurally, compositionally, and mood-wise." In the UK, Q gave it two stars, but arguably the most coruscating review came from Dorian Lynskey in the Guardian who, in also giving it two stars, described it as "a joyless collection of average ideas stretched desperately thin. If Daft Punk played this at your house, you'd chuck them out", referencing LCD Soundsystem's 'Daft Punk is Playing at My House' that came out a few weeks before 'Human After All'.

Today, 18 years on, there's been little appetite to reassess the album. And while the mood has tempered slightly – perhaps because what followed with their Pyramid shows a year later – the prevailing critical consensus would appear to be one of general indifference. 'Discovery', 'Human After All''s high-gloss predecessor also confounded some critics and listeners upon release, but it was immediately apparent that it was a significant album. 'Human After All', on the other hand, came out at a troubling time for dance and electronic music. In the wake of The Strokes and The White Stripes' energetic emergence a few years previously, rock music was supposedly where it was at.

Moreover, how we consumed music was changing. We weren't all streaming at this point, but in the age of Napster and Limewire, swathes of people were gleefully helping themselves to music online. Musical technology was changing too – how people made and presented music was rapidly shifting. It was a time when previously held truths were being torn asunder as humanity's vexed relationship with technology – a theme running through 'Human After All' - was going through one of its periodical transformations. No wonder people were unsure what was going on.

Looking back, Pedro Winter, Daft Punk's comrade and long-standing manager, remembers the period being a time of tumult for Thomas Bangalter and Guy-Man de Homem-Christo too.

"They were searching for the right equipment," he recalls. "Technology was changing, you know, the tools were changing so they had new equipment and stuff. Thomas was reading all the manuals and learning pretty fast of course. Once they had the full set up, [it was] let's record. I think in six weeks we got it. We loved this album..." His voice drops, pre-empting what followed: "The reviews were terrible."

> "They were searching for the right equipment. Technology was changing... Once they had the full set up, [it was] let's record. I think in six weeks we got it. We loved this album... the reviews were terrible."

"I was extremely harsh. I think I was cross with them."

Dorian Lynskey is reflecting upon *his* brutal Guardian review. As well as calling it joyless, he stated it recycled "a handful of familiar production tics – vocoders, processed rock guitars, snub-nosed beats – to the point of inanity". And in referring to the alleged time it took to write and record the album, he noted caustically. "[It] sounds like it took six days. Six short days. With long lunches."

"I think because they were so venerated from the start – and I was a fan. I saw them live around 'Homework', I loved 'Homework'," he says. "But they were worshipped by a culture that doesn't really exist anymore, you know, the likes of [style magazines] Sleazenation, The Face and so on. It was like they could do no wrong. Once someone was venerated... when they fell short I was just harsher because I didn't want to give them too much credit."

It wasn't blanket scorn though. James Pitt, then head of the dance department at Daft Punk's record label, Virgin, loved it. Coming from what he calls a "background of noise" citing Suicide, the Velvet Underground, Sonic Youth and Spacemen 3 as bands he adored, he was "absolutely over the fucking moon" when he heard it. "It was totally up my street. It was really punky."

Unfortunately, not everyone at the label shared his enthusiasm. Virgin were waiting for an album but Pitt says they didn't know the duo were recording a new one. "It was a surprise when it landed on my desk."

His surprise was marked by others' disappointment. "I was sitting in a room with radio pluggers and marketing people and there was less excitement because they didn't hear a hit. They were hoping they'd carry on where 'Discovery' left off. This was a lot more raw and less radio-friendly. So there wasn't as much action around the album as I would have expected."

Those charged with promoting the album might have emitted a sigh of disinterest, but Soulwax/2manydjs' David and Stephen Dewaele saw that the music was doing the business on dancefloors across the world.

"As DJs who were playing three or four times a week," remembers David, "there was so much in there that was working. We would play in front of crowds and they would go nuts for things like 'Robot Rock'."

According to Pitt this was always the intention. Following the demise of the superclub era and in the wake of electroclash, many electronic producers went back to basics and began marrying savage sounds – as if emulating the aesthetics of rock – to dance music's electronic pulse.

"The sound of the tracks was influenced by what was happening in the clubs at the time," recalls Pitt. "There were quite a lot of electro-sounding records that were doing well. I think they were mainly made for that. I think it was more that they wanted to make some harsh, angry sounding records to be played out in clubs."

Erol Alkan, a DJ who had made his name by not seeing a distinction between rock and dance, believes the album certainly chimed with some of that adventurous spirit that imbued the times.

"It was in line with a lot of other stuff that was happening," he explains. "Things getting noisier. You could tell it wasn't going to be as easy to get into as 'Discovery'. I thought it was brave."

"It's undeniable there was a thing in the air," remembers David Dewaele. "That we also manifested, and many people around, which was to bring the energy of rock into dance music. Obviously it's impossible for us to know what the impetus was. We've met them many times over the years and we've never had that conversation. But that idea, like LCD and other bands playing stuff you could dance to, that was very much alive."

Relishing this sonic volte face, Pitt organised a listening party for the album at London's fabric. Rather than journalists and radio pluggers listening to it for the first time on headphones after they'd received their watermarked CDs – the music industry was increasingly cautious in the mid-00s, petrified as it was by file-sharing sites like Napster – he wanted it heard in context.

"It was made to be heard on big fucking Marshall stacks," he laughs. "That's why I did it at fabric on that bouncy floor. I wanted people to feel the music. If people listened to it on the office stereo they would have thought about radio and commerciality – they wouldn't have thought about the power of the music."

He also invited lots of club DJs too. Those with a similar approach and outlook who he hoped would get it. "So if Erol was standing next to a journalist and he was excited, hopefully the journalist would pick up on that."

Unfortunately, while the evening itself went off pleasantly enough ("Looking back we could have probably put a bit more thought into it," Pitt says, "maybe a bit more staging, got some input from the band. There wasn't much going on other than literally playing the album – a few drinks") an incident followed that seriously soured the night. An incident that almost cost Pitt his job.

"My watermarked CD – the one that was played at the party – was leaked online the next day," he explains, an air of incredulity still apparent. "Someone during the playback managed to copy my CD. Virgin suspended me. I went into HR and was like: 'I'm one of the few people to give a fuck about this album. Why would I put it on the internet? I'm the one trying to make it a success.'"

After a couple of weeks protesting his innocence Pitt was eventually believed and allowed to return to work. Looking back, he doesn't think too much damage was done, although reviews at the time mention a leak (Erol admits he got sent a "moody link before it came out") and refer to disbelieving listeners arguing that this noisy, experimental music wasn't the work of the sonic perfectionists who had toiled over 'Discovery'.

"I think the increased security alongside the fact that it didn't sound like them and it did sound like other French artists might have fed some theories," laughs Pitt today.

It's not comforting, but if Daft Punk weren't breaking new ground artistically, they were one of the first casualties of online fake news.

When Daft Punk first emerged from Montmartre's creatively fertile and multicultural boulevards in the mid-90s much was made of their adopted moniker. It was funny. Provocative. Exciting. What it wasn't was accurate.

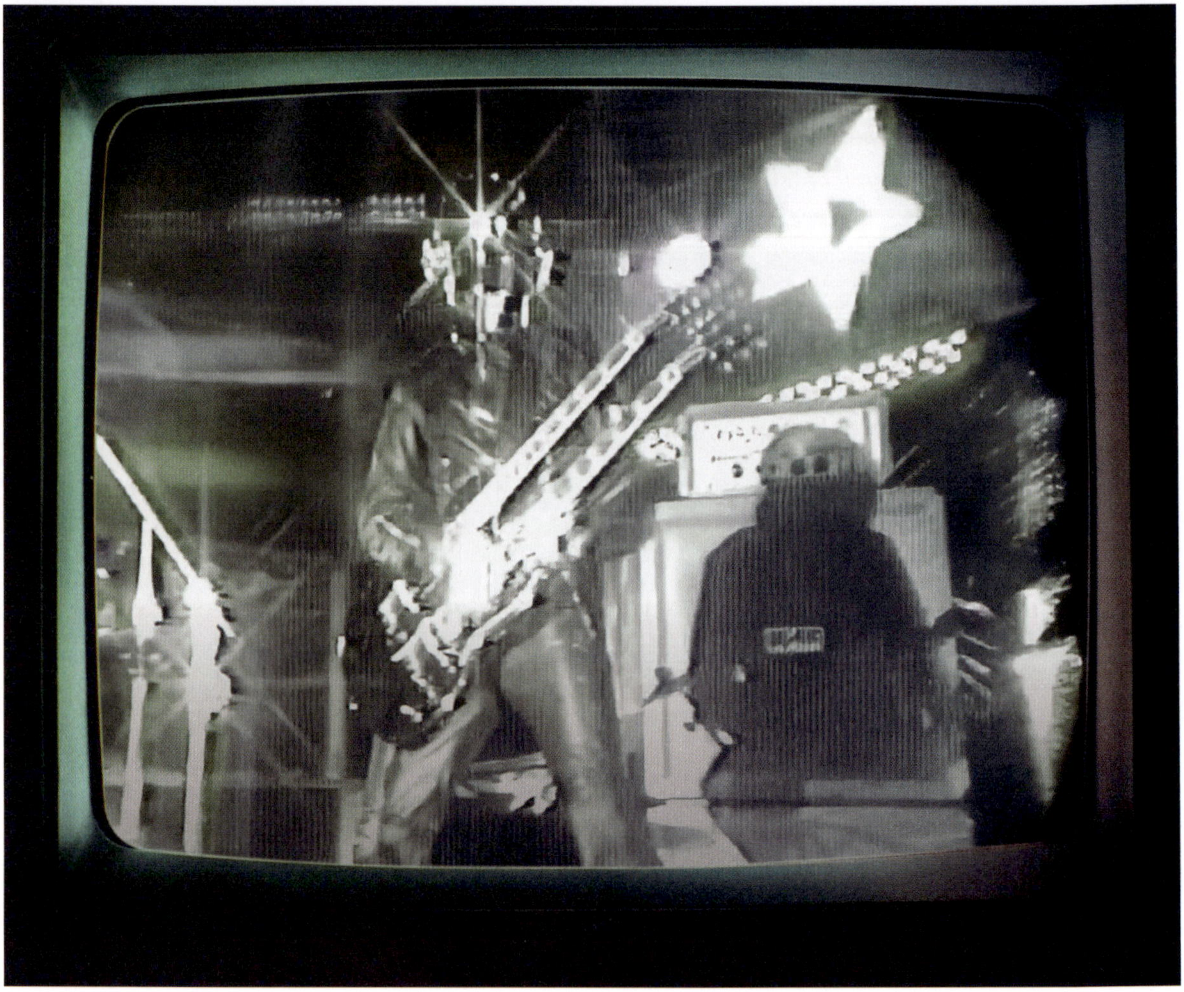

Their first releases breathed new life into the founding templates of Chicago house and Detroit techno – mixed with some typical French elan – culminating in the era-defining 'Homework'. 'Discovery''s synthesis of childhood nostalgia, alluring sci-fi futurism, elevated production and the emergence of the robots, meanwhile, turned everything up to 11.

The raw reset of 'Human After All', however, did sound like daft punk. Unquestionably unapologetic, certainly underdeveloped, possibly even unfinished, it sounds like the stylish robots had kidnapped Mark E Smith and staged a coup to take control of The Fall and transform the miserable Mancunians into a thrash band. Kicking off with the title track, the album begins with a crunching drum beat that moves at a fair lick and what sounds like the sonic equivalent of robots puking their shiny guts up, as if regurgitating the rotting corpse of dance music. An irreverent buzzsaw guitar – reminiscent of a heavily processed Link Wray – further signals the intent. The euphoric 'Digital Love' it certainly wasn't.

It doesn't get particularly nuanced or subtle thereafter either. 'Robot Rock' is an unholy alliance between AC/DC's guileless rock and Kiss's glam metal – where denim meets sequins. 'The Brainwasher' offers up the tantalising prospect of Lemmy on MDMA – another grinding, pounding repetitive groove, while the squelching 'Steam Machine' comes on like 'Da Funk''s cheeky street urchin cousin.

Only the breezy, Californian soft rock vibes of 'Make Love' and 'Emotion' – both pre-empting the chillwave phenomenon by a good couple of years – stand alone as aural relief. Over 10 (eight of them unrelenting) tracks – and clocking in at a healthy punk-like 45 minutes – the effect is disorientating. No wonder it bemused many expecting another 'Discovery'.

"'Random Access Memories' would have been a more logical follow up to 'Discovery'," says Lynskey. "You get bigger and lusher and more in tune with classic 70s production."

"'Homework' was two guys in a bedroom making this ground-breaking album," states David Dewaele. "Then on 'Discovery' it went wider – all the guitars, samples and disco stuff. What they did with 'Human After All' was narrow it down again. So for people looking at a trajectory it might have been a bit: 'Oh! This isn't building.'"

Both Pitt and Winter loved it for this very contrary nature.

"It's repetition as beauty," says Pitt. "It's transcendental to me. That harsh repetition, those minimal lyrics that some people thought were devoid of meaning, but after enough repetition they become something."

"I loved it," counters Winter. "Some people were saying that Daft Punk went too far on 'Discovery'. So what about going back to the roots? Are you ready for this? And then of course people were like: 'Whoa, whoa, whoa! Where is 'One More Time'?"

"I think Guy-Man said it was a stone left unworked in an interview," says Pitt. "It was definitely rough. Intentionally so. I think they were pissed off at how long it had taken them to do 'Discovery' – something like two-and-a-half years. So it was a response to that. To get something out there. When you create art you want something to happen quickly sometimes. It was a jam."

Never the most forthcoming interviewees, Daft Punk did scant promotion for the album – as if embracing the ambivalence that some at their record label displayed. So, we never got to know what they were thinking at the time – was the album really inspired by George Orwell's '1984'? Was the album meant to act as an alternative soundtrack to their directorial debut 'Electroma', which was released the following year?

The duo did offer some clues as time went on, however. Acknowledging the minimal, angry, almost paranoid aesthetic during an interview with Anthem magazine in 2007, Bangalter confided: "Our first two albums are really happy, they make you feel good and make you want to dance. It's a natural high. On the opposing side, both 'Human After All' and 'Electroma' are extremely tormented and sad and terrifying looks at technology, yet there can be some beauty and emoting from it."

The same year, Bangalter told The Fader quite simply: "It's not a fun record. It's not something intended to make you feel good."

In 2013, Guy-Man, revealing more than normal, told Dazed that each album they had written was closely linked to their lives at that time, before adding cryptically: "The internal, personal stuff Thomas went through during 'Human After All' made it closer to where he was at at the time."

Listening back today, Lynskey's opinions have mellowed slightly over time. He's adamant that some of it is still half-arsed and in need of finishing, but it's not worthless.

"As with all Daft Punk stuff they made deliberate choices," he says. "It was not a choice that I or most people enjoyed, but it kind of makes sense in context. And the best tracks when they were going for that sound really worked. They do sound amazing."

That context is of course the live shows that followed the release of 'Human After All', starting with the iconic Coachella performance. 'Human After All' might not have been the most conducive home listening experience for some, but transported to the live arena and it was a work of art transformed. As the accompanying album, 'Alive 2007', attests, the likes of 'Robot Rock', 'Technologic' and the title track, mixed ecstatically with tracks from 'Homework' and 'Discovery' bring the live experience to life.

"This album is the sparkle that makes Coachella and 'Alive 2007'," says Winter. "It's a triangular thing. They were missing a third one for the mix to be crazy. This album wasn't made with the live shows in mind, but when you step back you realise it was the missing piece to create the Pyramid."

It's a point that Soulwax hammer home.

"I remember when we watched the Pyramid show for the first time," remembers David. "We played right before them at Rockness, near the Loch Ness lake, and we both said: 'Right, now people will get the album.'"

For all his reservations, Lynskey admits that the live shows were where the record made most sense. He refers to a theory that did the rounds at the beginning of the third season of 'Succession'. Someone tweeted that 'Succession' reminded them of 'Breaking Bad' – that each season starts off with a tinge of disappointment because the show seems stuck and the best is in the past.

"And then by the end of the season you realise you're not cleverer than the show runner and the show runner knew what they were doing. I think that with this, when they did the live shows you realise they needed this heavier, harsher stuff. Live they combined the more tracky, abrasiveness of 'Homework' with the sounds and influences from 'Discovery' in a really productive way. This is the quintessential Daft Punk sound. Even if a lot of the tracks don't go anywhere, they sound great in small doses."

Pitt, unsurprisingly, relished how the album translated live and sees a deeper causal link between the two. 'Human After All', he surmises, was Thomas and Guy-Man scorching the Earth, leaving nothing of who we thought they were.

"Their ambition kicked in again," he suggests. "And I think the ambition of the show wouldn't have happened without the nihilism of this record. I think it reinvigorated their creative process."

Soulwax believe the album laid the groundwork for electronic music to transcend into hip hop – as was the case with Kanye West – and the wider American popular culture.

"It was like unleashing a monster," opines Stephen Dewaele. "Before that a lot of the gatekeepers were European. It was a really, really big moment. And this record kind of instigated it really. I do think there was another generation that comes up – the likes of Skrillex and all those kids that just went: 'Waaah!'

"A lot of these tracks, like 'Technologic' made sense in America after people saw it live. 'Oh, we can use this in a commercial. We can do this thing.' All of a sudden it does become part of the lexicon. It's a key that opened up America, and henceforth anything that comes after that."

## "It's repetition as beauty. It's transcendental. That repetition, those minimal lyrics that some thought were devoid of meaning, but after enough repetition they become something."

David concurs: "Bear in mind if you were to speak to someone in America right now and play them 'Da Funk' and 'Technologic', they would probably know 'Technologic'. Whereas in Europe, 'Da Funk' was the biggest hit. Something happens. It's the Year Zero for them [America]."

So where does that leave 'Human After All' today? The kneejerk reaction is still to refer to it disparagingly. But how many are merely aping supposed received wisdom? Granted, it's not perfect by any stretch, but listening back today, it's a riot. It's flawed, undoubtedly, but it's a riot. It's full of knowing street smarts and seditious acid house punk rock - which makes Jerry Lee Lewis' raucous 'Live at the Star Club, Hamburg' sound like a bunch of nursery rhymes performed by The Osmonds.

"It's interesting seeing the story in context," reflects Lynskey. "Seeing how it ends. That they

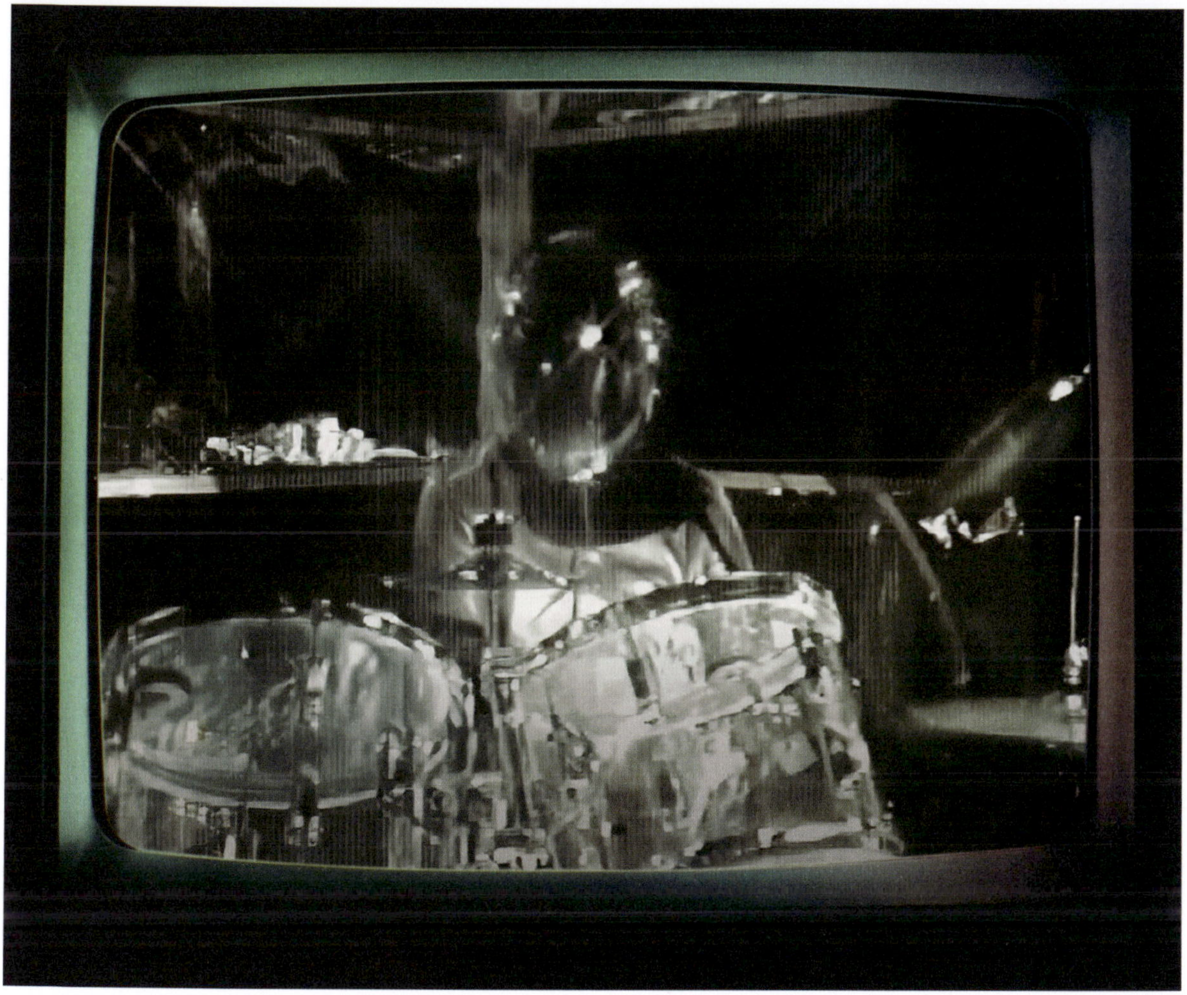

can do this soft-rocky, disco stuff or they can do this snarly, techno rock thing. But you always know it's Daft Punk. For an album to really fail it has to sound kind of anonymous. To lose the essence of what makes that band special. And there's a concentrated essence there. It's like the scaffolding for an amazing record. But they just didn't put the cladding on."

In this sense, 'Human After All' should be placed alongside other notable 'failures' (and that's used advisedly) like Lou Reed's 'Metal Machine Music', Joni Mitchell's 'Dog Eat Dog', Neil Young's 'Trans' and Bob Dylan's 'Self Portrait'.

"It makes me like their career more," Lynskey concludes. "The fact that it wasn't just four universally admired albums. When you judge an artist, a lot of the time you're looking at how do you respond to failure and Daft Punk's response was to act as though it wasn't a failure at all."

F. Scott Fitzgerald – no stranger to the idea of the flawed genius – once wrote: "Show me a hero and I'll show you a tragedy." Daft Punk's third album was the first tragedy of their astounding career. And while today it shouldn't be seen as such, what it does do is cleverly demonstrate that they were human. Human after all.

# MR NO

Between 1995 and 2008, no one got closer to Daft Punk than Pedro Winter. First as a friend and travelling companion and then as their manager with a fondness for the word no, Winter witnessed their dizzying ascent first-hand. Speaking to **John Burgess** he looks back fondly on the best time of his life...

Pierre Winter has adopted many names over the years. His nickname is Pedro, his stage nom de plume is Busy P, but when he managed Daft Punk for over a decade he became known as Mr No. As he reveals, he was the duo's naysayer, turning down offers for DJ gigs from clubs all over the world and declining remix offers from mega stars like Björk and George Michael.

A law student by day and Parisian mover and shaker by night, he joined the Daft crew in 1995, when Thomas and Guy-Man were already rising stars, assisting them on early jaunts around Europe. If a manager has many jobs one of the most important is being a buffer between the artist and the promoter and this is where Pedro would shine. He was always an affable chap; warm, fun and eager to talk whereas Daft Punk could be shy and unforthcoming. Leaving his law ambitions behind he learnt and honed his skills on the fly and was still managing Daft Punk when they played Coachella in 2006, a show he could finally say yes to.

With a desire to spin records rather than plates he left the Daft Camp soon after to focus on Ed Banger records, managing Justice and being an artist in his own right. Mr No became Very Busy P.

**When did you start working with Daft Punk?**

"I bought 'Da Funk' when it was on Soma and I met the guys in a radio station in Paris when they were promoting it. I was throwing my parties and we met like that. 'Ok, you're doing a record, I'm doing parties.' Literally, it happens like that. It was in 1995. I went to their studio and they were recording 'Around the World' and all those tracks. The music was done in total freedom as they had not signed with Virgin yet. It was the first step, so I think it was important. I started to work with them in 1996."

**Do you remember the very early touring period? How important was that in refining those early singles? Because 'Around the World' wouldn't have been played at that point, I don't think.**

"No, not at that point, in 1995 the track 'Alive' was the big thing. Of course, it was already released on Soma, but 'Alive' was the big rave track, you know, and so it was at the same time a rave track and a club track. And of course, 'Da Funk' started to make some noise. It was released in 1995 on Soma and a couple of years later we released it on Virgin. But at the time they were playing it live. In 1995 we started to hang out, I was part of this Daft friends zone and we were always travelling, six or seven friends together. They were not only doing this as a friendly thing, they were doing this because we were all carrying suitcases. The list of gear the boys were doing their first Daft Punk live show with was insane. They were bringing on stage the TR-909, sequencers, their classic Juno 106 and the SP-1200 belonging to Guy-Man. We were putting all this equipment into towels, into suitcases, so it was completely freestyle and unorganised. This is why we were all travelling together, because we needed hands to carry ten suitcases and boxes to plug all this in for Bugged Out! in Manchester or whatever. Today, when you do a live show, you come up on stage with just a laptop. They had no screen, they had no computer on stage."

**I'm surprised 'Da Funk' didn't end up as a fast track from those early live shows because everything was so banging – 'Rollin' and Scratchin'' for example. Do you remember them playing that?**

"Of course, yes. But 'Da Funk', you know, especially in France, I have a clear vision of what happened in France, it brought back this groove into the clubs."

**How significant was signing with Virgin?**

"Signing with Virgin had different meanings. Electronic music was suddenly something that interested major labels. It also meant that an independent label like Soma and an underground artist like Daft Punk could enter the big game of the music business and with the major label investment make sure they could reach the world."

**Can you describe in detail the studio where 'Homework' was made? Did the guys live there?**

"'Homework' was done in Thomas' bedroom. It's in the heart of Montmartre. Thomas' parents had an amazing apartment on two floors and on the first

Thomas and Pedro with American house royalty, Todd Terry

floor of the house they had a guest room and he took out the bed and did his own studio there. Very tiny, very small. No chairs. Thomas was working on the floor. On his knees. It was pretty well equipped for 1996, all the equipment cost a lot. To have a sampler, it was like thousands of francs, so it was not accessible to everyone. So, luckily he was coming from a wealthy family. Guy-Man was coming every day to the studio and then we decided to find an office. That was like five minutes away from the studio so we could do studio/office, studio/office. 'Discovery' was done in the same place. 'Human After All' was in another studio and also done in Thomas' first solo apartment, which is also in Montmartre. This time he didn't build a crazy studio, but he had a bigger room with a high ceiling. I'm sure that had chairs, though I have a vision of Thomas always on the floor. Always on the floor with his ankle bouncing. You know, he was on his knees and his ankles were touching each other on rhythm. I think first he liked it, and I'm sure the reason he was on the floor is also that he could plug and unplug the mixing stuff."

**How much influence did Thomas' father have on the early direction of your career as their manager?**
"Daniel was and has been there since day one. First around the band, then of course around me, because I suddenly became the one in between the band and Daniel. Daniel of course is the father of Thomas so I think Thomas was happy to have someone in between. Daniel was a great person to consult as he knew about the music business. He knew about success and also he was sharing with Thomas and Guy-Man what was the right and what was the wrong direction, or at least make them aware, as a father would do with his child. So Daniel was really helpful to me because I was 20 years old. I knew nothing about the music business. I wanted to become a lawyer and had been in law school for three months. To be honest, I didn't learn anything. Daniel was definitely the best teacher I had, because he shared with me all the keys of this business. After that, of course, you take the information, you digest it and I kept what I needed. I know some people try and say that Daniel was the master of puppets. This is not how it worked with Daft Punk. Of course he was sharing and giving a lot of information, but at the end, Thomas and Guy-Man were only picking up what they wanted to know."

**Was there a pivotal moment where you realised that 'Homework' had really broken through? Was there a moment on the second tour in 1997 when you thought, wow, this has gone crazy?**
"I was checking the sales of 'Homework' every week and of course, at some point when the album sales were more than one million, I thought: 'Ok, well, this is becoming serious.' But it wasn't what drove me. It was more about: 'What's next? What can we do with this? Ok, we sold one million. Ok, do we have enough money to make another video that costs 1 million francs?' Working with Spike Jonze and Michel Gondry, it was their own money. Of course, Virgin were helping, advancing the money, but they were advancing and three weeks later they get the money back from the sales."

**We used to call you the No Man back then.**
"Yes, of course. I was like the Mr No because of course we were saying no to Janet Jackson, no to Björk, no to George Michael... no to everything. It's funny, because after 10 years of working with Daft Punk in 2006 we said yes to Coachella. This yes means so much, of course, to Daft Punk and to

BIG
K mart

me personally. I wasn't a robot, but I was in fact saying no to everything. Sometimes I didn't even call Thomas or Guy-Man because I knew they will tell me no. This was my job, to get information and to quickly say to people, your project is amazing, wow, you have so much money, it's great. But they will say no to this.

"I remember in 2006 when I received this offer from the Daft Punk agent, the US agent at the time, Gerry Gerrard and he proposed us this slot for Coachella. Rather than reply automatically: 'Thank you, Gerry, but the band will not tour, they don't want to tour.' I took the information and for once I said: 'Ok, with this I will need to speak with the boys.' And I think it was the little sparkle that led us to sit down and discuss. Then of course Thomas and Guy-Man created the magic and came up with the Pyramid. It took me 10 years. It took me 10 years for them to say yes."

"I wasn't a robot, but I was... saying no to everything. Sometimes I didn't even call Thomas or Guy-Man because I knew they will tell me no."

**How much of a surprise was it to hear the different musical direction for 'Discovery'?**

"I was seeing them every day. They were not like: 'Hey, bye, we're on tour for the next three months. We'll call you from Houston or Phoenix.' They were next door. And the whole process, I can remember Thomas and Guy-Manuel came to the office often and shared what they were working on. They were sharing with us all this and so they were making the music, but they were also writing the animation because at the same time they had to finish the music to do the animation in Japan. I mean, they finished the music first, but the process of 'Discovery' was definitely a more ambitious and collective thing because of course we had to also include the Japanese people that will work on the animation."

**What did you think of 'One More Time' when you heard it? Did you hear that fully formed? Or was it in bits again?**

"I first heard it without the autotune. Then I was like: 'Wow, ok, it's very Cher, you know!' But when we started to play it, I remember we played it for the first time during a party and people went crazy. You know, if you ask me to choose one song, it will not be 'One More Time', even though it's the biggest today. We can say 'One More Time' is the biggest Daft Punk song along with 'Get Lucky'. But it was very ambitious and courageous for them to come back in 2001 with this. The ambition was to go somewhere else. They wanted to link again with their memories [from childhood], the music from the 80s, the music from the radio and you can hear it, of course. You can hear it in there."

**At the time the reviews were quite mixed. How did they take the poor ones?**

"Very badly. Because the feedback at the beginning was either, 'That's phenomenal' or 'Ok, you turn your back to the underground scene.' But then the 'Interstellar 5555' animation came out and people realised: 'Oh, that's the soundtrack for the animation.' Musically it makes sense."

**Can you remember how the collaborations with Sneak, Todd Edwards and Romanthony happened? Was it collaborative or did you just say: 'Here's your bit.'?**

"No, no, super collaborative. I wouldn't want it another way because I was contacting all of them at the moment. I was calling Sneak, I brought Todd to Paris. It was really collaborative, Todd Edwards is famous for his production and cut-up samples and they are calling him to sing. Sneak is famous for his clever beats and stuff and they are asking him to write the lyrics of 'Digital Love'."

**What were your thoughts when you first heard 'Human After All'?**
"I mean, I loved it, but the reviews were terrible. People were saying that Daft Punk went too far on 'Discovery' so what about going back to the roots? And then of course people were like: 'Whoa, where is 'One More Time'? I loved the rawness of this recording. But yes, the reviews as you know, were tough."

**Yes. How important do you think the album was in retrospect?**
"When you look back, this album is the sparkle that makes Coachella and Alive 2007. It's a triangular thing, they only have two albums and they were missing a third one for the mix to be crazy and when you have the vocals of 'Around the World' mixed with a bit of 'Robot Rock and the guitar of 'Aerodynamic', then you're killing everybody. It was the missing piece to create the Pyramid."

**It's got that rough, distorted Ed Banger/Justice sound so it was quite prescient.**
"It's true, Justice came right after with 'Waters of Nazareth'. 'Waters of Nazareth' could have been on 'Human After All' with this heavy metal vibe, but at the same time built for the club with repetitive beats. It influenced all the French scene, because you couldn't not be aware of what Daft Punk was doing. You could be a pure techno head but when you look at Daft Punk you say: 'Ok, it's good to play in a rave, but me too, I want to be played on radio.' I was still working with Daft Punk and Justice. But I remember pretty well in 2007 the Daft Punk tour in the US. I was doing a show with Daft Punk and then the next day I was flying to Los Angeles to do an Ed Banger party and then some time we were crossing in Toronto so it became too much to do both."

**What was the most difficult thing you ever had to do for them?**
"That's interesting. I don't know, it may be the fact I was saying no to everybody. At the beginning I wasn't thinking much, I was working for them. But the more I was doing, and I was growing and meeting more people, getting more confidence and sometimes I was like: 'Whoa, how come I can't influence you more?' You know, so that was probably the most difficult thing to realise, that even though you can get the closest to the biggest men ever, it's still a band, they are two, and there is no room for a third or fourth or fifth member. So maybe that was the most difficult to realise. They knew what they wanted to do. Of course, we were part of this amazing adventure, but creatively and artistically the magic came out of those two. Of course, when we are speaking together, they are telling me, no, you were part, you know, we were part of it together et cetera. But I know the magic was coming from those two brains."

**Did you ever say no for them and then later on they said: 'Oh, we wish we'd done that?'**
"That's a very interesting one. I don't think they ever mentioned it, but I'm sure there are plenty, you know, maybe it wasn't the right time. George Michael, how come we never... ? We should have done something. Björk, Thomas wasn't up for it. Thomas didn't even go to the meeting. It was me and Guy-Man. Some stuff like, opening for Madonna they say no, but it's not a drama. But George Michael and Björk for me are the ones which could have been amazing."

**You were still involved in the Coachella show?**
"Yes. We stopped working together in 2008. We came back from touring and we released 'Alive 2007', the album. We were working together for 12 years and like a teenager growing up it was time for me to have my own apartment. So, in a peaceful, friendly way, we decided to part ways. I moved in here (gestures around the Ed Banger office) and I was more focused on Ed Banger and with my own Busy P thing. I want to DJ, you know, this is my passion and so in 2008 I decided, ok, I will focus on my own thing."

**What did you learn most from your tenure with Daft Punk that helped you with Justice and Ed Banger?**
"Everything. The dynamic of what Daft Punk gave

me still drives me today. Of course, I'm confident now, you know, we did a pretty good job with Justice, with Mr Oizo and SebastiAn and more recently with Myd. I'm confident and we have our own mindset, our own creativity. But the seed is coming from my Daft Punk time. We grew up at a time where we had to scratch our heads, go digging for records, go digging for books, meet some older friends who may share with me their stories. Nowadays everything is immediate, you know, instant. With Daft Punk I have long passions, they often told me that, ok, if you say no now, you will see, it will come back later. I think Daft Punk is what they teach me the most: continue to do your thing and maybe it will not come back today but it will come back tomorrow. Honestly, it always came back. And with Ed Banger, this is the philosophy I learnt from them, and this is the philosophy of the label and the label is 20 years' old this year. Of course, you know, we are a French electronic music label so we have our sound, but I hope we are still relevant. And we can still make a connection here and there. I will owe Daft Punk for ever. That's a fact."

**Why do you think they split up when they did?**
"I think they split up because it was time to split up. There is of course a more personal decision which I'm sure you can imagine. But with Daft Punk they were not having the same vision. I think the last time they did music together was for The Weeknd, and this kind of direction musically was definitely more right for Guy-Man. Guy-Man was more attracted by this kind of sound than Thomas so I think it was a question of time. They started in 1993 and they split up in 2021 so a 28-year career is pretty nice. Again, it proves that they are consistent with their realness. A lot of people say: 'Why didn't they say nothing and then come back for Coachella for $6 million in five years?' But this is not Daft Punk."

**The four studio albums are a perfect collection and to go from 'Human After All', which is rough and ready and recorded quickly to working with top songwriters and session musicians on 'Random Access Memories', I don't know where they go from there, really.**
"I think this also, it was a question of time but also a question of what can they do after that? I learnt the news like everybody. Thomas called me at lunch, he called me and told me the news. When I received it I was like: 'Whoa, not true!' We spoke for an hour. And then I realised it was real – but I had to respect it. On a more personal level, for people who worked with them, it's a present, because even though I knew how precious and how lucky I was to have met and worked with them, today it's even more special, you know, because they don't exist anymore. So we lived the best moments, the golden moments with them. Of course the Grammys were amazing, but I believe the best moment was still the fax time, playing for free, carrying the suitcases, experimenting, growing up. That was definitely the best time of my life."

By the mid-2000s, it had been nearly a decade since Daft Punk had performed live and the duo seemed content with a life toiling in the studio. Until a big offer came in from Coachella that is. **Michaelangelo Matos** finds out how their iconic 2006 show and subsequent Alive tour came to be. And how it changed electronic live music forever...

# The Pyramid Scheme

"Everybody knew that Daft Punk were not touring anymore," Pedro Winter, the founder of Ed Banger Records and Daft Punk's long-time manager, said in 2013. "No one was proposing anything. Our agent, maybe once a year, would ask: 'Pedro, is Daft Punk going to tour?' And the boys were saying: 'No, no,' and walking out of the studio.

"Then Paul Tollett, who is the boss of Coachella, emailed me in 2006 with an offer for Daft Punk to play at the Sahara Tent. I got in touch with them and told them we had a serious offer to bring them back on stage. We sat down and the boys decided they wanted to take the money and do it. At the time, it was a big offer, something like $300,000. It seemed like a lot of money, obviously compared to now, it wouldn't be. But the band decided to take all that money and spend it on the production of the show, and they did the Pyramid. I'm sure you've heard about that."

As a matter of fact, we have.

Ask anyone active in the US dance music business in the mid-2000s about Daft Punk at Coachella. If they were there, they'll exult; if they weren't, they'll describe their phones blowing up with texts from their colleagues who were.

Daft Punk hadn't toured the US in nearly a decade. Their 1997 outing had been a success. It came during a busy autumn, often crossing paths with a trio of other tours (Big Top, Electric Highway, and Moonshine Over America) intended to put 'electronica' – as the US biz described it in the late-90s – on the map.

The show was simple: "Just the table and two samplers and the drum machines," as Guy-Manuel de Homem-Christo put it to Stop Smiling magazine in 2008 – as well as their own light show.

"Back then, it was difficult to put two DJs up with no show," says Winter. "It worked at a dance club – at least there were lights. But you couldn't take two DJs into a rock arena without production."

Even during the late-90s, as The Prodigy and The Chemical Brothers were blowing up in the States, the differences between how rock worked and how rave operated seemed insurmountable.

"With old school raves, you didn't know where they were until the day of the show," explains Tom Windish, founder of The Windish Agency, which books many electronic acts in the US. Dance promoters pay "a flat fee," while "you get a percentage" of the proceeds from a concert promoter. "Having relationships with both DJ promoters and live promoters is an awful lot to juggle," he says.

And most American rock bizzers couldn't be bothered. The Chemical Brothers and Orbital made huge waves as Glastonbury headliners, but in America most of the big festival tours kept their distance from electronic music – and when Lollapalooza included Orbital, The Prodigy and The Orb in its 1997 edition, the tour was a box-office failure, its final edition until 2003.

But that was a tour. It took until 1999 for European-style destination festivals to take root in America. That was the year Coachella debuted, and it immediately reset the US concert business. Big festivals no longer toured.

"Coachella is the most important gig of the year," says Windish. "It especially was then. The importance of the show kept elevating. Because of that, the artists kept on doing more and more to make their show better, to make it the best, and then they'd go tour that, or they'd do something even more special, more impressive there than on their tour, because it was so important."

By the mid-2000s, there was already a high bar for spectacle at Coachella. In 2004, The Flaming Lips debuted the giant plastic bubble that singer Wayne Coyne would get into and walk over the audiences. In 2005, when Bauhaus headlined, Peter Murphy came out upside-down, like a vampire.

Gerry Gerrard, Daft Punk's US booking agent from 1997 to 2006, had always done business with Coachella – Nine Inch Nails, The Chemical Brothers, Underworld and The Orb were among his clients. "I had a significant number of the headliners in the early days," he says. "My relationship with (the festival's promoters) Goldenvoice has always been friends, partners, like-minds."

Unfortunately, that didn't include his Parisian act. "They asked every year," he recalls. "From the early days they wanted Daft Punk." And always, they refused: "Daft Punk took 10 years off. They

hadn't played [live] since 1997. At one point in the 2000s, I took them over to Armand Van Helden's studio and said: 'You're breaking my heart. Are you ever going to go out?' The manager said: 'No. Here's what you tell people: Daft Punk are producers. Playing live is for losers. Daft Punk are not losers.' That was their position. It wasn't just Coachella that was asking for them every year. The whole country was asking for them."

Dance music has never 'died', but in the US you'd have been forgiven for thinking it had as the millennium began. The party crackdowns that began in August 2000 – when a New Orleans event put on by the promoter Disco Donnie Estopinal was busted by the DEA – had put a freeze on the entire scene. Except for LA.

"Even that lull in the mid-2000s, it was still kicking in Southern California. The rave culture never went away," says A&R woman and artist manager Sheneza Mohammed. "Everywhere in the East Coast had a big-time slowdown in the mid-2000s, but not Southern California."

But if raves were verboten, DJs were not. In New York, events like the Electroclash Festival in 2001 and parties like MisShapes were refashioning DJ culture for indie tastes. The latter's slogan was 'No Beatmatching'. (There was even a briefly popular T-shirt with that phrase.)

"I was playing at the MisShapes parties," says Steve Aoki, founder of Dim Mak Records and notorious (and retired) cake-thrower. "We were the LA contingent of what New York was doing – and Erol Alkan with Trash in London. Everyone doing the same thing had this network – it was pre-social media. There was a club called Vanity in Japan that did the same thing in Tokyo. I'd DJ that party, and I'd play with the girls from CSS, Klaxons... We were all interlinked. There was Revolver Club that Josh Menendez was doing. That progression led to the emergence of electro [the LA variant that came to be known as bloghouse]. It was Justice and 2manydjs leading the pack, and then Boys Noize, MSTRKRFT, the Bloody Beetroots holding down the flag. We were representing that sound in Los Angeles at the Dim Mak parties."

"People that did not give a shit about electronic music in the slightest were all excited about Daft Punk. I was like: 'Why do you care all of a sudden?'"

Dillon Francis, who was a regular at Aoki's parties at the original Cinespace beginning in 2001, recalls: "It was where Steve Aoki was doing mash-ups – playing The Rapture, electronic remixes, stuff like that. This was before any electronic music had blown up."

The Dim Mak parties began in 2004, when Aoki teamed up with promoter Franki Chan, bringing in rock musicians to spin records. "We were both contacting friends: 'Carlos D. from Interpol is coming to DJ. Yeah Yeah Yeahs' Nick Zinner is coming to DJ,'" says Aoki. "They would all come and make $100, and me and Franki would get $100 each. We had a killer, small party. For some reason it started happening all over. All of a sudden, we were the hipster kings of Hollywood."

And Hollywood was where Daft Punk had landed. "When you're in LA, for some reason, I don't know exactly why, you don't put too much limit (on things)," Guy-Man told Stop Smiling. "Maybe it's because we come from France and when we are there (in Los Angeles), we feel more creatively free in a way... Maybe we get more ideas, there's something more creative in the way you get inspiration."

The 'bonky electro' sound blanketing Cinespace – the phrase is Joshua Glazer's, the former editor of influential 90s and 00s American electronic magazine URB – made a clear impact on Daft Punk's third album, 'Human After All'. But that album's critical reception was, to put it nicely, muted. The album was said to have been made in a matter of weeks – hardly the patient perfectionism that had been the duo's hallmark until then. But the 'Human...' tracks, rough and full of distortion, would sound great live. But when?

As the 2006 edition of Coachella was being booked, Gerrard noticed a shortfall of his roster on the line-up. "I said: 'What the hell's going on? I used to have 10 acts on here. I've got two now? Why aren't I getting any love?' They said: 'We're going to give you some more love, but you're going to have to work for it. You've got to get Daft Punk.' I said: 'Well, you know where that goes. Send me the offer.' And the offer was spectacular. So I took it to them. They looked and said: 'Wow. Let us get back to you.' They mulled it over for a week and said: 'I think we're going to do it.'"

For most acts, that would have been that. Not Daft Punk. "Then they started to get unusual," Gerrard continues. "They said: 'Did you get a deposit? We need it.' I said: 'They send the deposit to me. I can't give it to you.' They said: 'Well, we need it to build the show.' I went back to the promoter and said: 'They need the money.' I think at this point they were only giving 10 per cent deposits. These guys wanted 25 per cent of the money, a huge amount, to put together the show. And they said: 'OK, give it to them.' They spent almost that whole guarantee on putting together that show."

Spending $300,000 on one show was unprecedented. "We knew we had to put on a proper show to make sure we could rock the big stage, to go inside the big rock festivals like Lollapalooza or Coachella," says Winter.

Though Winter was their manager, he had no input into the show's design. "Artistically, they knew exactly what they wanted to do," he says. "We have a really good production team around us. Artistically, they always drive their thing. I was there just to take care of the day-to-day business."

When the Coachella line-up was announced, no one – not even Madonna, who played the dance tent the night before – was buzzier than Daft Punk. "I remember being so surprised that year how many people were excited about Daft Punk," remembers Vivian Host, then editor of the US dance mag XLR8R. "I mean, people that did not give a shit about electronic music in the slightest were all excited about Daft Punk. I was like: 'Why do you care all of a sudden?'"

But this was Los Angeles, where, unlike the rest of America, dance music hadn't budged. "There was never a doubt in anybody's mind. This is the biggest thing ever," says LA artist manager Danny Johnson. "That's what you expect. This is going to be the most epic shit I've ever seen in dance music. It was the talk of the festival."

As was their way, Daft Punk kept everything completely secret until the last second. Danny Johnson was backstage. "I had my little access pass. I could move around the festival really easily. But you couldn't go anywhere near that (part of) backstage for that. I remember seeing (a friend) climb the side stage to see what was going on, and they were like: 'Everything's on lockdown. Complete lockdown.'"

No wonder: The infamous Pyramid – a cross between Parliament-Funkadelic's Mothership (which landed onstage every night on their 1977 tour), the spaceship from 'Close Encounters of the Third Kind' (whose theme opened the show), and the Egyptian pyramids, long a visual touchstone for the 70s R&B giants Earth, Wind & Fire – was unprecedented in dance music. The visuals were projection-mapped onto the Pyramid's surface and done so well that even the veteran lighting technicians in attendance were flummoxed. The duo's outfits were as lit up as the Pyramid – not cheap neon tubing, but as vivid and professional as the staging. Of course, Daft Punk were dressed as robots – they'd been doing it for the press for years – but this time they were also aliens.

Guy-Man would say: "I thought people really liked it all over the world, they didn't see it like a concert, more like an experience or a happening, which was really interesting to tourists. That it was not just a concert, but something different. Coachella asked us to do a concert, and that was an idea that was maybe behind our head for 10 years and at that time everything was right, everything fitted right to do this concert and we worked a lot on it."

Timing was also on their side. Daft Punk played after the main stage headliner, Depeche Mode, finished so there was a rush to the dance tent. "The impression they made was huge," says Windish. "People were blown away."

"People needed something to grab onto from dance music," says Vivian Host, who was also in the crowd. "If you're at Coachella and you're seeing a bunch of rock bands, they get up on stage, they do their rock band thing, that's nice. But a lot of them don't have any backdrop, they don't have any real stage setup. Then you get Daft Punk coming up there with their whole thing – and it's mysterious, and it's very patently not a rock band. 'Are they playing? Are they not playing? What are they doing? They're robots.' On top of that, it sounds completely refreshing after an entire day of guitar music."

Steve Aoki was another eyewitness. "It was one of the most life-changing moments," he recalls. "You're experiencing the feeling of the music around you and being part of a larger experiential feeling. I love 'Rollin' & Scratchin'' and all the songs that weren't the hits. They were mixing those with a cappellas of 'Around the World' and 'Prime Time of Your Life.' You'd keep hearing elements of them coming in. It just takes over your whole body. It's about absorbing all the music you've been listening to. That's a big part of what dance culture is. That was a really big moment to see that. It was a pinnacle – dance music finally broke out at Coachella."

But it wasn't just Coachella. It was also the Web. "In 2005, you started to see video on the internet," says Brian Long, founder of Astralwerks Records, The Chemical Brothers' US label. Specifically, YouTube had launched in February 2005. "A lot of people didn't have internet fast enough to stream video, so not everyone was watching video, but by 2006, it was having a much greater effect."

People attending the show didn't just text their friends about it. They also recorded it with their phones – and put the clips on YouTube. Better yet, someone took all those clips and made a "supercut" of the entire show. "The video clips of them playing with the Pyramid made a huge impact," says Long. It was akin to a tech-savvier version of The Beatles on 'The Ed Sullivan Show'.

Even Daft Punk were impressed by their fans' industriousness. When Stop Smiling asked if a DVD of the live show might be in the works, Guy-Man said: "It's not planned. I think what people did on YouTube is far more exciting than what we could do ourselves. And I think, yeah, the closest to what's happening in the show is what people shot on YouTube. It's much more lively than what we could do ourselves by shooting the show, and anyway, we didn't do it and the show is over now."

The Coachella show became the topic du jour all over the US festival circuit. "That's what everybody talked about," says Sam Fotias, who co-promotes Detroit's Movement Festival. "Those guys completely blew the roof off of dance music in the States. Before that, it was just guys on laptops, playing controllers. The entire visceral experience, the amazing visual thing, the music, the anonymity of them – they really hit the nail on the head across the board with everything. You'd be an idiot not to attribute dance music's growth in the United States to what they did with that performance and their tour. You had people that never listened to dance music before going to see that show just for the spectacle. And the music is extremely accessible."

The effect in the States was immediate. The LA nightspot Avalon, as Aoki puts it, "was holding down proper house music. In 2007-2008-2009, suddenly electro started going that route."

In 2007, the LA DJ and promoter Gary Richards (aka Destructo) put on a festival called Hard that spotlighted the electro sound. Danny Johnson, who worked on the festival with Richards, said: "Hard was a reaction to that: 'Oh, there's a market for this.'"

And that market was young. "The kids coming to those parties are 15. They are so small," Pedro Winter told Red Bull Music Academy in 2010. "You speak to them about '97, when 'Homework' was released: they were babies. So discovering Daft Punk, discovering this whole club energy, mixing, these guys who are 15, they don't have this whole question about there being a heavy metal guitar and an 808 beat. They don't understand that it's two different worlds getting together."

"The selling power of the dance acts just consistently increased," says Windish. "After the Daft Punk thing, as opposed to just steady, it was, (motions finger up) swish, and just kept steadily going up."

The impact of that show goes well beyond dance music. "Once you let that genie out of the bottle with very visually impressive production, a lot of artists want to kind of take a page out of that, especially artists who might have had a bit of fluency with the EDM space," says Eric Renner Brown, who covers the US concert industry for Pollstar magazine. "Like Tame Impala: Kevin Parker has spoken extensively about how influenced he is by Daft Punk. And you see that in the shows: it's about the spectacle as much as it is about music. I was at a Coldplay arena show last month and that felt like a similar thing, with the lasers and the confetti in the ring hanging from the ceiling and all the strobe lights."

Brown's reasoning is simple: "When a consumer is buying a ticket, especially with ticket prices going up, they're expecting a show beyond just the music that's being performed. Over the last 15 years, LEDs have become cheaper and easier to transport, which has then led to their wider adoption as well."

Even so, the reaction surprised even the band's inner circle. "When I met with Goldenvoice, I asked: 'How the hell did you know that it was such a huge phenomenon?' Paul Tollett said it was total gut," says Gerrard. "No one knew it was going to be as big, except Paul, god bless him."

"IT WAS LIKE WAL
PORTAL OF MY DE
AN INSTANT AND
ON MY PSYCHE. T
DELIVERING A FUL
EXPERIENCE WHIL
FROM A BAND ON
GAME-CHANGING
FOR ME BUT FOR A

Skrillex on watching the Alive 2006-07 tour/The Guardian/2021

ING INTO THE
TINY. IT LEFT
IDELIBLE MARK
E IDEA OF
CONCERT
DEPARTING
STAGE WAS
– NOT JUST
LL CREATORS."

# Stayin' Alive

By Jim Butler

The Park Hyatt hotel in Paris is an odd place. Furnished with a name that positively drips with otherworldly opulence and rightly located just off the exquisite Place Vendôme with its imposing column erected at the behest of Napoleon to celebrate the victory of Austerlitz in 1805, it should, by rights, be a monument to old school charm and cool.

Unfortunately, the disappointingly staid interiors paint a different picture. It's evident that money is no object, but inside the bland lobby, and non-descript bar and restaurant, what is revealed is a building that in trading on former glories now appears only to attract tourists for whom location is everything and style is nothing.

In other words, it's not a very Daft Punk-type of hotel. Or so you would have assumed, because downstairs Thomas Bangalter and Guy-Manuel de Homem-Christo are in a private meeting room preparing to field all manner of questions from various quarters of Her Majesty's press corps.

It transpires that Thomas and Guy-Man like this hotel because, according to one of their record company entourage, they're not disturbed and are allowed to get on with their business. Which, reading between the translucent lines, presumably means being able to walk around the hotel dressed as robots.

In reality, Daft Punk like confounding expectations – not least their own. And 2007 has seen them amaze and bewilder on a regular basis. You couldn't exactly herald 2007 a comeback in the manner of Sinatra or Elvis, but the year has seen their stock rise to arguably its highest point since the 'Homework' days of a decade ago.

Not only are they godfathers to the emergent rock'n'rave generation (Justice, Digitalism, Klaxons, Boys Noize et al) – a movement they're inextricably linked to through their manager Pedro Winter (head honcho of Ed Banger), but Kanye West has acknowledged their sonic genius by sampling them for his 'Stronger' single.

Nonetheless, the real reason for their current omnipotence has been their activities. Not only has their directorial debut, 'Electroma', been released to torrents of chin-stroking, analysis, befuddlement and wonder, but they have continued their triumphant return to the live arena with their mesmeric Alive 2007 tour. And now, as the year comes to an end, that's set to culminate with the release of their account of the tour, the live album, 'Alive 2007'. Oh, and they've been namechecked by the hilarious 'Flight of the Conchords'.

Perched on a sofa in their bland Park Hyatt lair, the robot suits safely packed away for another day, the duo begin to reflect upon their annus mirabilis.

"It's mainly been a lot of good surprises," reflects the stick-thin Thomas with characteristic understatement, as the notoriously silent Guy-Man sits beside him, no hint of emotion registering on his face. "I think the key to not being disappointed is not to have too much expectation."

Dance music has missed Daft Punk. To paraphrase Thomas Bangalter's most famous hit, music sounds better with them. With the release of their still-stunning debut album, 'Homework', in 1997, they forged a third path between aspects of the music tainted by rampant commercialism and the oft-anal proclivities of the underground. And by giving the music other qualities – aesthetic, cultural, political – that enabled it to look rock'n'roll squarely in the eye, Thomas and Guy-Man's restless creative spirit and sonic wanderlust has defined a decade-plus worthof sounds.

But their presence has been sorely missed in the live arena. Their early shows, whether it be their decks and fx dates or their incendiary 1997 tour in support of 'Homework', have passed into legend, so their return to the fray at the Coachella music festival last year, after a sojourn of nearly 10 years, was keenly anticipated. Thankfully, their Son et Lumière shows didn't disappoint. So why did they stay away for so long?

"It's simply about wanting to match our own expectations, not even the audiences," says the ever-thoughtful Thomas. "And we finally felt that we could do something that would match those expectations. We needed a lot of elements to come together."

At this juncture it's advisable to note that when Thomas is in the room, Guy-Man is conspicuously mute. Much has been made of the pair's sullen and reticent interview technique in the past, and much of it has focussed upon Guy-Man's ability to sit in a room for an hour and give absolutely nothing.

Today seems to be going to script then, but when Thomas receives a phone call that he feels compelled to answer and leaves the room, Guy-Man suddenly becomes animated. He explains that they never intended to stop playing live for so long but being renowned perfectionists they were waiting for technology to catch up with their imagination.

"'Discovery' (their 2001 album) was hard to express live," he says, "whereas 'Homework' was more minimal and more simple to do. Now all the software and technology can allow us to replicate these songs live. We can manipulate the songs, have fun with them, mix them together: this is one of the aspects that made us want to come back and do the live shows."

Suddenly, this minute 33-year-old, perfectly framed by a mass of black hair and accompanied by black T-shirt and black jeans, has come alive. Although it's apparent he's comfortable to cede speaking duties to his long-time friend (Thomas is a year younger) when the pair of them are together, it's pleasing to note that his antipathy towards the fourth estate has either mellowed or was over-played.

"Everything is much more concentrated now," he continues. "With a laptop you can do everything. Back then all our gear was our home studio. We put all of this onstage so it took three or four drum machines, a lot of samplers, frequencers, synthesisers... whereas now you can do it all in a laptop. Virtual machines – compressors, synthesisers and sequencers – everything can be there in a laptop.

"So that's a big difference - what you can do: one big example of what we couldn't do from before is pitching. Having the same pitch – taking two totally different tracks, for example you take 'Da Funk' from 'Homework' and 'Robot Rock' from 'Human After All' and you can sync them at the same tone. So now we can take any song that we've done from our past albums and we can blend them, mix them together, or chop it up all on the laptop."

And that's just what they've done on 'Alive 2007'. A synapse-shattering patchwork quilt of music from their three albums, it veers from pounding, Jeff Mills-like techno to fluid house dynamism as tracks such as 'Robot Rock' and 'Oh Yeah'; 'Around the World' and 'Harder, Better, Faster, Stronger'; and 'Da Funk' and 'Daftendireckt', segue into each other as they would in a euphoric DJ set.

And while it's an uncomfortable truism that most live albums, irrespective of genre, fail to satisfy because they can neither match the experience of 'being there' nor replicate the lush studio offering of the conventional album, 'Alive 2007' circumvents these pitfalls by deconstructing the original versions to offer something fresh and vital. And to their credit they've included those all-important rapturous crowd noises – all the necessary whoops and hollers, those moments of ecstatic recognition – to supply the requisite atmosphere.

## "With a laptop you can do everything. Back then all our gear was our home studio... Virtual machines... everything can be there in a laptop."

The recording itself is taken from their homecoming show in Paris this summer. Although the temptation must have been immense to go with this show for sentimental reasons, Thomas and Guy-Man waited until the last possible moment to decide which gig to go with.

"Yes, all the shows have been recorded," explains Thomas. "But the Bercy show was the best performance to sum up the whole tour. Of course it was also symbolically right too, but musically it was the one show that really stood out."

So did the pair miss the thrill of playing live? Contrarily enough, no, they didn't.

"Maybe not having played for so long is what makes these performances and this meeting with the audiences so special. It might not have been this regathering otherwise," says Thomas in typically abstract fashion. "But at the same time it's true, you know, all of these years, all our creative life has been shaped by so many surprises and good things that we can fully appreciate the moments right now without any of the arrogance or blasé feeling that you might get if you are younger and not fully grasping it." Although by way of an existential caveat he adds: "At the same time we are fully detached from it,

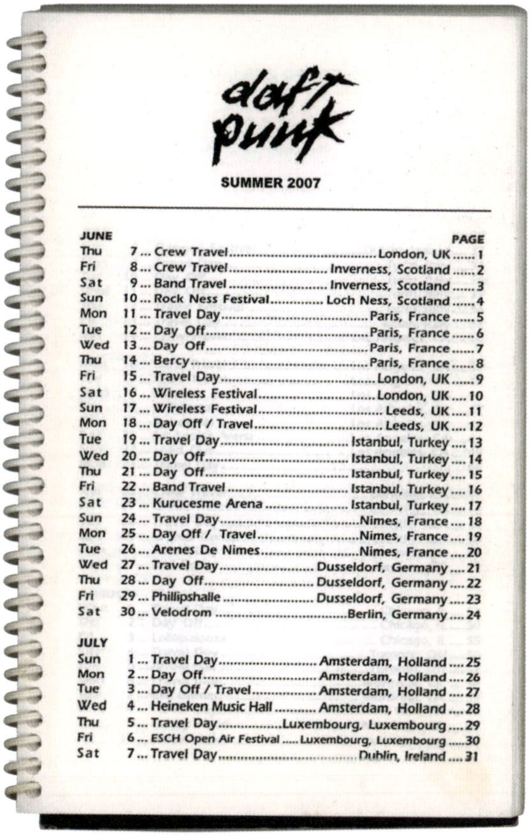

daft punk

SUMMER 2007

| JUNE | | | | PAGE |
|---|---|---|---|---|
| Thu | 7 | Crew Travel | London, UK | 1 |
| Fri | 8 | Crew Travel | Inverness, Scotland | 2 |
| Sat | 9 | Band Travel | Inverness, Scotland | 3 |
| Sun | 10 | Rock Ness Festival | Loch Ness, Scotland | 4 |
| Mon | 11 | Travel Day | Paris, France | 5 |
| Tue | 12 | Day Off | Paris, France | 6 |
| Wed | 13 | Day Off | Paris, France | 7 |
| Thu | 14 | Bercy | Paris, France | 8 |
| Fri | 15 | Travel Day | London, UK | 9 |
| Sat | 16 | Wireless Festival | London, UK | 10 |
| Sun | 17 | Wireless Festival | Leeds, UK | 11 |
| Mon | 18 | Day Off / Travel | Leeds, UK | 12 |
| Tue | 19 | Travel Day | Istanbul, Turkey | 13 |
| Wed | 20 | Day Off | Istanbul, Turkey | 14 |
| Thu | 21 | Day Off | Istanbul, Turkey | 15 |
| Fri | 22 | Band Travel | Istanbul, Turkey | 16 |
| Sat | 23 | Kurucesme Arena | Istanbul, Turkey | 17 |
| Sun | 24 | Travel Day | Nimes, France | 18 |
| Mon | 25 | Day Off / Travel | Nimes, France | 19 |
| Tue | 26 | Arenes De Nimes | Nimes, France | 20 |
| Wed | 27 | Travel Day | Dusseldorf, Germany | 21 |
| Thu | 28 | Day Off | Dusseldorf, Germany | 22 |
| Fri | 29 | Phillipshalle | Dusseldorf, Germany | 23 |
| Sat | 30 | Velodrom | Berlin, Germany | 24 |
| JULY | | | | |
| Sun | 1 | Travel Day | Amsterdam, Holland | 25 |
| Mon | 2 | Day Off | Amsterdam, Holland | 26 |
| Tue | 3 | Day Off / Travel | Amsterdam, Holland | 27 |
| Wed | 4 | Heineken Music Hall | Amsterdam, Holland | 28 |
| Thu | 5 | Travel Day | Luxembourg, Luxembourg | 29 |
| Fri | 6 | ESCH Open Air Festival | Luxembourg, Luxembourg | 30 |
| Sat | 7 | Travel Day | Dublin, Ireland | 31 |

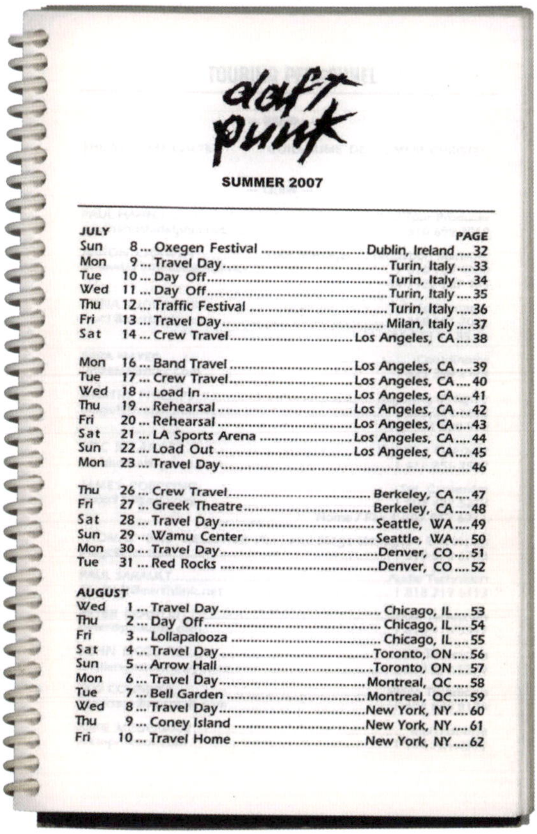

daft punk

SUMMER 2007

| JULY | | | | PAGE |
|---|---|---|---|---|
| Sun | 8 | Oxegen Festival | Dublin, Ireland | 32 |
| Mon | 9 | Travel Day | Turin, Italy | 33 |
| Tue | 10 | Day Off | Turin, Italy | 34 |
| Wed | 11 | Day Off | Turin, Italy | 35 |
| Thu | 12 | Traffic Festival | Turin, Italy | 36 |
| Fri | 13 | Travel Day | Milan, Italy | 37 |
| Sat | 14 | Crew Travel | Los Angeles, CA | 38 |
| Mon | 16 | Band Travel | Los Angeles, CA | 39 |
| Tue | 17 | Crew Travel | Los Angeles, CA | 40 |
| Wed | 18 | Load In | Los Angeles, CA | 41 |
| Thu | 19 | Rehearsal | Los Angeles, CA | 42 |
| Fri | 20 | Rehearsal | Los Angeles, CA | 43 |
| Sat | 21 | LA Sports Arena | Los Angeles, CA | 44 |
| Sun | 22 | Load Out | Los Angeles, CA | 45 |
| Mon | 23 | Travel Day | | 46 |
| Thu | 26 | Crew Travel | Berkeley, CA | 47 |
| Fri | 27 | Greek Theatre | Berkeley, CA | 48 |
| Sat | 28 | Travel Day | Seattle, WA | 49 |
| Sun | 29 | Wamu Center | Seattle, WA | 50 |
| Mon | 30 | Travel Day | Denver, CO | 51 |
| Tue | 31 | Red Rocks | Denver, CO | 52 |
| AUGUST | | | | |
| Wed | 1 | Travel Day | Chicago, IL | 53 |
| Thu | 2 | Day Off | Chicago, IL | 54 |
| Fri | 3 | Lollapalooza | Chicago, IL | 55 |
| Sat | 4 | Travel Day | Toronto, ON | 56 |
| Sun | 5 | Arrow Hall | Toronto, ON | 57 |
| Mon | 6 | Travel Day | Montreal, QC | 58 |
| Tue | 7 | Bell Garden | Montreal, QC | 59 |
| Wed | 8 | Travel Day | New York, NY | 60 |
| Thu | 9 | Coney Island | New York, NY | 61 |
| Fri | 10 | Travel Home | New York, NY | 62 |

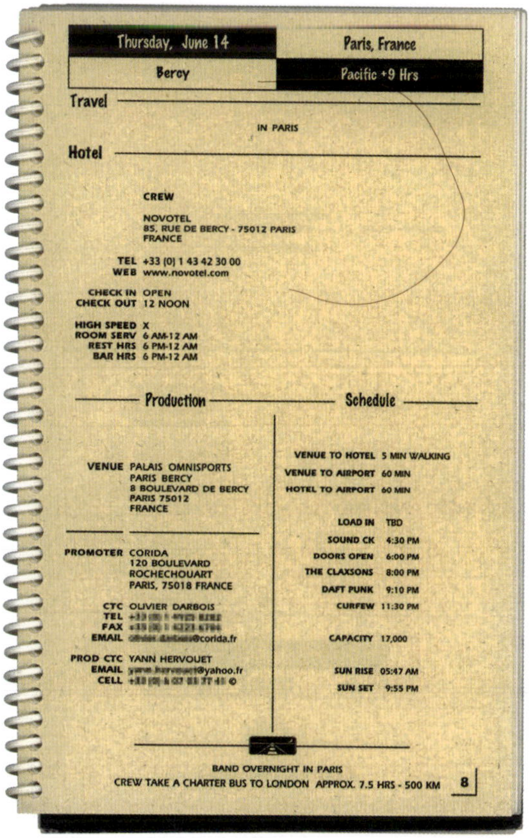

Thursday, June 14 | Paris, France
Bercy | Pacific +9 Hrs

Travel

IN PARIS

Hotel

CREW

NOVOTEL
85, RUE DE BERCY - 75012 PARIS
FRANCE

TEL +33 (0) 1 43 42 30 00
WEB www.novotel.com

CHECK IN OPEN
CHECK OUT 12 NOON

HIGH SPEED X
ROOM SERV 6 AM-12 AM
REST HRS 6 PM-12 AM
BAR HRS 6 PM-12 AM

Production

VENUE PALAIS OMNISPORTS
PARIS BERCY
8 BOULEVARD DE BERCY
PARIS 75012
FRANCE

PROMOTER CORIDA
120 BOULEVARD
ROCHECHOUART
PARIS, 75018 FRANCE

CTC OLIVIER DARBOIS
TEL
FAX
EMAIL @corida.fr

PROD CTC YANN HERVOUET
EMAIL @yahoo.fr
CELL

Schedule

VENUE TO HOTEL 5 MIN WALKING
VENUE TO AIRPORT 60 MIN
HOTEL TO AIRPORT 60 MIN

LOAD IN TBD
SOUND CK 4:30 PM
DOORS OPEN 6:00 PM
THE CLAXSONS 8:00 PM
DAFT PUNK 9:10 PM
CURFEW 11:30 PM

CAPACITY 17,000

SUN RISE 05:47 AM
SUN SET 9:55 PM

BAND OVERNIGHT IN PARIS
CREW TAKE A CHARTER BUS TO LONDON APPROX. 7.5 HRS - 500 KM 8

Alive Tour 2007, summer itineraries

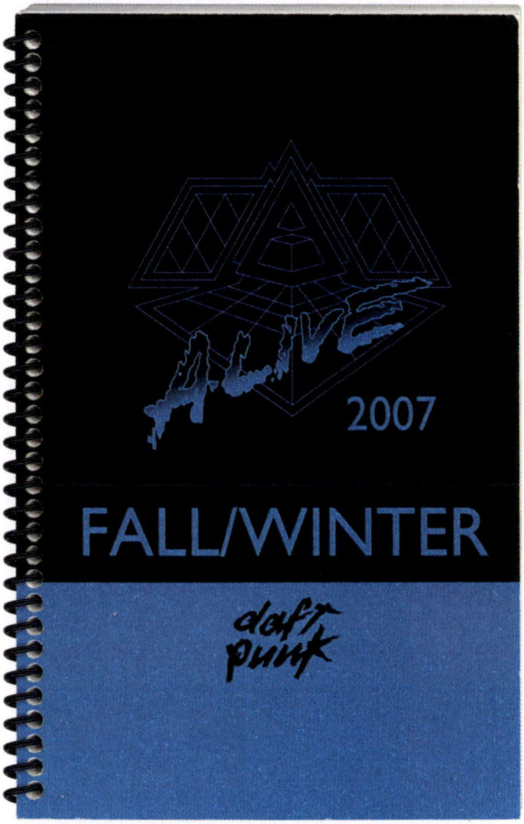


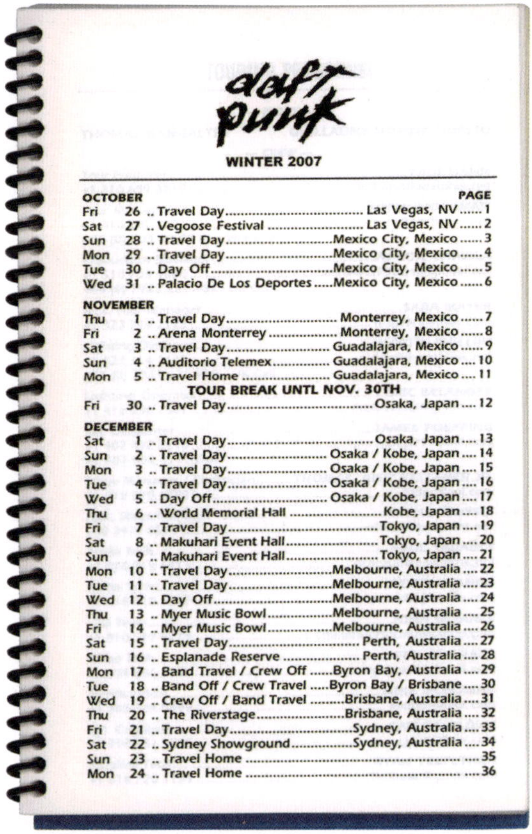

daft punk

WINTER 2007

| | | | | PAGE |
|---|---|---|---|---|
| **OCTOBER** | | | | |
| Fri | 26 | .. Travel Day | Las Vegas, NV | 1 |
| Sat | 27 | .. Vegoose Festival | Las Vegas, NV | 2 |
| Sun | 28 | .. Travel Day | Mexico City, Mexico | 3 |
| Mon | 29 | .. Travel Day | Mexico City, Mexico | 4 |
| Tue | 30 | .. Day Off | Mexico City, Mexico | 5 |
| Wed | 31 | .. Palacio De Los Deportes | Mexico City, Mexico | 6 |
| **NOVEMBER** | | | | |
| Thu | 1 | .. Travel Day | Monterrey, Mexico | 7 |
| Fri | 2 | .. Arena Monterrey | Monterrey, Mexico | 8 |
| Sat | 3 | .. Travel Day | Guadalajara, Mexico | 9 |
| Sun | 4 | .. Auditorio Telemex | Guadalajara, Mexico | 10 |
| Mon | 5 | .. Travel Home | Guadalajara, Mexico | 11 |
| | | **TOUR BREAK UNTL NOV. 30TH** | | |
| Fri | 30 | .. Travel Day | Osaka, Japan | 12 |
| **DECEMBER** | | | | |
| Sat | 1 | .. Travel Day | Osaka, Japan | 13 |
| Sun | 2 | .. Travel Day | Osaka / Kobe, Japan | 14 |
| Mon | 3 | .. Travel Day | Osaka / Kobe, Japan | 15 |
| Tue | 4 | .. Travel Day | Osaka / Kobe, Japan | 16 |
| Wed | 5 | .. Day Off | Osaka / Kobe, Japan | 17 |
| Thu | 6 | .. World Memorial Hall | Kobe, Japan | 18 |
| Fri | 7 | .. Travel Day | Tokyo, Japan | 19 |
| Sat | 8 | .. Makuhari Event Hall | Tokyo, Japan | 20 |
| Sun | 9 | .. Makuhari Event Hall | Tokyo, Japan | 21 |
| Mon | 10 | .. Travel Day | Melbourne, Australia | 22 |
| Tue | 11 | .. Travel Day | Melbourne, Australia | 23 |
| Wed | 12 | .. Day Off | Melbourne, Australia | 24 |
| Thu | 13 | .. Myer Music Bowl | Melbourne, Australia | 25 |
| Fri | 14 | .. Myer Music Bowl | Melbourne, Australia | 26 |
| Sat | 15 | .. Travel Day | Perth, Australia | 27 |
| Sun | 16 | .. Esplanade Reserve | Perth, Australia | 28 |
| Mon | 17 | .. Band Travel / Crew Off | Byron Bay, Australia | 29 |
| Tue | 18 | .. Band Off / Crew Travel | Byron Bay / Brisbane | 30 |
| Wed | 19 | .. Crew Off / Band Travel | Brisbane, Australia | 31 |
| Thu | 20 | .. The Riverstage | Brisbane, Australia | 32 |
| Fri | 21 | .. Travel Day | Sydney, Australia | 33 |
| Sat | 22 | .. Sydney Showground | Sydney, Australia | 34 |
| Sun | 23 | .. Travel Home | | 35 |
| Mon | 24 | .. Travel Home | | 36 |

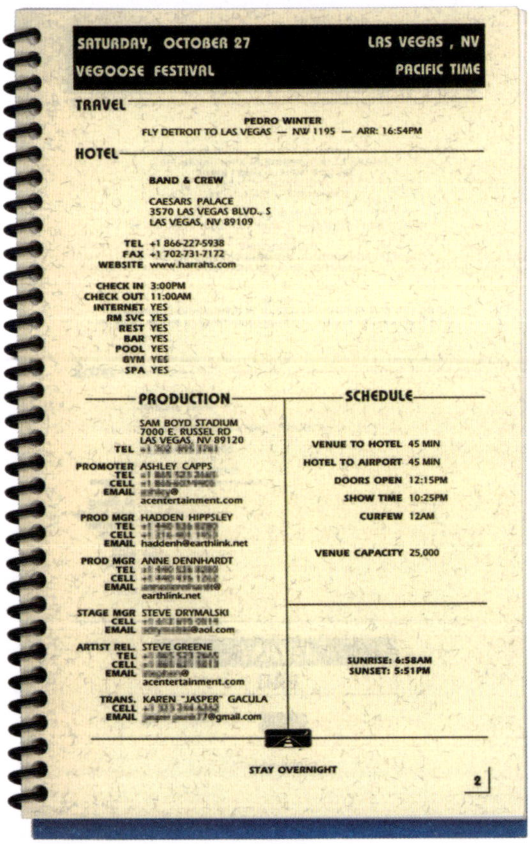

SATURDAY, OCTOBER 27 — LAS VEGAS , NV
VEGOOSE FESTIVAL — PACIFIC TIME

TRAVEL
PEDRO WINTER
FLY DETROIT TO LAS VEGAS — NW 1195 — ARR: 16:54PM

HOTEL
BAND & CREW
CAESARS PALACE
3570 LAS VEGAS BLVD., S
LAS VEGAS, NV 89109
TEL +1 866-227-5938
FAX +1 702-731-7172
WEBSITE www.harrahs.com
CHECK IN 3:00PM
CHECK OUT 11:00AM
INTERNET YES
RM SVC YES
REST YES
BAR YES
POOL YES
GYM YES
SPA YES

PRODUCTION
SAM BOYD STADIUM
7000 E. RUSSEL RD
LAS VEGAS, NV 89120
TEL [redacted]
PROMOTER ASHLEY CAPPS
TEL [redacted]
CELL [redacted]
EMAIL [redacted]@acentertainment.com
PROD MGR HADDEN HIPPSLEY
TEL [redacted]
CELL [redacted]
EMAIL haddenh@earthlink.net
PROD MGR ANNE DENNHARDT
TEL [redacted]
CELL [redacted]
EMAIL [redacted]@earthlink.net
STAGE MGR STEVE DRYMALSKI
CELL [redacted]
EMAIL [redacted]@aol.com
ARTIST REL. STEVE GREENE
TEL [redacted]
CELL [redacted]
EMAIL [redacted]@acentertainment.com
TRANS. KAREN "JASPER" GACULA
CELL [redacted]
EMAIL [redacted]@gmail.com

SCHEDULE
VENUE TO HOTEL 45 MIN
HOTEL TO AIRPORT 45 MIN
DOORS OPEN 12:15PM
SHOW TIME 10:25PM
CURFEW 12AM
VENUE CAPACITY 25,000
SUNRISE: 6:58AM
SUNSET: 5:51PM

STAY OVERNIGHT

2

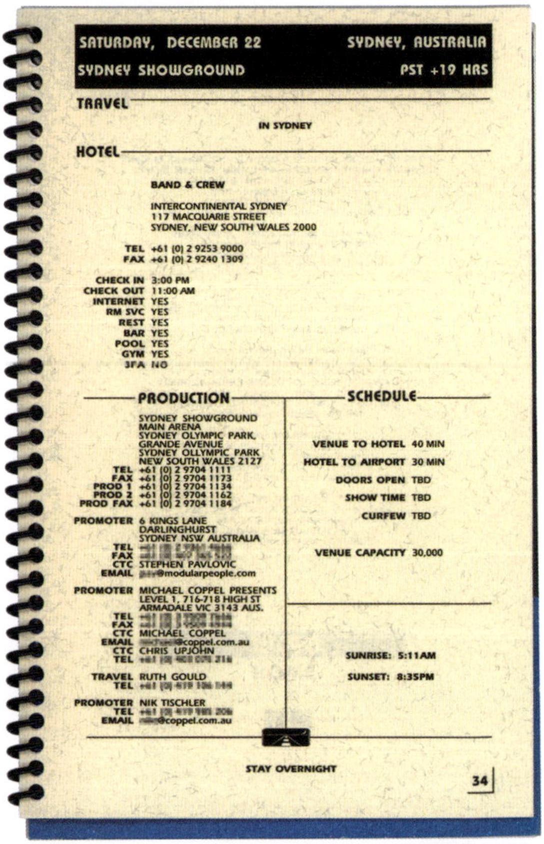

SATURDAY, DECEMBER 22 — SYDNEY, AUSTRALIA
SYDNEY SHOWGROUND — PST +19 HRS

TRAVEL
IN SYDNEY

HOTEL
BAND & CREW
INTERCONTINENTAL SYDNEY
117 MACQUARIE STREET
SYDNEY, NEW SOUTH WALES 2000
TEL +61 (0) 2 9253 9000
FAX +61 (0) 2 9240 1309
CHECK IN 3:00 PM
CHECK OUT 11:00 AM
INTERNET YES
RM SVC YES
REST YES
BAR YES
POOL YES
GYM YES
3FA NO

PRODUCTION
SYDNEY SHOWGROUND
MAIN ARENA
SYDNEY OLYMPIC PARK,
GRANDE AVENUE
SYDNEY OLLYMPIC PARK
NEW SOUTH WALES 2127
TEL +61 (0) 2 9704 1111
FAX +61 (0) 2 9704 1173
PROD 1 +61 (0) 2 9704 1134
PROD 2 +61 (0) 2 9704 1162
PROD FAX +61 (0) 2 9704 1184
PROMOTER 6 KINGS LANE
DARLINGHURST
SYDNEY NSW AUSTRALIA
TEL [redacted]
FAX [redacted]
CTC STEPHEN PAVLOVIC
EMAIL [redacted]@modularpeople.com
PROMOTER MICHAEL COPPEL PRESENTS
LEVEL 1, 716-718 HIGH ST
ARMADALE VIC 3143 AUS.
TEL [redacted]
FAX [redacted]
CTC MICHAEL COPPEL
EMAIL [redacted]@coppel.com.au
CTC CHRIS UPJOHN
TEL [redacted]
TRAVEL RUTH GOULD
TEL [redacted]
PROMOTER NIK TISCHLER
TEL [redacted]
EMAIL [redacted]@coppel.com.au

SCHEDULE
VENUE TO HOTEL 40 MIN
HOTEL TO AIRPORT 30 MIN
DOORS OPEN TBD
SHOW TIME TBD
CURFEW TBD
VENUE CAPACITY 30,000
SUNRISE: 5:11AM
SUNSET: 8:35PM

STAY OVERNIGHT

34

Alive Tour 2007, autumn/winter itineraries

> "All the life that comes from this dream machine we are operating comes from the audience itself. It comes together in a fusion."

and we are amused by the surprise of still being able to generate that connection."

What they don't downplay, however, is the audience's key role in the performance, and, even more specifically, the entire experience itself. Rather than the passive crowd of yore – not that a crowd can be passive at a Daft Punk concert – where the barriers between the audience spectating and the artist performing were clearly marked, Thomas generously insists that crowd participation at their shows is paramount.

"Yes! The audience is a very important factor in this show, much more than perhaps an unplugged thing, where you can have a guy with a piano, and it doesn't matter whether there's ten people or ten thousand people in the audience. I don't think it's the same here, we try really to combine technology and machines, and all the life that comes from this dream machine that we are operating comes from the audience itself. And it comes together in a fusion."

So the audience are similar to actors in this show, then?

"Yes, and that's what's cool because it's staged without being completely staged, because it's not theatre and it's not real life. It's really about presenting a story without words. It's a new format, so it's hard to describe, but it's like a happening. It's about a spaceship that lands in your city for two hours and then leaves."

And it's Thomas' belief that it's not just acting within the audience that acts as a catalyst for this spectacle. When talks turns, as it must, to the thorny issue of how 'live' their gigs actually are, he begins to explain that their performances are analogous to the shows that one might see in the West End or Broadway.

"There is a sense of showmanship and that's also something unique to this show. It's like if you go to see 'Phantom of the Opera' or 'Les Misérables' there is a level of improvisation that you want to achieve, but at the same time there is a level of similarity that we're aiming for."

In layman's terms this means that, yes, there are cues which Thomas and Guy-Man must hit for this multi-media extravaganza to proceed, but there are parts of the show which allow for improvisation. Beneath their stylish robot suits – and yes, it is them up there on stage, they've heard the rumours that they've been replaced by actors, perhaps the ones that appear in 'Electroma', but as they laugh, why would they deny themselves the opportunity to perform in front of 50,000 enthusiastic fans? – they can communicate by radio intercom.

"It's a performance and we try to make it evolve," says Thomas. "But there is a sense of staging that we completely acknowledge, because it's conceptually part of this show, which is a completely different concept to the last show that we did and possibly different from the next show that we might do."

Thomas also admits that coming to the show with a rock aesthetic in mind is something of a vexed notion. Some areas work and adhere to such a dynamic ("We try to work on an energy that is similar to a rock experience"), but because of the reliance upon technology ("It's almost like a plane. A plane obviously had better not crash once there are people on board"), he concedes that their brief involves curation as much as performance.

"I think that stands for a lot of electronic artists," he says. "We are not virtuoso players, and I don't think we could have made a lot of records without the help of technology. We have a very integrated relationship with technology – very love/hate – that we try to express in the records, especially with the last album or in the movie. And the show is that idea too. The show is this idea that things cannot happen without us operating the equipment and us being on stage.

"At the same time we have nine or ten G5 computers and we rely on those circuit boards to do those things because it's not like an Oasis or Coldplay-thing where if the whole thing shuts down you could have Chris Martin on the piano. So this dependency upon technology, people can see it as an easy thing sometimes, which means that people think the computers do everything, but appearing in front of I-don't-know-how-many-people and having to rely on technology I can assure you is not an easy thing."

The heart of the Pyramid

As noted, another aspect of Thomas and Guy-Man's re-hijacking of the cultural zeitgeist has been their effect upon the next wave of producers and bands looking to shift dance and/or electronic music into exciting new terrains. Indeed, any act under the rock'n'rave aegis owes Daft Punk a huge debt. What is surprising though is that it's taken nigh-on-ten years for their influence to really seep through back into the mainstream. Thomas thinks he knows why.

"Ours is an influence that isn't linked to how many records you sell," he notes. "So it takes time to be accepted. It's not necessarily linked to the music industry, which is imploding anyway, because it's not about being number one or selling records. Of course it's flattering and very pleasing, but sometimes I think because we've never really explained what we are doing, we are really relying on the audience to take the time to assimilate things, and this can take longer."

But do Daft Punk even consider themselves dance artists anymore? Their last album, 'Human After All', was made without any synthesisers, and while this can be seen as an aesthetic approach rather than a qualitative one (the pair are often at pains to point out that they don't like repeating themselves), will their music ever speak so fluently to a dancefloor again?

"I can imagine that as we get older, we want to express ourselves musically in different ways," Thomas explains. "Sometimes we feel old in the electronic music world, which is often geared around the young. We are 33 now, but as artists in the general culture we feel young. We're just starting to do things."

He then laughs and adds: "However, if we feel like dancing at 60, then why not? I think that we have very broad tastes and maybe broader than the audience, so we might be doing things that the audience might not be into so we might be left alone with our own ideas.

"Which is fine because dance music has sometimes been political and had a big statement – especially in the mid-90s when it was not accepted as much. But today it is different because it is not so political because it has been accepted. Musically it's still exciting, sometimes it's exciting just as a pure style of music, but we might not feel so much because we like to try and do things that are meaningful, whether aesthetically, or musically."

This has meant their drift into other creative areas. Always a three-dimensional outfit with a nod and a wink to the visual – early videos came from Spike Jonze and Michel Gondry, today's maverick cinema auteurs – the drip-drip release of their contentious directorial debut, 'Electroma', has sealed their desire to widen their holistic creative approach.

Expanding upon the loose theme of man's paradoxical relationship with technology – a motif that began with the release of 'Discovery' – 'Electroma' is a provocative piece of abstract cinema. You'd be hard pushed to call it entertaining: the wafer thin plot concerns two robots (the Daft Punk robots) wishing to alter their identity, an act that provokes huge resistance from their peers. As a result the stylish pair are forced to leave town and walk across the desert for what seems like forever. A good half-an-hour of cinema time in fact. In all, the film lasts for 70 minutes and contains no dialogue.

"It's music for the eyes," Thomas explains of their ambitious project. "We were fascinated by exploring ideas without text or even sub-text."

And yet, as pretentious as that sounds, the movie works, remaining with you for days after. And that in a nutshell is Daft Punk. At times as baffling and infuriating as they are joyous and accessible, they have proved time and again to be a singular presence in our cultural landscape. We're fortunate to have them and it's great to have them back.

"At the start we decided that we would only do what we wanted," concludes Thomas. "Whereas sometimes people think they only have to do whatever it takes to get somewhere – to get famous, to get respected, to get recognised, whatever. But we decided to do the opposite, and I think the rewarding and gratifying thing is that apparently we took the right decision."

*Originally published in DJ, 2007*

# DAFT PUNK: ENCORE!

By Rod Stanley

If you look closely at the back of a circuit board, that tightly-packed grid of lines and soldering points looks a lot like a top-down view of a futuristic city. At least, it must have seemed that way to director Steven Lisberger in the late-70s, around the time he moved his small animation studio to Los Angeles.

Inspired by his experience of the first video game 'Pong', Lisberger had a vision of the future – a utopian virtual world that existed inside computer space, populated by avatars of programs and the people that created them, and enabled by a new form of animation that swapped paintbrushes for pixels. He called it 'Tron'.

Los Angeles, 2010. The world's entertainment centre stretches out beneath the wings of the computer-controlled Airbus, continuing its automated descent to LAX. Around 18 million people live here in an area that runs to the horizon in a scarcely interrupted grid of light, their flow within it determined by a ceaseless, automated blinking – red, green, red.

And somewhere in it sits a cluster of people busy reactivating the 'Tron' universe for the first time since 1982, for a next-generation 3D spectacle they hope will be the ultimate film thrill ride. Daft Punk, robot overlords of the digital disco, provide the soundtrack to this immersive vision of a futuristic electronic society – except, in typical Daft Punk style, nothing is quite what it seems.

In an eminent Hollywood mastering studio, Thomas Bangalter relaxes on a sofa, smiling at the sounds filling the room. The door opens and Guy-Manuel de Homem-Christo enters, nodding a greeting. He expresses pleasure at the overall sound balance, and the engineer continues clicking her mouse, offering a breakneck overview of what this pair have spent the last two years

working on. And one thing that is abundantly clear, notwithstanding snatches of crisply edited beats and haunting synth riffs, is that much of the music is orchestral.

Some 17 years after they struck the UK dance scene like a glitterball comet, Daft Punk remain probably the most successful electronic music act in the world. As they discuss cutting a couple of reference CDs to take away, the film's music mixer Alan Meyerson jokes that they don't want to leave many of those lying around: "These guys have some pretty sophisticated fans who will try anything to get hold of this."

Thomas laughs and relays a story about a fan who got in touch with sequel director Joseph Kosinski, claiming to be Thomas and asking him to send over all the tracks by email. Meyerson puts down his headphones: "And then there are the not-so-sophisticated."

The blacked-out BMW pulls into traffic, and their manager adjusts the volume of the music. "Daft Punk EQ'd my car stereo," he smiles, sounding very much like the great LCD Soundsystem song that never was. Six weeks after Dazed first met up with them in London, as they were about to record with an orchestra at AIR Lyndhurst (built by Beatles producer George Martin in a Victorian chapel), Daft Punk are sitting in the back of the car, looking tired but relaxed.

"We feel good," shrugs Thomas. "There is more work to be done, but we've more or less finished."

"This project is by far the most challenging and complex thing we have ever been involved with," he continues. "Coming from our background of making electronic music in a small bedroom, and ending up having our music performed by a 90-piece orchestra, with some of the best musicians in the world... We are lucky to have had the opportunity to experience some powerful moments artistically over the years, but recording this orchestra was a very intense experience."

A few days later, the completed soundtrack album is played through at their studio, and Daft Punk's skill as composers is clear. Dance has flirted with classical in the past, and composers from Hans Zimmer to original 'Tron' scorer Wendy Carlos have incorporated electronic music into film themes, but this score is a new form of cybernetically enhanced organism, seamlessly merging emotional strings and horns with pulsing bass and sci-fi synth. There's an electronic version of the main theme that fuses with the instruments so completely that it somehow seems to be originating from within that same high-domed Victorian chapel – it's crazy and beautiful, a classical orchestra cutting shapes at a 90s warehouse rave.

Thomas nods, saying they spent about six months just experimenting with the sound. Recording was very pure, he adds, and they limited themselves to six or seven digital sounds, embedded like virtual instruments within the orchestra. He namechecks Max Steiner, Bernard Herrmann, John Carpenter, Vangelis and Maurice Jarre as soundtrack composers that have been inspirational to them.

A gate glides open automatically, and the car pulls into their studio base. In their upstairs production offices, one wall is covered in a giant space scene, a red electric guitar on the floor. A few people tap away at computers, sheltered from the oppressive heat. It's a hint at the preparation needed to record with an orchestra, not to mention the pressures of working with one of the world's biggest film studios – after all, Daft Punk are notoriously protective of their creative control.

"The most pressure we feel is always from ourselves, even in a project like this," says Thomas. "I think that is why we took so much time before we jumped on board, so we could guarantee our freedom and room for experimentation in this environment – it's a dream factory. Hollywood is at the corner of imagination and industry."

The roots of this particular journey lie in Daft Punk's 2007 world tour, when director Kosinski and another producer met with them and asked if they would be interested in working on a 'Tron' sequel. The film had not been approved at that point, but a shared affinity for the world of the original became clear.

"As soon as we saw the filmmaker was not trying to copy the first, but expand it after almost

"The most pressure we feel is always from ourselves. That is why we took so much time before we jumped on board... Hollywood is at the corner of imagination and industry."

30 years, we thought it was interesting," says Thomas. "Then we questioned ourselves to whether or not it was something we could actually do."

Before introspection, however, there was the matter of completing the tour, an audio-visual epic with Daft Punk triumphantly atop an illuminated pyramid in front of delirious crowds of up to 60,000.

"It's a big blur," smiles Guy-Man, visibly lighting up at the memory. "Always a crazy reaction. Everybody was giving so much back to us... a party every night."

"Just seeing that the music and robots still mean things on a deep level to people was definitely an affirmation we received with a lot of humility," adds Thomas. "That tour gave us the energy and enthusiasm to keep on doing unexpected things. So, after we finished, we thought the idea of an audio-visual odyssey in 3D in the IMAX, with a partner as unexpected as Disney, seemed a good way to build something new."

Already with experience in film, from working on their own videos to directing 2006 robot road-movie 'Electroma', the pair detail their involvement with the filmmaking process, and how they set about learning film scoring from scratch.

"This movie was cut to the music," explains Guy-Man proudly. "Usually, composers come in at the end when everything is done." If they did a score again, would they work this way? "We won't take two years again! We learned enough this time to start more quickly."

This dedicated approach has clearly earned admiration from the filmmakers. A couple of days later, at an open day for the film in Venice Beach, Steven Lisberger is the most compelling character, baffling the assembled American entertainment journalists with his passionate exposition of his original utopian vision.

"There are no mining colonies on planets, no vampires, no apocalypse... but we are all users now," he thunders, referring to the original film's notion of individuals interacting in cyberspace. "Our world has divided into the analogue and the digital, but we seek wholeness. That's the image of the disc. Are we going to use technology to bring us together or keep us apart?"

In his notes for this soundtrack release, Lisberger writes: "Daft Punk has increased 'Tron: Legacy''s bandwidth, adding depth to the low end, the Soul, and expanding the high end, the Spirit. They have decompressed the 'Tron' universe and created a new form of cyber-opera."

"'Tron' left a strong imprint as a kid," reflects Guy-Man. "I was eight, he was seven. Maybe I only saw it two or three times in my entire life, but the feel of it is so strong even now, that I think the imprint of the first one will not be erased by the new one. It has a real visionary quality to it."

On its release in 1982, 'Tron' defined an entire visual language, setting the parameters for something that at that time had only been glimpsed – the computer world. To a generation growing up with the first video games, the idea of being able to go inside a game was an incredibly powerful one, and its pioneering computer-generated imagery ensured its aesthetic was 'imprinted' on the minds of a generation – one that would later use computers to create dance music. Early rave was preoccupied with the idea of using technology to create an alternate society, a kind of cyber-pagan utopia that can be traced back to the world of 'Tron'.

"There was a naïve quality in 1982 around technology and the start of video games," agrees Thomas. "And that's like the start of electronic music – there was this statement, and ideologically these things to fight for. But these thoughts are outdated now – socially and artistically irrelevant. So, as always, what can you do next?"

Guy-Man pinpoints the roots of their creative approach to one specific choice they made 17 years ago. "I think there was a turn, right when we started," he says thoughtfully. "We'd made 'Da Funk'. And in England and Scotland, where our label was, there was big pressure and big attention on us… especially when you are 17. It went crazy on us so fast. And we actually did a 'Da Funk 2' in the studio. I think we've never talked about it… We really thought there was a formula," he laughs, miming playing a synth, *"Parp parp paaarp parp PARP!* I remember feeling we have to kill that stuff and go the other way. There were two roads there, and we took the road doing totally the opposite – we did 'Rollin' And Scratchin'' instead. And we consciously killed 'Da Funk 2'. It's always about following the unexpected."

"We knew from the start that there was no way we were going to do this film score with two synthesisers and a drum machine," adds Thomas, by way of conclusion.

Of course, many will be expecting exactly that, and both admit that the filmmakers were originally expecting a purely electronic score. Daft Punk's musical melting pot, from disco to funk and metal, has long been discussed, but perhaps there are classical elements that have gone less remarked.

"Yeah, the baroque quality," nods Guy-Man, adding passionately that he hopes this soundtrack encourages their fans to explore classical music. "The soul and emotion of it is so *powerful* that to like it is so easy – it's just people think you need to be educated. I thought that myself for a long time, until I had listened to so many kinds of music, that one day I just tried it.

Best
Western
SUNSET PLAZA HOT
Sunset

But it's not about learning... it's about learning that it's just there."

"The end of 'Aerodynamic' is *completely* baroque music, a classical composition we put into synthetic form," says Thomas. "This film was the opposite – we wanted to make it timeless. A cello was there 400 years ago and will still be here in 400 years. But synthesisers that were invented 20 years ago will probably be gone in the next 20. Synths are a very low level of artificial intelligence," he smiles, "whereas you have a Stradivarius that will live for a thousand years. In the past, we have worked with clashing genres like disco and heavy metal, and here we would do it with film scores... this idea of the ultimate retro-futurism."

Retro-futurism is one of Thomas's favourite words, and it's no accident that some of the most powerful moments in sci-fi film have been set to classical music, such as the space docking scene in Stanley Kubrick's '2001', played out to 'The Blue Danube' by Johann Strauss.

"Daft Punk would not exist if there was no technology," says Thomas. "So here was a way of saying: 'Ok – if there was no technology, let's see what we could have done.' This is what Daft Punk would have done in 1750!"

A music theatre, downtown. As members of the mechanical orchestra slowly assemble themselves, two robot figures have taken to the stage. Thomas sits down calmly at the grand piano, lights reflecting off his silver head and hands, and plays a Bach prelude amid the faded grandeur of the empty theatre. Guy-Man stands beside him, curved visor impassively facing front, and the few people present fall silent. It's a powerful moment, evoking both the dispassionate nature of technology and the humanity of live performance. These robots have provided an elegant nexus for Daft Punk's ideas about art, technology and humanity for over a decade, and that technologic transformation back in 1999 created two genuine pop icons for the 21st century. The robots also make an appearance in the new film, surely a childhood fantasy fulfilled.

"Last week we were with Steven," Thomas

outlines. "We played him the soundtrack, and he was so moved by it, and appreciative." He later reveals Lisberger wept during playback. "That is the kind of moment when you feel it is really worth it, to have the ability to give back to someone that inspired you. And the rest is fun! It is as fun as being in 'Star Wars'," he says, referring to last year's Adidas commercial, "when we were in the cantina with C3PO and R2D2."

Guy-Man chuckles: "We are lucky."

Given their reputation for elusiveness, Daft Punk are surprisingly open, except about plans for the future: a subject that results in the visors sliding down every time. More film scores? Maybe. New Daft Punk material? Perhaps. Touring this soundtrack live with a 90-piece orchestra on a floating electronic city with players parachuting in from the edge of space? They rule nothing out.

"One thing for sure is that we have been creating a lot of music," Guy-Man says, teasingly. "The energy we got from the tour has been put back into this movie, and some other stuff too."

"Electronic music has definitely taken over America," says Thomas, discussing their ongoing association with rap megastars from Kanye to Pharrell. "There is more and more interaction with hip hop."

Do they simply find dance music less appealing at the moment? The only real dancefloor number here, 'Derezzed', clocks in at one minute and fifty seconds, after all. "For us, yes," he says. "We are definitely excited by music, but just trying to constantly experiment. And sometimes that means going with other art forms, because you think there's more latitude to experiment with an orchestra than an 808 drum machine and synth."

Throughout their career, Daft Punk have not been afraid to make mistakes, and while not every creative choice has been welcomed with open arms, people have usually come round to their way of thinking. "When 'Homework' came out, people said it was a sell out and the death of techno," laughs Thomas. "We're definitely ready for whatever happens with this and feel very happy about it on a personal level. We have plenty of experience of ups and downs."

Despite this insistence on never repeating themselves, Daft Punk have also somehow remained a permanent fixture in music's fast-revolving firmament; three hours after our arrival in LA, a DJ had already played 'Robot Rock'.

"It is puzzling," says Thomas. "Especially tracks like that off 'Human After All' that were not so much appreciated – I mean, we were very happy with that record. But in electronic music, having been around for 17 years and to not have been tagged 'uncool' is surprising." How have they done that? "We have no idea."

"And if we knew, we wouldn't tell you," laughs Guy-Man. "No, I think it is just because we are dedicated, and we are passionate. We met when we were kids. And it is about taking your brain out – you just feel, and you enjoy. It is like two kids playing, and if something makes you laugh or is exciting, then you keep on. It's doing things not for fame, success or money, but enjoying the journey rather than the goal."

Pool party, an LA rooftop. Acres of tanned flesh in the 40° heat, relentlessly locking step to a machine groove that has become a kind of aural wallpaper. Technology can set you free, or it can become a prison – that was what Steven Lisberger saw 30 years ago when he gazed at a circuit board and saw the possibilities that lay beyond it. Will we use technology to bring us together, or keep us apart? In their ongoing mission to make us feel emotion in the midst of the most synthetic spectacle, Daft Punk are a celebration of humanity in a robot world, not just in art and music, but the way we live.

"Technology is an interesting subject, people thinking: how much good, and how much bad, does it inherently carry?" said Thomas. "And I think our way of participating in that debate is to have made an album with real people, and not so much with computers. Maybe that's what we feel right now, surrounded by all this technology," and he smiles, "whether subconscious or not."

*Originally published in Dazed and Confused, December 2010*

# RANDOMLY ACCESSED MEMORIES

When Daft Punk returned in 2013 with their first studio album since 2005's 'Human After All', the intervening years had seen the duo become one of the primary inspirations for a global dance music explosion. **Kevin EG Perry** – who interviewed the duo for an NME cover feature at the time – remembers the buzz around one of the most anticipated albums of the 21st century and asks if its legacy matches the hype?

The whole thing was hush-hush from the very start. When I was called into the NME editor's office at the start of March 2013, nobody would even tell me what the meeting was about. I guessed that meant I was going to be bollocked, or fired, or both. Instead it was something quite the opposite. They wanted me to go to Paris to interview Daft Punk, where legendary NME photographer Dean Chalkley would be shooting them for an upcoming cover story. I couldn't say 'oui' fast enough.

By then, anticipation for Thomas Bangalter and Guy-Manuel de Homem-Christo's new record 'Random Access Memories' was already at fever pitch. At the end of February, the official Daft Punk website announced that after years of apparent inactivity they'd signed to the storied Sony Music label Columbia Records. Then, on March 2, an enigmatic 15-second clip aired during an episode of 'Saturday Night Live'. It featured the Daft Punk logo, their robotic helmets, and an irresistibly funky guitar riff which Chic guitarist Nile Rodgers soon confirmed was his distinctive handiwork.

At that moment, it felt as if everyone on the planet was united in their desperation to hear what the duo had been working on behind closed doors for the last half-decade. It already seemed clear they had no intention of returning to the electronic sound they had thoroughly explored on their first three records, and this notion was confirmed when I arrived at Sony Music in Kensington for a clandestine listening session ahead of the interview. The level of secrecy verged on the ludicrous. Although I would be allowed to hear the album once (and once only), nobody could tell me what any of the tracks were called. Only a few tantalising nuggets of information were made available: No computers had been used in the record's production, and the music had apparently been influenced by disco, pop rock and Steely Dan. "No EDM," I hastily scribbled down. "Just dance."

I was also told that the record had been built around an underlying, unifying theme: "It's a homage to memories, and music's power to evoke them." That sounded suitably vague and mysterious until the album surged into life and it became clear just how deliberately Daft Punk had set about drawing out the musical memories we all share through popular culture. On opening track 'Give Life Back to Music', Rodgers, creator of countless disco hits with Chic, trades fluid grooves with Paul Jackson Jr, whose inimitable guitar sound can't help but bring to mind his work with Michael Jackson on era-defining albums like 'Thriller', 'Bad' and 'Dangerous'. With that superlative backing, the vocoder-synthesised robotic vocals imploring us to: "Let the music of your life, give life back to music" are clearly meant to be taken entirely literally. It's a statement of intent for the record as a whole. Daft Punk had brought together two of the most successful and influential guitarists in pop music history for the express purpose of breathing new meaning and purpose into dance music.

As Rodgers himself put it: "They went back to go forward." De Homem-Christo, meanwhile, would later confirm the lyric's implication that they found the rest of the contemporary music scene dull, vapid and lifeless was very much intentional.

It wasn't just popular music history that Daft Punk were revisiting and reimagining on 'Random Access Memories', but their own too. Three minutes and 15 seconds into 'Give Life Back to Music' we hear the sound of a gathering crowd, ready to party, a nod back to 'Revolution 909', from their 1997 debut album 'Homework', which opens with the sound of a rave being broken up by the police.

In many ways, 'Random Access Memories' represents the moment Daft Punk came full circle to make the record they were always destined to create. On 'Homework', at the start of their careers, they'd sampled upbeat 70s hits like Barry White's 'I'm Gonna Love You Just a Little More Baby', Elton John and Kiki Dee's 'Don't Go Breaking My Heart' and Billy Joel's 'Just the Way You Are'. Now, 16 years on, they were making their own versions of that freewheeling, ecstatic music, often using the same equipment, the same studios and even the same musicians who had first inspired them. No wonder it sounded like they were having the time of their lives.

For Bangalter, the distinctive sound of that era holds a particular familial significance. His father, who released music under the name Daniel Vangarde, wrote and produced a string of 70s dance hits including Ottawan's 'D.I.S.C.O.' and the Gibson Brothers' 'Cuba'. While Daft Punk didn't sample Vangarde directly on 'Random Access Memories', they did recruit the father of disco himself, Giorgio Moroder, to relate his own journey to becoming a musician on the innovative track, 'Giorgio by Moroder', a micro-documentary dressed up as a song and another obvious homage to how intertwined music is with memory.

If 'Random Access Memories' is a trip back into Daft Punk's musical memory banks, then they weren't going to stop at 'Homework'. That period in their lives before they were DJs, when they were two-thirds of indie rock band Darlin' (alongside Laurent Brancowitz, later of Phoenix) is thrillingly referenced on 'Instant Crush', their collaboration with Julian Casablancas of The Strokes, the apotheosis of indie rock frontmen.

At the heart of 'Random Access Memories' sits 'Touch', a monumental collaboration with the songwriter and composer Paul Williams which sees Bangalter and de Homem-Christo pursuing their trip down memory lane all the way back to childhood. As boys growing up in Paris, they had both been obsessed with Brian De Palma's 1974 slapstick rock opera 'Phantom of the Paradise', and in particular with Williams' performance as ageless impresario Swan. Working with Williams, who also wrote music for 'The Muppets' and the cult 1976 musical 'Bugsy Malone', was both a chance for Daft Punk to work with a hero of theirs and a way to guide listeners back towards their own earliest musical memories. The lushly arranged song, which features the repeated refrain: "Hold on, if love is the answer, you're home", clearly carries great significance for the band. When they announced their split with the video 'Epilogue' in February 2021, it was 'Touch' that they chose to play themselves out with.

A couple of days after hearing the album for the first time, I got an email from NME telling me that instead of Paris, the interview would be happening at "the Bing Crosby mansion" in Palm Springs, where the band would be staying during the first weekend of Coachella in April. Having heard the record, moving the interview to California seemed perfectly logical. After all, much of the album had been recorded in Los Angeles, and it was hard to miss how much the 70s-influenced sound was intended to conjure up the hazy heyday of the Sunset Strip.

Months earlier, the pedal steel guitar player Greg Leisz, who has played with everyone from Joni Mitchell to Bruce Springsteen, had also been lured to Los Angeles by a mysterious message from Daft Punk. He spent a day recording at the Jim Henson Studios, a historic Hollywood space, originally built by Charlie Chaplin. While Leisz was never told exactly why he'd been hired, he got the sense from working with Bangalter and de Homem-Christo that there was a particular sound they wanted to pay tribute to.

"They wanted the pedal steel guitar in their music, not only for the instrumentation but also because they were interested in a particular era," Leisz told me recently. "They would refer to people like the Eagles, and other bands that were super popular in the 70s, who had an element of Americana in their music."

Leisz also remembered the duo referring to how much their musical vision for 'Random Access Memories' had been shaped by their experience working with a 90-piece orchestra for their 2010 film score 'Tron: Legacy'.

"We did talk quite a bit on the session, and they explained that the whole idea of using musicians on the record came from them working with that orchestra in London," he says. "I remember Thomas saying that had opened up their minds to the idea of doing it, because all of a sudden they realised there was something there emotionally that was coming in because these were real people playing real instruments. They took that and moved it into the concept for their next album."

The decision to make a fully analogue record with live instruments was Daft Punk's way of stepping away from an electronic music scene that had been largely shaped by the gargantuan influence of their first two records, 'Homework' and 'Discovery'. By the early 2010s there were a rash of imitators churning out electronic music, which, was now being identified by the initialism 'EDM', and the genre was quickly becoming a punchline.

Bangalter and de Homem-Christo had initially embraced the ease with which new songs could be created on a computer, but they were starting to wonder whether the trick had lost its sparkle now that everyone with a laptop could pull it off. 'Random Access Memories' was their analogue reaction against this digital homogeneity.

When I arrived in LA, the veil of mystery surrounding 'Random Access Memories' was drawn back – but only a little. A publicist finally consented to tell me what the songs were called. Sitting outside a bar on the Sunset Strip, she handed me a scrap of paper with a list of 13 song titles written on it in pencil. "We're not allowed to send it electronically," said the PR. "I'm sure you understand." It seemed absurd until I realised I was dealing with something like Van Halen's M&Ms. David Lee Roth once explained that the band's rider request to be provided with a bowl full of M&Ms minus all the brown ones was actually a way to make sure venues were reading the small print, ensuring complex technical and logistical requirements were met. This was similar: a deliberately over-the-top instruction from Daft Punk to remind their label that loose lips sink spaceships.

That Friday I was making my way towards the main stage at Coachella to catch the Yeah Yeah Yeahs when all hell broke loose. On the big screens around the festival a deafening crackle of static was interrupted by the unmistakable sound of 'Get Lucky', as the screen displayed, for the first time anywhere, the sight of Pharrell and Nile Rodgers, in matching glitterball jackets, backed up by the robots themselves on bass and drums. The rumour mill had already been abuzz with stories that Daft Punk might play an unannounced set at the festival, but it turned out this was all they needed. A video clip that lasted less than two minutes generated more excitement than pretty much anyone who actually turned up to play. (Certainly more than The Stone Roses, who headlined the festival that night in front of a bemused crowd scattered across a largely empty venue.)

On Sunday lunchtime, I made my way to Bing Crosby's estate in Palm Springs for my audience with Bangalter and de Homem-Christo. I had a sprawling list of questions for them, which Bangalter answered loquaciously while de Homem-Christo sat mostly silent, the picture of Gallic cool, waiting for the opportune moment to drop a bon mot. It was easy to see how their brains worked in tandem, spliced together like the helmets on their album cover.

The pair were on fine form, relaxed and confident that with 'Random Access Memories' they had taken a huge leap in a new musical direction. The only time they appeared exasperated was when asked whether they would tour the album. They said it might come later, but as it turned out it never did. It was only in 2021, when Daft Punk finally announced their split, that I finally gave up hope of one day seeing 'Random Access Memories' played live. It would have been a hell of an undertaking to get it right, but if anyone had been capable of doing it then it would have been Daft Punk. The experience of seeing them on the Alive tour in 2007 had been like your first taste of ecstasy – the sort of high you can chase for a lifetime.

'Get Lucky' was released the Friday after Coachella and spent four consecutive weeks at the top of the UK charts. When 'Random Access Memories' finally arrived the following month, it was heralded by a sea of ecstatic reviews that couldn't help but be influenced by the enormous hype the record had generated. As the only member of NME staff who had heard the album outside of a music industry listening party at The Shard, I was put in the unusual position of having to write the review at the same time as the cover story and gave it a delirious score of 10/10. Several other publications joined me in giving the album full marks. It was a commercial hit, giving Daft Punk their first ever number one records in France, the UK and the USA, and selling over 3.2 million copies within its first 12 months.

In recent years, with the hype now long subsided, some critics have begun to reassess its impact. In 2021, Pitchfork published a piece revising the scores awarded to several of their reviews. At the same time as elevating 'Discovery' from a 6.4 to a 10, they downgraded 'Random Access Memories' from 8.8 to 6.8. Their initial review had predicted 'RAM' would become as influential as their earlier work, but critic Philip Sherburne felt time had been less kind to it. "It's not that people aren't listening to it; the album has racked up nearly 1.5 billion plays on Spotify alone," he wrote. "'RAM' has some jams, but it doesn't feel pivotal in the same way that 'Discovery' did."

It's hard to argue too much with that assessment, but perhaps it was always inevitable that 'Random Access Memories' wouldn't be replicated and homaged in the same way that 'Discovery' was by a generation of young laptop producers. That was sort of the point. Daft Punk set out to make a grand, expensive, expansive, landmark of an album, one that could only be achieved with their combination of ingenuity, idiosyncratic taste and limitless resources. It stands now as a worthy final statement from a pair of musical mavericks who did far more than just get lucky.

"THE FIRST THING
HEARD IT WAS: 'C
THAT'S AN INTERE
THE TONGUE. THE
DESCRIBE IT IS KU
THEY TAKE YOU B
AND THEN THEY T
THE FUTURE."

Paul Williams on 'Random Access Memories'/The Guardian/201

SAID WHEN I
AN I SEE IT AGAIN?'
STING SLIP OF
BEST WAY I CAN
RICK'S '2001'.
CK IN TIME
AKE YOU INTO

# SAMPLE IT, LOOP IT, F*CK IT AND EAT IT

From cutting up Barry Manilow and Sister Sledge on 'Homework' and 'Discovery' to being sampled on one of the biggest hip hop records of all time, the art of sampling was always a key component of the Daft Punk story. **Ben Cardew** finds out how the duo's deft use of other people's sounds helped create some of the most iconic dance records of all time...

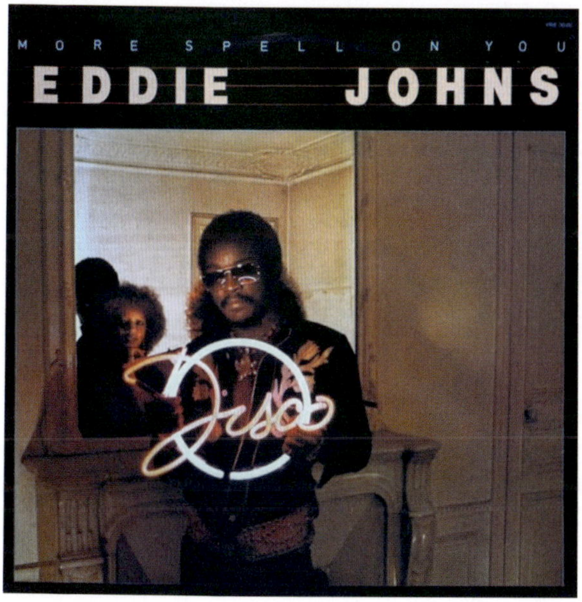


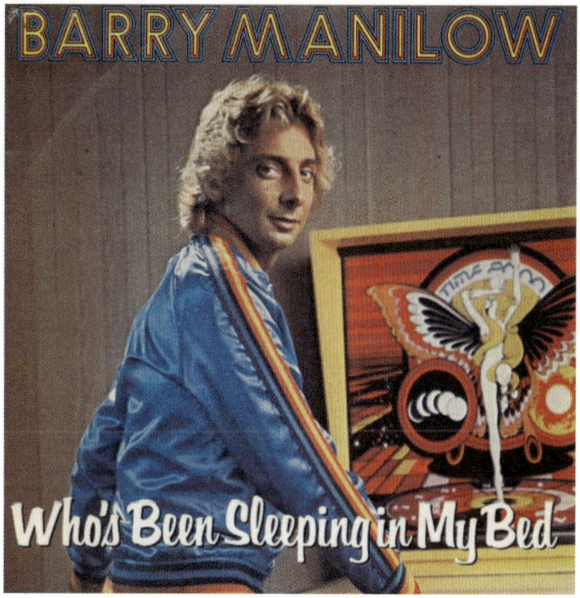


Sampling has been a vital piece in the multifarious jigsaw of modern music since the birth of hip hop in the 70s. But it remains a fundamentally misunderstood art, liable to provoke furious disbelief and outright rage among certain sectors of the 'real-music' brigade when examples of the practice are discovered. Daft Punk, as an act that has made relatively prominent use of sampling, are far from immune to this controversy. One of the biggest Daft Punk news stories in the year following their split was an LA Times article from May 2021, whose headline screamed in unforgiving 24 point font: "A homeless L.A. musician helped create a Daft Punk classic. So why hasn't he seen a dime?"

Predictably, there was outrage at the article, which relates the story of Eddie Johns, a musician whose 1979 track 'More Spell on You' Daft Punk sampled on 'One More Time', their biggest hit until 'Get Lucky'. Daft Punk may have done nothing legally wrong in the case – a representative for the group confirmed to the LA Times that they were paying royalties twice a year to "the producer and owner of 'More Spell on You'" – but the story certainly didn't look good for them, with the journalist comparing Daft Punk's night of glitz at the 2014 Grammys with Johns bedding down in an LA shelter.

Of course, nobody wants to see a musician like Johns go unrewarded for his work. And you could argue that Daft Punk – for all the royalties they pay to the owner of 'One More Time' – were hoist by their own secretive petard here. Johns didn't receive a credit on the sleeve of 'Discovery', the duo's second album on which 'One More Time' features, and Daft Punk hadn't acknowledged the use of the sample until the LA Times story came out, despite the existence of several YouTube videos that show exactly how they chopped and rearranged the ebullient horn section from 'More Spell on You' into the basis of 'One More Time'. You can, in fact, find similar videos for several Daft Punk tracks, which purport to show how they sampled everything from Tavares to Karen Young, with little regard to the official line on the matter.

At the same time, it feels unfortunate that this controversy should centre on Daft Punk, a band who used sampling but never leaned on it as a crutch (well, perhaps, once, in the case of 'Robot Rock'); who were clever in deconstructing their source material and contributed significantly towards advancing the art of sampling.

The fact is, for a band rooted in house music, Daft Punk didn't actually sample that much. (To insert a brief, legal-tinged notice, I once asked a music industry lawyer about sampling

credits and he told me that artists can, in some circumstances, legally sample a record without crediting it in the sleeve notes. It depends on the agreement. So Daft Punk may – or may not – have sampled more records than the ones that are publicly acknowledged on their records. As I wasn't in the studio with them, I simply don't know. So I am going to be basing myself here, in the large, on the records that Daft Punk specifically said they sampled.)

'Homework' lists one sample among its 16 tracks. The sleeve of 'Discovery' mentions four, plus we have the Eddie Johns sample on 'One More Time'. 'Human After All' sports one sample and 'Random Access Memories' has two, both of them on 'Contact', a song that had been knocking around in some form since the early 2000s. These are not particularly large numbers. What's more, on 'Discovery' Daft Punk were often sampling themselves, recording their own loops on guitar and synth which they then played through samplers.

When Daft Punk did sample, they did it well, too, with love for their source material that never spilled over into stifling reverence. Daft Punk were never diggers, scouring second-hand stores for the obscurest songs to plunder. Their sample material isn't obvious, exactly (particularly in the case of Barry Manilow's 'Who's Been Sleeping in My Bed', which they use on 'Superheroes'). But it's not that far out, either, largely based around funk/disco records from the late-70s and early-80s. Their skill, then, came in what they did with their samples, the illuminating ways that they manipulated their source material to create something genuinely new.

Take 'One More Time': Daft Punk didn't just lift the song's strident horn riff from 'More Spell on You'; they took three small samples from the song, chopped them out and rearranged them to make something very different, a transformative use of sampling that takes the base elements and innovates with them. This is not to downplay the importance of 'More Spell on You' in the creation of 'One More Time'. But Daft Punk's own creativity should not be denied.

'Harder, Better, Faster, Stronger' is similar. On many online forums you will find people claiming to be shocked to the core that Daft Punk have lifted a section of Edwin Birdsong's 'Cola Bottle Baby' in making their song. But this is a ridiculous reaction. True, one part of 'Harder, Better, Faster, Stronger' does use a lengthy and very recognisable stretch of 'Cola Bottle Baby'. But Daft Punk also employed a series of shorter samples from the song, which they rearranged in counter-intuitive ways to make their own musical riffs.

Daft Punk's use of sampling on 'Harder, Better, Faster, Stronger' comes close to the microsampling technique that Daft Punk collaborator Todd Edwards learned from MK and later made entirely his own. You can hear this technique at play on 'Face to Face' from 'Discovery' and – to a lesser extent – on 'RAM''s 'Fragments of Time', the two songs that Edwards produced with Daft Punk. Edwards takes tens, if not hundreds, of tiny samples and creates gorgeously staccato rhythmical patterns with them in a way that entirely transforms his source material, each sample like a key on a piano or an instrument in an orchestra. The result is both incredibly innovative and – in Edwards' hands at least – entirely funky, the kind of innovation that slips down like a gulp of sugary tea on a cold winter's day.

If you were feeling particularly critical, you might make hay of the fact that the most innovative sampling on a Daft Punk record comes from Todd Edwards, rather than Daft Punk themselves. But, as Edwards tells it, the group plunged head-first into microsampling while making 'Face to Face'. He selected 70 samples for the song; Daft Punk took another 70, and they produced the track together. Besides, Daft Punk were excellent collaborators and are to be congratulated for letting Todd Edwards work in this way on their record. 'Face to Face' ended up at the perfect intersection of the two acts' typical sounds, while 'Fragments of Time' somehow managed to pull off a combination of microsampled chorus and soft rock verses. (And yes, in a way, the 140+ samples on 'Face to Face' does slightly contradict the idea above that Daft Punk didn't sample that much. But 'Face to Face' and 'Fragments of Time' are two songs amid the 102 that Daft Punk released. And these samples are tiny.)

Daft Punk's other innovation in sampling is perhaps more tenuous, given that it found its apotheosis in 'So Much Love to Give' by Together, the duo formed by Thomas Bangalter and DJ Falcon. But the utter extreme minimalism that Together pioneered found its reflection on 'RAM''s

'Contact' (on which DJ Falcon is credited) so it does have a space here. This technique is, in many ways, the polar opposite of microsampling, in that it involves taking a sample and looping it to extreme new lengths, while toying with the loop's sonic make-up. In the case of 'Contact', the band use two four-bar samples taken from The Sherb's 1982 single 'We Ride Tonight'; while 'So Much Love to Give' uses one loop from The Real Thing's 'Love's Such a Wonderful Thing'.

Like so many things in electronic music, this is a technique that is deceptive in its simplicity. It sounds incredibly simple to find one loop and keep hammering it home; but precisely choosing the right sample, one that you can play around with for 10 minutes (in the case of 'So Much Love to Give') without the audience howling at the moon in frustration is incredibly difficult. Which perhaps explains why such extreme minimalism never really took off in house music and why Together remains almost a one-off. I like the efficiency of this technique too; like the producers have wrung every last drop of soul from their sample; the Boxing Day sandwiches and New Year's Eve soup from the Christmas turkey of sampling.

You can hear this kind of brutal efficiency in 'Robot Rock', the lead single from 'Human After All'. I love 'Robot Rock'. But it is the one moment

"Sampling was a bridge... the connection between electronic music and hip hop; and Daft Punk's leg up into global musical immortality."

in Daft Punk's career where I concede that they relied a bit too heavily on the song's main sample, which is taken from 'Release the Beast' by US funk rock band Breakwater.

Large sections of 'Robot Rock' are essentially just one sample from 'Release the Beast', with Daft Punk adding the song's robotic – and very simple – two-word vocal over the top. Unlike the flawless technological gleam of 'So Much Love to Give', 'Robot Rock' sounds to me a little unfinished, like a demo that is still waiting forlornly in the rain for another lick of paint.

Sampling other acts was important for Daft Punk, then. But so too was being sampled. I would argue, in fact, that without Daft Punk's music being sampled by hip hop producers, the duo might not have made their US breakthrough; and the country that birthed house and techno might never have seen these two genres have their commercial moment in the sun on their home turf.

That might sound like an outrageous claim. But it comes with a historical context. House music and hip hop spring from the same roots (largely funk and disco) and, initially at least, they got along famously, with rappers like the Jungle Brothers hopping onto house beats. By the time Daft Punk emerged, however, hip hop was at mortal odds with house music and electronic sounds as a whole. (It didn't exactly help with the frequently homophobic world of 90s hip hop that house had emerged from the gay clubs of Chicago.)

In a country like the US, where hip hop was (and is) the dominant cultural force, this was a big problem for house music producers looking to break into the mainstream. Hip hop wasn't just the leading musical force; it dominated fashion and cultural discourse. What hip hop said, went. And if hip hop said that dance music wasn't cool, then that was the dominant narrative. The US electronica mini boom of the late-90s, for example, took place largely among rock audiences, who were more receptive to electronic sounds.

Twenty years ago, a credible hip hop act sampling a European house music record was pretty much unheard of. But that was precisely what happened in 2000, when Slum Village, led by J Dilla, sampled Thomas Bangalter's 'Extra Dry' on their song 'Raise It Up'. At the time the move seemed utterly incredible to house music fans but – while it did lead to Slum Village remixing Daft Punk's 'Aerodynamic' – the impact on the wider world was limited.

Far more important for the mainstream was Swizz Beatz's decision to sample the hook from Daft Punk's 'Technologic' on Busta Rhymes' 2005 single 'Touch It'. This was the Holy Grail of talented producer plus respected artist plus big chart hit, with the song reaching 16 in the US Billboard Hot 100. Perhaps more importantly, it was this that led Kanye West to sample 'Harder, Better, Faster, Stronger' on his vast worldwide hit single 'Stronger'.

A-Trak, who was West's tour DJ at the time, told Genius that 'Touch It' was West's introduction to Daft Punk, after he heard it on tour in Europe in 2006. One year later 'Stronger' dropped, with a hefty – and instantly recognisable – sample from 'Harder, Better, Faster, Stronger', Daft Punk in the video and cartoon drawings of the Daft Punk robots on the single's sleeve, the kind of ultra-mainstream exposure Daft Punk had never before enjoyed, particularly in the States.

It's hard to overemphasise how important this sample would be for Daft Punk and electronic music as a whole. True, Daft Punk had already played their legendary Coachella 2006 set by this time, which helped them on their way to their global touring success with Alive. But 'Stronger' was a planet-sized hit, selling five million copies in the US alone and hitting number one on the Billboard chart. It was credible, too, coming from Kanye West then arguably at his commercial peak and close to his critical summit. Kanye has probably been the most important figure over the last two decades of hip hop, helping with the crossover between hip hop and fashion, as well as the rise of autotune. His thumbs up to Daft Punk was like a hip hop benediction: if Kanye said Daft Punk were OK; then hip hop would agree. And if hip hop agreed; then the US public as a whole was not going to argue.

'Stronger' was a hit. But it was also a proof of concept: proof that the electronic sounds of Daft Punk in particular – and dance music in general – could work well with hip hop beats and rapping. The next few years would see an explosion in rap songs that sampled electronic music and by 2013, Complex magazine was able to list its Top 10 hip hop songs that sampled Daft Punk, from Lil B to Wiley. By the end of the 2010s, David Guetta was one of the biggest producers in commercial rap music, something that would have been inconceivable 10 years previously.

It wasn't just the obvious Daft Punk hooks that got sampled, either. Janet Jackson sampled Homework's 'Daftendirekt' on 'So Much Betta'; Chance The Rapper employed lovelorn masterpiece 'Something About Us' from 'Discovery' on his unreleased song of the same name; Jazmine Sullivan sampled the dreamy 'Veridis Quo', also from 'Discovery' on 'Dream Big'. And so on.

After Kanye released 'Stronger', it became fairly standard practice for hip hop producers to sample Daft Punk, a cliché even. Perhaps more importantly, Daft Punk themselves were ushered into the world of hip hop production, working on songs for Kanye West, N.E.R.D. and the Weeknd, resulting in huge chart hits, while Jay-Z contributed a rap to a (sadly unreleased) song for Daft Punk's 'Tron' soundtrack.

Without Swizz Beatz and 'Touch It', it is likely that none of this would have happened. Sampling was a bridge between Daft Punk and Kanye West; the connection between electronic music and hip hop; and Daft Punk's leg up into Billboard chart success and global musical immortality.

# Instant Crush

No act in electronic music elicits fan devotion like Daft Punk. As the legend of the robots grew, so too did online fan communities, where devotees could pore over every detail of the duo's output. Some even turned their passion for Daft Punk into thriving businesses, providing fan merch and Daft Punk paraphernalia to the community. **Sean Griffiths** meets the Daft Punk super fans...

**DAFT PUNK SUPER FAN**

# LUKE PEREZ

Luke Perez first became obsessed with Daft Punk after catching their much talked about minute-long promo for 'Random Access Memories', screened during the ad break for 'Saturday Night Live' in 2013.

"I was about 15 at the time," they explain. "And it just grabbed me straight away. There was so much attention to detail and it was like nothing else around at that point. You could tell it was a real labour of love." Following their initial exposure, Luke set about finding out more and more, and found themselves in a rabbit hole, discovering the group's previous albums and music videos on YouTube.

"I can be quite an obsessive person," they say. "So very quickly it became about knowing everything about them. And with Daft Punk, they're mysterious and there's a lot of hidden history, which makes it a lot more fun to delve into. I like the challenge of researching something mysterious."

Luke's growing enthusiasm for the robots eventually led them to set up the Daft Punk Historian blog (a fan site that collects together archived interviews, discography and filmography and an in-depth history of the group) and YouTube channel in 2018.

**What is so special about Daft Punk?**

"I think their mystique is a big part of it as it really draws people in. And the music is great, obviously, but there has to be something else there besides the music to create the kind of fandom Daft Punk have. I have Asperger's and that's a very obsessive mindset and Daft Punk is a great subject to obsess over as you can really go down a rabbit hole with them. I've connected with a lot of other big Daft Punk fans online and it's something quite a few of us share."

**What made you make the leap from being a fan to setting up the Daft Punk Historian site and YouTube channel?**

"I started the Twitter account first, in 2015, and then the site in 2018. A lot of older people will know this stuff already, but I was doing all this research on Daft Punk and learning it for the first time, and really just wanted to share that with people. My mission statement for the site is to archive my own research into Daft Punk and provide fans with information. There's 400 articles about Daft Punk on the site - which I took from Tumblr accounts and defunct fan forums - plus an in-depth history of the group and a discography. I get a lot of people thanking me for running the site as it means they don't have to trawl the internet for hours to find obscure information about Daft Punk. It's all there for them."

**What's your favourite Daft Punk album?**
"I love 'Random Access Memories' as that was my entry point, 'Discovery' is a close second. That's a real classic album and one a lot of people consider to be one of the best and most important albums of this century. I've also got a lot of appreciation for 'Human After All' too, which a lot of people don't really like. Daft Punk led me on to a lot of other great music too like Justice, SebastiAn, Gesaffelstein and that whole French electronic scene."

**You've got a fairly sizable Daft Punk merch collection. Can you talk us through it?**
"I started out with CDs and then moved on to vinyl. Then I moved on to posters and I've got a whole corner of the room filled with cardboard tubes of posters as I haven't got enough room on the walls for all of them! I've got a lot of old magazines too with Daft Punk in, maybe around 30, and my closet is full of Daft Punk shirts and jackets. A lot of Daft Punk collectors will focus on one thing, like collecting every cassette or piece of vinyl they released, but my collection is more general. The most expensive thing in my collection is my Daft Punk varsity jacket which I bought for $780 from their website at the end of 2017. Altogether the collection's worth around $15,000."

**How did you feel when they split up?**
"They'd wound down and liquidated some of their companies a few years earlier so there were some signs that they might be ending things. In some ways it was a little cathartic, in that it means you're not constantly living in hope of them releasing new material or touring. I've had to come to terms with never seeing them live though. I take solace in the fact their Coachella show inspired so many electronic live shows to come. It's like there's a little part of Daft Punk in every live show you go to."

*To find out more visit thedaftpunkhistorian.weebly.com*

## DAFT PUNK SUPER FAN
# ARTEM MEDVEDEV

When Artem Medvedev discovered Daft Punk as a pre-teen in Russia, he knew there was little chance of them ever coming to his home country to perform, or little chance of him getting his hands on some much coveted Daft Punk merch. So he set about designing and building his own replica Daft Punk helmets, with some help from his parents and grandparents and whatever DIY supplies he could get his hands on. Just over a decade later, he's the premier supplier of wearable Daft Punk replica helmets.

**How did you fall for Daft Punk?**
"It was when 'Tron: Legacy' was coming out and I must have been 11 or 12. I saw a promo video on YouTube and it just grabbed me. I then realised I knew some of their songs already. I'd say the music grabbed me first and then the aesthetic which is really unique. Within three months I'd started work on building my first helmet."

**What did that entail?**
"I'm from Russia but live in Georgia in the US now. But when I first discovered Daft Punk and was living in Russia, I knew they were never going to show up and do a concert there and there wasn't much merch I could get my hands on. I wanted to have something Daft Punk that I could hold and building something for myself seemed like the only way."

**How did you go about it?**
"My father and grandfather are quite practical people who fix their own cars and radios and things like that so I'd picked up skills from them. They taught me how to sand things down with sandpaper and some basic electrical help and from there it was just a case of spending hours and hours on it. In the summer holidays when everyone was out playing I was just working on the helmet non-stop. I'd moved to America by the time I finished it!"

**How did it grow from there into a business?**
"I put the first one on eBay and sold it for around $500. When you consider how much work I'd put into it, it wasn't a huge amount of money but I needed the cash to rebuy supplies and invest in making more helmets. I had friends in Russia who had no access to Daft Punk merch and wanted something so I asked them to send me $50 each as a deposit to make more. From there I made a mould to help create the helmets and began developing the idea of turning them into kits people could assemble themselves at home. Now each kit costs around $400."

**How many have you sold altogether?**
"Between 1,500 and 2,000. When 'Random Access Memories' came out I had a huge spike in sales and was only 13 at the time! Then it dipped a bit but sales picked up when they split. It's strange because it dips to a point where I consider not doing it anymore and then it rises again to a point where it's almost too much work for me to manage!"

**Has it led to other work? Is this something you want to pursue professionally outside of building the helmets?**
"I worked with the band Purity Ring and made helmets for the music video for their track 'heartsigh'. That's over two million plays on YouTube now which is amazing. And the coolest thing that happened was Tony Gardner who designed the Daft Punk helmets getting in touch with me in 2020. It was such an honour to talk to Tony as he's such a legend and he wanted to buy some kits from me which was amazing. He told me the whole team loved them which was great."

**Do you think Daft Punk have seen the helmets?**
"I think they must have from a legal perspective or from friends or family pointing them out to them. But I've not heard anything from them."

**The Daft Punk fan community seems like a nice and supportive place. Do you ever meet up with other Daft Punk super fans in person?**
"I've had some meet ups. I actually went to MegaCon, the comic book and sci-fi convention in Florida, with a friend I made through the community. We dressed up as Daft Punk, he was Thomas and I was Guy-Man because I'm shorter, and as soon as we walked in we were just mobbed all day and constantly having our pictures taken with people. It was an amazing experience."

**Do you have a favourite Daft Punk album or track?**
"I loved 'Random Access Memories'. I think that's an amazing album and the only one I was around for the whole campaign - I can remember all the buzz and excitement of it. When that came out I just thought: 'They're not messing around here.' It was them returning in all their glory. But it depends too on how I feel on a certain day. 'Discovery' is almost like a greatest hits, there's so

many amazing tracks on it. Then I think 'Human After All' gets unfairly treated. I really like it and it's supposed to sound super raw."

**How did you feel when they split?**
"I've had so many dreams about what they're going to look like in the future, or what they're going to sound like, but now I know they're just dreams. If they ever make something again I'll be immensely happy but I'm not sitting around waiting for it to happen. I think Thomas is mostly a family man now while Guy-Man is just doing his thing, like he always does."

*Find out more at artyomprops.com*

## DAFT PUNK SUPER FAN
# ARIEL ANAYA

Discovering Daft Punk as a 14-year-old, Ariel Anaya turned his interest in the duo into a thriving business when he wanted to furnish a Daft Punk denim jacket he had bought with patches and badges but found there wasn't much on offer online.

"I never wanted to just bootleg stuff they'd already officially released," he explains. "But I wanted to put my own spin on it and create something new for all the Daft Punk fans out there."

Since launching in 2017, Veridis Quo Design has become a veritable treasure trove of Daft Punk paraphernalia including patches, badges, art prints and jewellery with custom growing exponentially in the wake of the robots split.

**How did your interest in Daft Punk begin?**
"I remember downloading 'Around the World' on Limewire around the age of 14, but it was when Kanye came out and sampled 'Harder, Better, Faster, Stronger' in 2007 that they really grabbed me. That's when I first saw them and the robot personas really drew me in. I'm a huge fan of 'Tron' and that whole aesthetic, so from there I was just hooked. The robot outfits make them almost like comic book heroes or something, and

that's something that really enticed me. I downloaded every image of them I could find and downloaded all their music on MP3 too.

**You run a business selling unofficial Daft Punk merch. Tell us about that.**
"It began after their performance with The Weeknd at The Grammys in 2017. They did this pop-up shop in LA and I saw pictures of people queuing up outside. I live in San Francisco and didn't go – to this day I say: 'What was I thinking?' Anyway, I went straight to their website and managed to buy the denim jacket they were selling at the shop. I actually bought three and am keeping two completely fresh and unworn. Once I got the jacket, I thought I'd like to add some Daft Punk pins to it so started searching around to find some. I found a few designs online but not many, so I decided to design something myself. I never got to see the live show so the Pyramid feels really iconic and that was where I started. I designed it, had 100 made and started the Instagram account. They sold out so fast I was like: 'Wow, people really love Daft Punk!' The next pin I did was one of the helmets where it's split

down the middle and you can see half the helmet and half of their face. That sold out really fast too - it's just grown from there."

**Do you have a background in design?**
"Not really, I'm just self-taught. I did the first design in Microsoft Excel!"

**How has the business grown since 2018?**
"Well the real catalyst was when they split. My followers on social media doubled that day. I woke up at 7am, saw a Facebook alert to say they'd posted a video and thought: 'Holy shit, they're releasing new music.' Then when I saw it was a retirement video I actually cried briefly. But then I started getting notifications on the store and sales were just pouring in. Stuff was selling out and I had to contact the manufacturers to make sure we could do another run of this stuff ASAP."

**What is the range of products on the site?**
"The Anthology Back Patch is the best-selling product. That's the Daft Punk logo but combines the designs and colourways from each of their albums. I was going to just keep that to a limited edition run of 400, but people wanted them so much I had to make more. Then we did the Epilogue Necklace to mark their retirement and that sold out really quickly. There's around 40 products on the site and it's generally pins, patches and art prints. I've done some designs of artists like Gesaffelstein too."

**How do you manage to run it on top of your day-job?**
"It's just myself and my wife so it can be tough! I do all the designs and my wife contributes ideas then once we have the products we pack them all and ship them ourselves. I remember after the retirement our entire apartment was just completely covered with orders. That was an amazing sight for us!"

**Is your wife a huge fan as well?**
"You know what, she kind of makes fun of me for it. I have an obsessive personality which a lot of the other Daft Punk super fans I know have too. But she gets excited for me. When 'Random Access Memories' dropped we listened to it together and when they did The Grammys she was cheering along with me."

**Do you have your own personal Daft Punk merch collection too?**
"I got really into vinyl before the pandemic so have amassed a lot of the records Daft Punk released. I even have the Darlin' release on vinyl, which I bought from a big collector. I also bought two replica helmets which I paid $2,500 a piece for. It's a lot but they are just done so well! Whenever I'm bored I look on eBay to see what Daft Punk memorabilia there is. Altogether I've spent around $25K on Daft Punk merch and collector's items which is a lot."

**How did you feel when they split?**
"I mean, I was sad and disappointed but, at the same time, they went out at the top. I think 'Random Access Memories' was an amazing album and was recognised across all genres. I'm an audiophile and in general, they've given us some of the best sounding albums of all time. I think there's an amazing opportunity for them to come back and do one more tour at some point, but in general I've made peace with not seeing them live."

*Find out more at veridisquodesign.com*

VERIDIS
QUO
DESIGN
VERIDIS
QUO
DESIGN
robot
rock
HARDER
BETTER
FASTER
daft
punk

As the hype around 'Random Access Memories' subsided, Daft Punk's stock was at an all-time high. But for all the rumours of even more ambitious live shows and new albums, the light seemed to slowly dim on the Daft Punk project over the next eight years, before the duo finally pulled the plug in 2021. What exactly happened in those final years? asks **Ben Cardew**. And where do they go next?

# ONE MORE TIME?

When Daft Punk finished 'Random Access Memories' they could have done anything. Interest in the duo, as a live act, recording artists, film composers and external producers, was at an all-time high and it was generally assumed that Daft Punk would go from strength-to-imperial strength over the next few years. Live dates, surely, would be in the works, with rumours flying around the possibility of a numerically convenient Alive 2017 tour, while Daft Punk fans had their radars permanently attuned to any hint of a new album.

As it turned out, though, the eight years between the release of 'RAM' and the announcement of the group's split in February 2021, were, if not exactly a damp squib, then considerably less fiery than most people had expected. There was no tour – although Omar Hakim, who played drums on 'RAM', told French magazine Society that Daft Punk's management did give him a call about the possibility, with rumours of some kind of hologram set-up also in the works. And there was no new music released, despite the duo having a Paris studio set-up where they worked away diligently.

Looking back now, post-split, it is tempting to see this as evidence of a group who had trapped themselves in a creative gold cage with the success of the Alive 2006/07 tour and 'RAM'. With the cold light of hindsight, it seems obvious that Daft Punk would never top the opulent chart smash disco of 'Random Access Memories' or improve on their epochal Alive 2006/07 tour. Because where, frankly, could they go? If Daft Punk returned to their roots with a set of DJ dates and head-shredding techno, it would be seen as underwhelming, confusing and possibly elitist. But going *even bigger* than 'Random Access Memories' and 'Alive' would mean the duo sacrificing some degree of creative control. Staying in the same place, meanwhile, was never an option for Daft Punk.

But this is to see things with hindsight. There were, perhaps, clues towards the end of the 2010s that Daft Punk were soon to be no more. In 2018 the duo dissolved their Daft Arts production company that had been key to their later business and the same year Bangalter apparently stepped down as co-manager of Daft Music, the company they had created in 1996. At the same time, the gap between records was getting worryingly long. But Daft Punk fans were used to an enigmatic silence from the duo. What's more, the interviews that Daft Punk gave around the time of 'RAM' suggested they were content with their position in the music world, as they edged towards their 40s. Guy-Man said little in interviews. But Guy-Man *always* said little in interviews.

Besides, the work that Daft Punk did post-'RAM' was both an artistic and a commercial success. There was, it is true, no grand concept behind their various production and soundtrack works. But it seemed to follow the duo's twin interests in the commercial and the avant-garde, in music and cinema. And if Daft Punk had followed their four production credits on Kanye West's 2013 album 'Yeezus' - for 'On Sight', 'Black Skinhead', 'I Am A God' and 'Send It Up' – and two 2016 collaborations with The Weeknd ('Starboy' and 'I Feel It Coming') with a new album that reflected their interest in hip hop and R&B, their post-'RAM' productions would have been seen as part of a grand master scheme that Daft Punk had pulled off.

That didn't happen, of course. But these two projects proved massive commercial hits, with 'Yeezus' topping sales and critical polls around the world in 2013 and 'Starboy' with its two billion (and counting) Spotify plays, a number that dwarfs any Daft Punk tune. We tend to overlook these kinds of feats because Daft Punk were so universally acclaimed. But 20 years ago, the idea that a French house music duo would score major hits with some of the North American hip hop and R&B elite would have seemed utterly fanciful.

Daft Punk also lent their production skills to Australian electro pop group Parcels, for their 'RAM'-lite 2017 single 'Overnight', while Bangalter was one of a handful of producers on Arcade Fire's 2017 album 'Everything Now'. Keeping up his keen interest in cinema (see 'Electroma', 'Tron' et al) Bangalter also lent his previously unreleased 1995 track 'Sangria' to Gaspar Noé's 2018 film 'Climax', and 'Riga (Take 5)' to the rather mysterious 2017 Latvian movie 'Riga (Take 1)', both songs sitting towards the ear-bleed techno side of the Daft Punk spectrum.

In hindsight, again, these dual moves – towards hip hop/pop production on the one hand and avant-garde cinema on the other – seem telling, given what would emerge after the duo split. On 22 February, 2021, a video appeared on Daft Punk's official YouTube channel entitled 'Epilogue'. Using footage from 'Electroma', the duo's art-house film, we see the two Daft Punk robots walk slowly into the desert, where Guy-Man's robot activates a bomb strapped to robot Thomas' back. A Daft Punk logo appears on the screen, underneath which reads '1993 – 2021', as 'RAM''s 'Touch' drifts slowly into life. Daft Punk's US publicist Kathryn Frazier confirmed that the band had split but no more official information was given.

Daft Punk's friends were slightly more forthcoming. Todd Edwards, who had worked with them on 'Discovery' and 'RAM', said he wasn't surprised by the news, with Bangalter getting increasingly into film, while Guy-Man was more interested in producing hip hop.

"And that wasn't really Thomas's thing," Edwards told me, when I interviewed him in 2021 for my book on Daft Punk's 'Discovery'. "That was a divergent path for the two of them."

French magazine Society then published a (seemingly well-sourced) article in July 2021, a few months after the split, which put more meat on the bone. It painted a picture of a duo who, while still friends, had grown apart artistically in the 28 years since they formed; of two men in their 40s who were perhaps out of time in the world of TikTok and iPhones and were smart enough to know it. There were revelations for Daft Punk fans in the article – that Guy-Man had allegedly got divorced in 2010, for example – but the duo's split seemed affable and, perhaps, inevitable.

Interest in Daft Punk went through the roof after the split was announced. Social media was full of people relating their Daft Punk memories. Spotify reported a 500% jump in Daft Punk streams, while both the Financial Times and the French Defence Ministry – neither notable fans of jackin' Chicago house – saluted Daft Punk's achievements. Two books about Daft Punk have been published since they split – you're reading one and I wrote the other – with more in the works.

Speculation was fevered as to what they might do next. We didn't have long to wait: in July 2021 it was announced that Thomas Bangalter would be scoring 'Mythologies', a new ballet co-produced by the Opéra National de Bordeaux and Ballet Preljocaj (the orchestral score to 'Mythologies' was released in April 2023). The ballet seems a suitably high-brow project for Bangalter – always the most intellectual of the duo – to kick off his post-Daft Punk life, as well as a fitting tribute to his mother, who was herself a dancer. As for Guy-Man, for the moment nothing is known, although the announcement of every high-profile new rap or R&B album brings a wave of excitement among Daft Punk fans, who speculate whether the more taciturn half of Daft Punk might be involved.

Other Daft Punk fans will tell you that the split is just a temporary stop gap or even part of an elaborate marketing hoax; that Daft Punk *will* return for Coachella 2024/2025/2026 (delete as appropriate) or surprise release a new album. It's not, of course, impossible. Everyone seems to get back together in the end (bar The Smiths and Talking Heads) and why wouldn't Thomas and Guy-Man want to reap what they had sown in the form of lucrative festival gigs and acclaim?

For the moment, though, that doesn't seem likely. The one-year anniversary of Daft Punk's split brought frantic speculation as the group revamped their website, re-launched their social media channels and launched an official Twitch channel. But no reunion or new album was forthcoming. Instead, Daft Punk streamed

footage of their 1997 gig at the Mayan Theater in LA, on Twitch and announced the reissue of 'Homework', in a nifty 25th anniversary edition, and the 'Alive 97' album. Welcome additions to the Daft Punk canon, sure. But not really new.

And maybe that's how it should be. With Alive 2006/07 and 'Random Access Memories', Daft Punk cemented their reputation at the top of the electronic music tree, perhaps the most important electronic music act since Kraftwerk. And this acclaim has only increased since they split. The influence of Daft Punk's music is everywhere – from Ariana Grande's pop house to 100 Gecs' frantic hyperpop – and they have been proved right time and again in their decision making, from protecting their identities in robot outfits before social media hit, to realising the power of music as a visual media with 'Interstella 5555' and 'Tron'. What, frankly, is there left for Daft Punk to do?

Besides, if the last image we have of Daft Punk is a robot striding off slowly into the desert, as 'Touch''s tear-jerking choir sings stories of love, isn't that a beautiful way to end a profound musical relationship, one forged in the bourgeois schools of Paris, raised by the clubs of Chicago and consummated with some of the most gloriously life-affirming house music ever to reach our eardrums? Daft Punk are dead; but their spirit lives on, in glory, wonder and a pounding house beat.

**DISCOGRAPHY:** Darlin' **'Darlin''** 1993 // Darlin' **'Cindy So Loud'** 1993 // Darlin' **'Untitled'** (18) 1993 // Darlin' **'Untitled'** (33) 1993 // Daft Punk **'The New Wave'** 1994 // Daft Punk **'Alive'** 1994 // Daft Punk **'Assault'** 1994 // Daft Punk **'Drive'** 1994 // Daft Punk (feat. DJ Kevin) **'ß Wax'** 1995 // Daft Punk **'Da Funk'** 1995 // Daft Punk **'Rollin' & Scratchin''** 1995 // The Micronauts **'Get Funky Get Down' (Daft Punk Remix)** 1995 // The Chemical Brothers **'Life is Sweet' (Daft Punk Remix)** 1995 // Daft Punk **'Indo Silver Club (Part One)'** 1996 // Daft Punk **'Indo Silver Club (Part Two)' [album version]** 1996 // I:Cube **'Disco Cubism' (Daft Punk Remix)** 1996 // Gabrielle **'Forget About the World' (Daft Punk Mix)** 1996 // Ian Pooley **'Chord Memory' (Daft Punk Remix)** 1996 // Daft Punk **'Daftendirekt'** 1997 // Daft Punk **'WDPK 83.7 FM'** 1997 // Daft Punk **'Revolution 909'** 1997 // Daft Punk **'Phoenix'** 1997 // Daft Punk **'Fresh'** 1997 // Daft Punk **'Around the World'** 1997 // Daft Punk **'Teachers'** 1997 // Daft Punk **'High Fidelity'** 1997 // Daft Punk **'Rock'nRoll'** 1997 // Daft Punk **'Oh Yeah'** 1997 // Daft Punk **'Burnin''** 1997 // Daft Punk **'Funk Ad'** 1997 // Daft Punk **'Musique'** 1997 // Scott Grooves (feat. Parliament & Funkadelic) **'Mothership Reconnection' (Daft Punk Remix)** 1998 // Daft Punk **'One More Time'** 2000 // Daft Punk **'Aerodynamic'** 2001 // Daft Punk **'Digital Love'** 2001 // Daft Punk **Harder, Better, Faster, Stronger'** 2001 // Daft Punk **'Crescendolls'** 2001 // Daft Punk **'Nightvision'** 2001 // Daft Punk '**Superheroes**' 2001 // Daft Punk **'High Life'** 2001 // Daft Punk **'Something About Us'** 2001 // Daft Punk **'Voyager'** 2001 // Daft Punk **'Veridis Quo'** 2001 // Daft Punk **'Short Circuit'** 2001 // Daft Punk **'Face to Face'** 2001 // Daft Punk **'Too Long'** 2001 // Daft Punk **'Aerodynamite'** 2001 // Daft Punk **'Alive 1997'** 2001 // Daft Punk **'Ouverature'** 2003 // Daft Punk **'Aerodynamic' (Daft Punk Remix)** 2003 // Franz Ferdinand **'Take Me Out' (Daft Punk Remix)** 2004 // Daft Punk **'Human After All'** 2005 // Daft Punk **'The Prime Time of Your Life'** 2005 // Daft Punk **'Robot Rock'** 2005 // Daft Punk **'Steam Machine'** 2005 // Daft Punk **'Make Love'** 2005 // Daft Punk **'The Brainwasher'** 2005 // Daft Punk **'On/Off'** 2005 // Daft Punk **'Television Rules the Nation'** 2005 // Daft Punk **'Technologic'** 2005 // Daft Punk **'Emotion'** 2005 // Daft Punk **'Robot Rock' (Maximum Overdrive)** 2005 // Teriyaki Boyz **'Heartbreaker' (Produced by Daft Punk)** 2005 // Daft Punk **'Robot Rock'/'Oh Yeah'** 2007 // Daft Punk **'Touch It'/'Technologic'** 2007 // Daft Punk **'Television Rules the Nation'/'Crescendolls'** 2007 // Daft Punk **'Too Long'/'Steam Machine'** 2007 // Daft Punk **'Around the World'/'Harder, Better, Faster, Stronger'** 2007 // Daft Punk **'Burnin''/'Too Long'** 2007 // Daft Punk **'Face to**

**Face'/'Short Circuit'** 2007 // Daft Punk **'One More Time'/'Aerodynamic'** 2007 // Daft Punk **'Aerodynamic Beats'/'Forget About the World'** 2007 // Daft Punk **'The Prime Time of Your Life'/'The Brainwasher'/'Rollin' & Scratchin''/'Alive'** 2007 // Daft Punk **'Da Funk'/'Daftendirekt'** 2007 // Daft Punk **'Superheroes'/'Human After All'/'Rock'nRoll'** 2007 // Daft Punk **'Human After All'/'Together'/'One More Time (Reprise)'/'Music Sounds Better With You'** 2007 // Daft Punk **'Harder, Better, Faster, Stronger' (Alive 2007)** 2007 // N.E.R.D. **'Hypnotize U' (Produced by Daft Punk)** 2010 // Daft Punk **'Overature'** 2010 // Daft Punk **'The Grid'** 2010 // Daft Punk **'The Son of Flynn'** 2010 // Daft Punk **'Recognizer'** 2010 // Daft Punk **'Armory'** 2010 // Daft Punk **'Arena'** 2010 // Daft Punk **'Rinzler'** 2010 // Daft Punk **'The Game Has Changed'** 2010 // Daft Punk **'Outlands'** 2010 // Daft Punk **'Adagio For TRON'** 2010 // Daft Punk **'Nocturne'** 2010 // Daft Punk **'End of Line'** 2010 // Daft Punk **'Derezzed'** 2010 // Daft Punk **'Fall'** 2010 // Daft Punk **'Solar Sailer'** 2010 // Daft Punk **'Rectifier'** 2010 // Daft Punk **'Disc Wars'** 2010 // Daft Punk **'C.L.U.'** 2010 // Daft Punk **'Arrival'** 2010 // Daft Punk **'Flynn Lives'** 2010 // Daft Punk **'TRON Legacy (End Titles)'** 2010 // Daft Punk **'Finale'** 2010 // Daft Punk **'ENCOM, Part I'** 2010 // Daft Punk **'ENCOM, Part II'** 2010 // Daft Punk **'Round One'** 2010 // Daft Punk **'Castor'** 2010 // Daft Punk **'Reflections'** 2010 // Daft Punk **'Father and Son'** 2010 // Daft Punk **'Outlands, Part II'** 2010 // Daft Punk **'Sea of Simulation'** 2010 // Daft Punk **'Sunrise Prelude'** 2010 // Daft Punk **'Computerized' (unreleased)** 2010 // Junior Kimbrough **'I Gotta Try You Girl' (Daft Punk Edit)** 2012 // Daft Punk **'Give Life Back to Music'** 2013 // Daft Punk **'The Game of Love'** 2013 // Daft Punk **'Giorgio by Moroder'** 2013 // Daft Punk **'Within'** 2013 // Daft Punk **'Instant Crush'** 2013 // Daft Punk **'Lose Yourself to Dance'** 2013 // Daft Punk **'Touch'** 2013 // Daft Punk **'Get Lucky'** 2013 // Daft Punk **'Beyond'** 2013 // Daft Punk **'Motherboard'** 2013 // Daft Punk **'Fragments of Time'** 2013 // Daft Punk **'Doin' It Right'** 2013 // Daft Punk **'Contact'** 2013 // Daft Punk **'Horizon'** 2013 // Daft Punk **'Get Lucky' (Daft Punk Remix)** 2013 // Kanye West **'On Sight' (Produced by Daft Punk)** 2013 // Kanye West **'Black Skinhead' (Produced by Daft Punk)** 2013 // Kanye West **'I Am a God' (Produced by Daft Punk)** 2013 // Kanye West **'Send It Up' (Produced by Daft Punk)** 2013 // Pharrell Williams **'Gust of Wind' (Co-written/vocals by Daft Punk)** 2014 // The Weeknd **'Starboy' (feat. Daft Punk)** 2016 // The Weeknd **I Feel It Coming (feat. Daft Punk)** 2016 // Parcels **Overnight (Produced by Daft Punk)** 2017

COMPILED BY LUKE PEREZ

**THOMAS DISCOGRAPHY:** Thomas Bangalter **'On Da Rocks'** 1995 // Thomas Bangalter **'Roulé Boulé'** 1995 // Thomas Bangalter **'What To Do'** 1995 // Thomas Bangalter **'Outrun'** 1995 // Thomas Bangalter **'Ventura'** 1995 // Manu Le Malin + Thomas Bangalter **'M18'** 1995 // Spring **'True Elegance'** 1995 // Spring **'Thimble Theatre'** 1995 // Spring **'Funeral Cowboy Tremolo'** 1995 // Thomas Bangalter **'Sangria'** 1995 // Thomas Bangalter **'Spinal Scratch'** 1996 // Thomas Bangalter **'Spinal Beats'** 1996 // Alan Braxe **'Vertigo' (Virgo Edit)** 1997 // Roy Davis Jr **'Rock Shock' (Thomas Bangalter's Start-Stop Mix)** 1998 // Thomas Bangalter **'Club Soda'** 1998 // Thomas Bangalter **'Extra Dry'** 1998 // Thomas Bangalter **'Shuffle!'** 1998 // Thomas Bangalter **'Colossus'** 1998 // Thomas Bangalter **'Turbo'** 1998 // Stardust **'Music Sounds Better With You'** 1998 // Thomas Bangalter vs. Bob Sinclar **'Gym Tonic'** 1998 // Phoenix **'Embuscade'** 2000 // Phoenix **'If I Ever Feel Better (Edit)'** 2000 // Together **'Together'** 2000 // Together **'So Much Love to Give'** 2002 // Thomas Bangalter **'Irréversible'** 2002 // Thomas Bangalter **'Tempus Edax Rerum'** 2002 // Thomas Bangalter **'Rectum'** 2002 // Thomas Bangalter **'Night Beats'** 2002 // Thomas Bangalter **'Stress'** 2002 // Thomas Bangalter **'Paris By Night'** 2002 // Thomas Bangalter **'Outrage'** 2002 // Thomas Bangalter **'Désaccords'** 2002 // Thomas Bangalter **'Ventura'/'Into the Tunnel'** 2002 // Thomas Bangalter **'The End'** 2002 // 113 vs. Thomas Bangalter **'113 Fout La Merde'** 2002 // AIR **'Don't Be Light' (Edit)** 2002 // Scenario Rock **'Skitzo Dancer' (Remixed By Justice)** 2004 // Hell **'Let No Man Jack' (Busy P Stotter Mix)** 2005 // DJ Mehdi **'Signatune' (Thomas Bangalter Edit)** 2006 // Richard Phillips **'First Point' (Short film score)** 2012 // Arcade Fire **'Everything Now'** 2017 // Arcade Fire **'Signs of Life'** 2017 // Arcade Fire **'Electric Blue'** 2017 // Arcade Fire **'Put Your Money On Me'** 2017 // Thomas Bangalter **'Riga (Take 5)'** 2017 // -M- **'Lettre Infinie'** 2019 // -M- **'Supercherie'** 2018 // -M- **'Massaï'** 2019 // -M- **'Logique Est Ton Écho'** 2019 // -M- **'Grand Petit Con'** 2019 // -M- **'L.O.Ï.C.A.'** 2019 // -M- **'Adieu Mon Amour'** 2019 // -M- **'L'Alchimiste'** 2019 // -M- **'Thérapie'** 2019 // -M- **'Une Seule Corde'** 2019 // -M- **'Si Près Si...'** 2019 // -M- **'L'Autre Paradis'** 2019 //-M- **'Billie'** 2019 // Hofesh Shechter **'That Night in Brazil'** 2022

**GUY-MAN DISCOGRAPHY:** Le Knight Club **'Santa Claus'** 1997 // Le Knight Club **'Holiday On Ice'** 1997 // Le Knight Club **'On The Air' (unreleased track)** 1997 // Le Knight Club **'Troobador'** 1998 // Le Knight Club **'Mirage'** 1998 // Le Knight Club vs. DJ Sneak **'Intergalactik Disko'** 1998 // Le Knight Club **'Boogie Shell'** 1999 // Le Knight Club **'Coco Girlz'** 1999 // Le Knight Club **'Mosquito'** 1999 // Le Knight Club **'Coral Twist'** 1999 // Le Knight Club **'Hysteria'** 1999 // Le Knight Club **'Hysteriall'** 1999 // Raw Man **'Number7' (Le Knight Club Remix)** 1999 // Deelat vs. Le Knight Club **'Wet Indiez'** 1999 // Deelat vs. Le Knight Club **'G.M.F.'** 1999 // Deelat vs. Le Knight Club **'Wetness Anthem'** 1999 // Le Knight Club vs. DJ Sneak **'Think Love Not Hate' (unreleased track)** 1999 // Play Paul **'Spaced Out'** 2000 // Play Paul **'Spaced Out II'** 2000 // Play Paul **'Holy Ghostz'** 2000 // Phoenix **'Too Young' (Le Knight Club Remix)** 2000 // Le Knight Club **'Gator'** 2001 // Le Knight Club **'Chérie D'Amoure'** 2001 // Le Knight Club **'Soul Bells'** 2002 // Le Knight Club **'Palm Beat'** 2002 // Le Knight Club **'Tropicall'** 2002 // Le Knight Club **'Nymphae Song'** 2002 // Le Knight Club **'Rhumba'** 2002 // Crydajam **'Playground'** 2002 // Fantastic Plastic **'Machine Philosphy' (Le Knight Club Remix)** 2003 // Syndicated People **'Be Right!' (Dirty Grandpa Mix by Le Knight Club vs. Play Paul)** 2003 // Cassius **'20 Years (How Do You See Me Now)' (Le Knight Club Remix)** 2003 // Zoot Woman **'Taken It All' (Le Knight Club Remix)** 2004 // David Guetta **'Stay' (Le Knight Club Remix)** 2004 // Aloud **'Undersea' (Le Knight Club Edit)** 2004 // Daft Punk **'Technologic' (LeKnight Club Remix)** 2005 // Cassius **'See Me Now'** 2006 // Sébastien Tellier **'Roche'** 2008 // Sébastien Tellier **'Kilometer'** 2008 // Sébastien Tellier **'Look'** 2008 // Sébastien Tellier **'Divine'** 2008 // Sébastien Tellier **'Pomme'** 2008 // Sébastien Tellier **'Une Heure'** 2008 // Sébastien Tellier **'Sexual Sportwear'** 2008 // Sébastien Tellier **'Elle'** 2008 // Sébastien Tellier **'Fingers Of Steel'** 2008 // Sébastien Tellier **'Manty'** 2008 // Sébastien Tellier **'L'Amoure Et La Violence'** 2008 // Kavinsky **'Nightcall'** 2010 // Sébastien Tellier **'My Poseidon'** 2012 // Le Knight Club **'The Fight'** 2014 // Charlotte Gainsbourg **'Rest'** 2017 // The Weeknd **'Hurt You'** 2018

COMPILED BY LUKE PEREZ

**SET HISTORY:** Darlin' 1992 Event Unknown France // Darlin' 09/92 Caves du Chapelet (Extralight) France (Paris) // Daft Punk 01/04/94 Blues Du Nord (Alive Party) France (Paris) // Daft Punk 28/05/94 Gymnase Jemmapes (LUVYOU Rave) France (Paris) // Guy-Manuel de Homem-Christo 22/07/94 Pumpking Party France // Daft Punk 02/03/95 Trolleybus France (Marseille) // Daft Punk 21/06/95 L'American Center (Global Tekno) France // Daft Punk 07/07/95 L'An-Fer (Respect Party) France (Dijon) // Daft Punk 01/08/95 Fuse Belgium (Brussels) // Daft Punk 05/08/95 Prophecy (Carros) France // Daft Punk 04/09/95 Paradise Factory Back To Basics (In The City) England (Manchester) // Daft Punk 05/09/95 The Orbit England (Leeds) // Daft Punk 09/09/95 Deux Alpes France (Isère) // Daft Punk 16/09/95 Chrisalyd France (Toulouse) // Daft Punk 22/09/95 Hellscrack France (Nantes) // Daft Punk 23/09/95 Le Zenith De Paris (STORM) (Soirée CODA) France (Paris) // Daft Punk 29/09/95 The Ministry Of Sound England (London) // Daft Punk 30/09/95 The Renfrew Ferry (Never Get Out The Boat) Scotland (Glasgow) // Daft Punk 06/10/95 Pelican Club Scotland (Aberdeen) // Daft Punk 07/10/95 The Pleasure Rooms (Back To Basics) England (Leeds) // Daft Punk 07/10/95 The Orbit (After Dark) England (Leeds) // Daft Punk 08/10/95 Smithfields (Sunday Social) England (London) // Daft Punk 12/10/95 Astoria Theatre England (London) // Daft Punk 13/10/95 Sankeys Soap (Bugged Out!) England (Manchester) // Daft Punk 14/10/95 The Pleasure Rooms (Back To Basics) England (Leeds) // Daft Punk 14/10/95 The Orbit England (Leeds) // Daft Punk 19/10/95 Keele University (Skool Disco) England (Stoke-on-Trent) // Daft Punk 04/11/95 Planet Rose (Dance Night) Netherlands (Nijmegen) // Daft Punk 10/11/95 Voorhuit (I Love Techno) Belgium (Gent) // Daft Punk 17/11/95 Soirée Dauphine Aquaboulevard France (Dauphiné) // Daft Punk 18/11/95 Le Privé Club France (Avignon) // Daft Punk 02/12/95 Transmusicales France (Rennes) // Daft Punk 1995 L'Espace France // Daft Punk 1995 Carmès France (Toulouse) // Daft Punk 1995 Rex Club France (Paris) // Daft Punk 1995 Le Palace (Happy House) France (Paris) // Daft Punk 03/02/96 Le Privé Club France (Avignon) // Daft Punk 16/02/96 Heavenly Social England (Nottingham) // Daft Punk 17/02/96 London After Midnight England (London) // Daft Punk 24/02/96 Club L'Espace (Leave Earth) France (Rennes) // Thomas Bangalter 03/04/96 Warm Up (DJ'z Contest) France (Paris) // Daft Punk 06/04/96 Unknown Festival (Techno Spirit Stage) France (Paris) // Daft Punk 19/04/96 Printemps De Bourges (Rave Sir.Cus Cybernaut System) France (Bourges) // Daft Punk 26/05/96 Even Furthur USA (Wisconsin) // Daft Punk 24/06/96 Rex Club France (Paris) // Daft Punk 29/06/96 Tribal Gathering England (Oxford) // Daft Punk 06/07/96 Presqu'île De Malsaucy (Eurockéennes) France (Bercy) // Daft Punk & Slam 31/08/96 The Renfrew Ferry (Never Get Out The Boat) Scotland (Glasgow) // Daft Punk 02/10/96 Queen Club (Respect) France (Paris) // Daft Punk 15/11/96 Neuss Tribehouse Germany (Neuss) // Daft Punk 16/11/96 Tresor Germany (Berlin) // Daft Punk 23/11/96 L'An-Fer France (Dijon) // Daft Punk 07/12/96 Transmusicales France (Rennes) // Daft Punk/Thomas Bangalter/Guy-Manuel de Homem Christo 11/12/96 Queen Club (Respect Party) France (Paris) // Daft Punk 1996 Club Canecao France (Montpellier) // Daft Punk 1996 Le Palace France (Paris) // Daft Punk 1996 Unknown Warehouse Party France (Marseille) // Daft Punk 17/01/97 Sankeys Soap (Bugged Out!) England (Manchester) // Daft Punk 18/01/97 The Stage England (Stoke-on-Trent) // Daft Punk 19/01/97 Plastic People England (London) // Daft Punk 20/01/97 The Escape England (Brighton) // Daft Punk 22/01/97 The End (Soma 50 Party) England (London) // Daft Punk 24/01/97 The Arches (Slam Event) Scotland (Glasgow) // Daft Punk 25/01/97 Back To Basics (Dave Beer Birthday Celebration) England (Leeds) // Daft Punk 11/02/97 Route 66 Roller Skate Rink (Dust Traxx Party) USA (Chicago) // Daft Punk 15/02/97 Leave Earth France (Rennes) // Daft Punk 02/97 Centrale Country/City Unknown // Daft Punk 24/03/97 Cameo Theater (W.M.C.) USA (Miami) // Daft Punk 1997 Event Unknown USA (Philadelphia) // Daft Punk 28/03/97 Twilo (Respect Party) USA (New York) // Daft Punk 29/03/97 Funky Tekno Tribe USA (San Francisco) // Daft Punk 03/04/97 House of Blues (The Saint Premiere Party) USA (Los Angeles) // Daft Punk 03/04/97 Bossa Nova USA (Santa Monica) // Daft Punk 04/04/97 HiFi USA (Minneapolis) // Daft Punk 05/04/97 Metropolis (Channel 1st Year Anniversary) Canada (Montreal) // Daft Punk 10/04/97 The Shelter Club USA (Chicago) // Daft Punk 11/04/97 We Are Family (Route 66) USA (Chicago) // Daft Punk 12/04/97 The Industry Club Canada (Toronto) // Daft Punk 07/05/97 Flanders Expo (I Love Techno) Belgium (Gent) // Daft Punk 15/05/97 Rex Club France (Paris) // Daft Punk 24/05/97 Tribal Gathering England (Luton) // Daft Punk 30/05/97 Liquid Room Japan (Tokyo) // Daft Punk 31/05/97 Rockets Japan (Osaka) // Daft Punk 07/06/97 Rimini (Dance Festival) Italy (Rimini) // Daft Punk 12/06/97 Sónar Festival Spain (Barcelona) // Daft Punk 14/06/97 Hultsfredfestivalen Sweden (Hultsfred) // Daft Punk 21/06/97 New Frontier Festival Netherlands (Holland) // Daft Punk 22/06/97 Hurricane Festival Germany (Scheeßel) // Daft Punk 28/06/97 Roskilde Festival Denmark (Roskilde) // Daft Punk 29/06/97 Glastonbury England (Somerset) // Daft Punk 01/07/97 Rock Torhout Festival Belgium (Torhout) // Daft Punk 02/07/97 Quart Festival Norway (Quart) // Daft Punk 05/07/97 Rock Werchter Festival Belgium (Werchter) // Daft Punk 07/07/97 Dance & Levi's Festival Israel (לוכשא) // Armand Van Helden & Daft Punk 09/07/97 Queen Club (Respect Surprise Party!) France (Paris) // Daft Punk 12/07/97 T in the Park Festival Scotland (Balado) // Daft Punk 09/08/97 Borealis Festival France (Montpellier) // Daft Punk 14/08/97 Privilege Ibiza Spain (Ibiza) // Daft Punk 08/97 Ku Spain (Ibiza) // Daft Punk 16/08/97 V97 Festival England (Leeds) // Daft Punk 17/08/97 V97 Festival England (Chelmsford) // Daft Punk 31/08/97 Parc Jarry (Cream Festival) Canada (Montreal) // Daft Punk 01/09/97 The Warehouse Canada (Toronto) // Daft Punk 03/09/97 Roseland Ballroom (CMJ Music Marathon) USA (Manhattan) // Daft Punk 04/09/97 The Metro USA (Chicago) // Daft Punk 06/09/97 The Showbox USA (Seattle) (WA) // Daft Punk 07/09/97 The Rage Canada (Vancouver) // Daft Punk 09/09/97 The Fillmore USA (San Francisco) // Daft Punk 10/09/97 El Rey Theatre USA (Long Beach) // Daft Punk 12/09/97 The Fillmore USA (San Francisco) // Daft Punk 17/09/97 Ogden Theatre USA (Denver) // Daft Punk 19/09/97 Hard Rock Hotel USA (Las Vegas) // Daft Punk 20/09/97 Snow Summit Resort USA (Big Bear Lake) // Daft Punk 23/09/97 Irving Plaza USA (New York) // Daft Punk 24/09/97 The Cameo Theatre USA (Miami) // Daft Punk 25/09/97 The Fillmore USA (San Francisco) // Daft Punk 27/09/97 American Legion Hall USA (Los Angeles) // Daft Punk 28/09/97 DV8 USA (Seattle) // Daft Punk 02/10/97 Paradiso Nedtherlands (Amsterdam) // Daft Punk 03/10/97 L'Aeronef France (Lille) // Daft Punk 04/10/97 Ancienne Belgique Belgium (Brussels) // Daft Punk 06/10/97 Garage Germany (Saarbrücken) // Daft Punk 07/10/97 Live Music Hall Germany (Cologne) // Daft Punk 08/10/97 Soundgarden Germany (Dortmund) // Daft Punk 09/10/97 Große Freiheit 36 Germany (Hamburg) // Daft Punk 11/10/97 Huxley's Germany (Berlin) // Daft Punk 12/10/97 LKA Germany (Stuttgart) // Daft Punk 13/10/97 La Laiterie France (Strasbourg) // Daft Punk 17/10/97 Espace événement France (Paris) // Daft Punk 18/10/97 Le Zénith De Nancy (Nancy Jazz Pulsations) France (Nancy) // Daft Punk 20/10/97 Exo 7 France (Rouen) // Daft Punk 21/10/97 Le Liberté France (Rennes) // Daft Punk 24/10/97 Guilldhall England (Southampton) // Daft Punk 26/10/97 Red Box Ireland (Dublin) // Daft Punk 28/10/97 Newcastle Mayfair England (Newcastle) // Daft Punk 30/10/97 Town & Country England (Leeds) // Daft Punk 31/10/97 Barrowland Ballroom Scotland (Glasgow) // Daft Punk 01/11/97 Academy England (Manchester) // Daft Punk 03/11/97 Corn Exchange England (Cambridge // Daft Punk 05/11/97 Astoria Theatre England (London) // Daft Punk 06/11/97 Astoria Theatre England (London) // Daft Punk 08/11/97 Que Club England (Birmingham) // Daft Punk 09/11/97 Rock City England (Nottingham) // Daft Punk 10/11/97 The Event England (Brighton) // Daft Punk 12/11/97 Hall Penfeld France (Brest) // Daft Punk 14/11/97 Sala Aqualung Spain (Madrid) // Daft Punk 15/11/97 Sala Zeléste Spain (Barcelona) // Daft Punk 17/11/97 Espace Médoquine France (Bordeaux) // Daft Punk 18/11/97 Le Confluent France (Toulouse) // Daft Punk 20/11/97 Dome France (Marseille) // Daft Punk 20/11/97 Dome (After Concert Party) France (Marseille) // Daft Punk 21/11/97 Le Palladium Switzerland (Geneva) // Daft Punk 22/11/97 Transbordeur France (Lyon) // Daft Punk 24/11/97 Rolling Stone Italy (Milan) // Daft Punk 25/11/97 Tenax Italy (Florence) // Daft Punk 26/11/97 Frontiers Italy (Rome) // Daft Punk 29/11/97 Jail Switzerland (Zurich) // Daft Punk 30/11/97 Libo Music Hall Austria (Vienna) // Daft Punk 01/12/97 Nachtwerk Germany (Munich) // Daft Punk 03/12/97 Capitol Germany (Hanover) // Daft Punk 04/12/97 MS Conection Germany (Mannheim) // Daft Punk 07/12/97 Planète France (Rennes) // Daft Punk 08/12/97 Elis Mon Paris France (Paris) // Daft Punk 08/12/97 Rex Club (Daft Club) France (Paris) // Stardust 11/12/97 Rex Club France (Paris) // Daft Punk 17/12/97 The Mayan Theatre USA (Los Angeles) // Daft Punk 20/12/97 Hammerstein Ballroom USA (Manhattan) // Daft Punk 1997 Citrus Club Scotland (Edinburgh) // Guy-Manuel de Homem Christo 22/01/98 Rex Club (Hometown Night) France (Paris) // Thomas Bangalter 07/02/98 Apollo Festival Australia (Sydney) // Thomas Bangalter 14/02/98 Apollo Festival Australia (Melbourne) // Daft Punk 06/03/98 W.M.C. 1998 USA (Miami) // Daft Punk 08/03/98 Raleigh Hotal (W.M.C.) USA (Miami) // Stardust 03/98 Unknown (W.M.C. 1998) USA (Miami) // Daft Punk 11/03/98 Liquid (Respect Party) USA (Miami) // Thomas Bangalter 06/04/98 Metro (Dust

Traxx Records Party) **USA (Chicago)** // Daft Punk **10/04/98** The Arches (The Final Night Party) **Scotland (Glasgow)** // Daft Punk **15/04/98** Queen Club (Respect Party) **France (Paris)** // Daft Punk **02/05/98** Creamfields **England (Winchester)** // Daft Punk **02/07/98** Arena Festival (Amphithéâtre Du Zénith) **France (Nancy)** // Stardust **08/98** Borealis Festival (Le Rockstore) **France (Montpellier)** // Le Knight Club **08/98** Borealis Festival **France (Montpellier)** // Cassius & Thomas Bangalter **09/08/98** Borealis Festival **France (Montpellier)** // Thomas Bangalter **1998** Space **Spain (Ibiza)** // Thomas Bangalter **02/10/98** Gibus Club (Global House) **France (Paris)** // Daft Punk **16/10/98** Twilo (Respect Party) **USA (New York)** // Le Knight Club **29/10/98** Rex Club (Intergalactic Disko Release Party) **France (Paris)** // Thomas Bangalter & DJ Sneak **05/11/98** Industry Club **Canada (Toronto)** // Daft Punk **20/11/98** Grande Halle De La Villette (Global Tekno) **France (Paris)** // Daft Punk/ Thomas Bangalter **27/11/98** Cream (Bugged Out! 4th Birthday) **England (Liverpool)** // Daft Punk **12/11/98** The Queen Club (Respect Au Daft Club) **France (Paris)** // Daft Punk/Le Knight Club/Stardust **16/12/98** Queen Club (Respect Party) **France (Paris)** // Da Glads/Daft Punk **1998** Queen Club (Respect Party) **France (Paris)** // Daft Punk **1998** Festival de Champéry **Switzerland (Champéry)** // Guy-Manuel de Homem-Christo **1998** // Le CALAO (HomeTown Party) **France (Paris)** // Le Knight Club/Thomas Bangalter **20/02/99** The Junction **England (Brixton)** // Daft Punk **13/03/99** Cameo Theatre **USA (Miami)** // Daft Punk & DJ Sneak **15/03/98** The Mission (W.M.C. 1999) **USA (Miami)** // Daft Punk **16/03/99** 1st Annual WMC Boat Party **USA (Miami)** // Thomas Bangalter **03/99** (W.M.C. 1999) **USA (Miami)** // Daft Punk **19/03/99** Liquid Room **Japan (Tokyo)** // Daft Punk **20/03/99** Grand Cafe **Japan (Osaka)** // Daft Punk **21/03/99** Club Metro **Japan (Kyoto)** // Thomas Bangalter **29/05/99** Salle Wagram (T.G.V.) **France (Paris)** // Le Knight Club **26/06/99** The Arches (Pressure) **Scotland (Glasgow)** // Thomas Bangalter **14/08/99** Astropolis **France (Bretagne)** // Daft Punk & DJ Sneak **15/08/99** El Divino **Spain (Ibiza)** // Daft Punk **08/99** Space (Manumission Carry On) **Spain (Ibiza)** // Daft Punk **21/08/99** Amnesia (Bugged Out!/Jockey Slut Party) **Spain (Ibiza)** // Daft Punk **04/09/99** Hyperactive **Canada (Toronto)** // Daft Punk **05/09/99** Olympic Stadium (Cream Festival) **Canada (Montreal)** // Thomas Bangalter **09/09/99** MTV VMA After Party **USA (New York)** // Daft Punk **10/99** Mass Club **England (Brixton)** // Thomas Bangalter **09/10/99** Dolton Expo Center (WE) **USA (Chicago)** // Thomas Bangalter **23/10/99** Halloween Tribal Massive (Funky Tekno Tribe) **USA (San Francisco)** // Thomas Bangalter **24/10/99** Phoenix Hotel **USA (San Francisco)** // Daft Punk **05/11/99** fabric (Bugged Out!) **England (London)** // Thomas Bangalter **19/11/99** Elysee Montmartre **France (Paris)** // Daft Punk **22/12/99** Robin Des Bains **France (Paris)** // Daft Punk **1999** (Basement Jaxx Gig) **France (Paris)** // Daft Punk **01/29/00** Elysee Montmartre **France (Paris)** // Daft Punk **19/04/00** L'Hôtel Ivoire **France (Paris)** // Le Knight Club **13/10/00** Temple Bar **Italy (Piacenza)** // Le Knight Club **01/12/00** Cirque Zig Zag **France (Paris)** // Le Knight Club **2000** Event Unknown **Belgium** // Le Knight Club **14/07/01** Matilda **Italy (Jesolo)** // Daft Punk **17/12/01** fabric (Crisis In Afghanistan) **England (London)** // Daft Punk **2001** Champs Elysées (Daft Club) **France (Paris)** // Le Knight Club **21/02/02** Rex Club **France (Paris)** // Cassius & Thomas Bangalter/Daft Punk **23/03/02** Nikki Beach Club (W.M.C. 2002) **USA (Miami)** // Le Knight Club **13/04/02** Liquid Club **Germany (Dortmund)** // Le Knight Club **20/06/02** Module (Crydamoure & Daft Crew Japan Tour 2002) **Japan (Tokyo)** // Le Knight Club **21/06/02** Underlounge (Crydamoure & Daft Crew Japan Tour 2002) **Japan (Osaka)** // Le Knight Club **22/06/02** O/D (Crydamoure & Daft Crew Japan Tour 2002) **Japan (Fukuoka)** // Le Knight Club **26/06/02** Luners (Crydamoure & Daft Crew Japan Tour 2002) **Japan (Tokyo)** // Cassius & Thomas Bangalter **26/06/02** Concorde Atlantique (Respect Été D'Amour) **France (Paris)** // Le Knight Club **27/06/02** King Xmhu (Crydamoure & Daft Crew Japan Tour 2002) **Japan (Sapporo)** // Le Knight Club **04/07/02** Faith Club (The Daft Crew / Crydamoure Asia Tour 2002) **Thailand (Sumkhumvit)** // Le Knight Club **30/08/02** Chaos (Crydamoure World Tour) **USA (New York)** // Thomas Bangalter **09/02** Villette Numérique **France (Paris)** // Together & Cassius **19/10/02** Paradiso (Amsterdam Dance Event) **Netherlands (Amsterdam)** // Together & Cassius **25/10/02** X-Tra Limmathaus **Switzerland (Zürich)** // Together & Cassius **26/10/02** GrooveLift (Couleur 3 20th Birthday Party) **Switzerland (Geneva)** // Together & Cassius **28/10/02** Goldclub lounge **Canada (Toronto)** // Together & Cassius **29/10/02** Sona **Canada (Montreal)** // Together & Cassius (unsure if Thomas was present) **31/10/02** Centro-Fly **USA (New York)** // Together & Cassius (unsure if Thomas was present) **01/11/02** Avalon Ballroom **USA (Boston)** // Together & Cassius (unsure if Thomas was present) **02/11/02** Hammerstein Ballroom **USA (New York)** // Together & Cassius (unsure if Thomas was present) **04/11/02** Zentra **USA (Chicago)** // Together & Cassius (unsure if Thomas was present) **08/11/02** Tribal Sessions (Tribal Gathering) **England (Southport)** // Together & Cassius [no Thomas (he had an ear infection)] **09/11/02** The End **England (London)** // Together & Cassius (no Thomas) **10/11/02** La Dune **France (Montpellier)** // Together & Cassius (no Thomas) **15/11/02** Fish **France (Lyon)** // Together & Cassius (no Thomas) **16/11/02** Tenax **Italy (Florence)** // Together & Cassius (no Thomas) **21/11/02** Event Unknown **France (Paris)** // Together & Cassius (no Thomas) **23/11/02** Pay & Go Groove City **Belgium (Bruxelles)** // Together & Cassius (no Thomas) **24/11/02** Docks Des Suds **France (Marseille)** // Together & Cassius (no Thomas) **29/11/02** The Arches (Pressure 4th Birthday) **Scotland (Glasgow)** // Together & Cassius (no Thomas) **30/11/02** Spitit **Ireland (Dublin)** // Daft Punk **2002/2003** Respect **France (Paris)** // Together & Cassius (no Thomas) **16/08/03** Pacha (Fuck Me I'm Famous Party) **Spain (Ibiza)** // Together & Cassius (no Thomas) **25/11/04** Pacha **Spain (Barcelona)** // Daft Punk **29/04/06** Coachella Valley Music and Arts Festival **USA (Indio)** // Daft Punk **30/06/06** Eurockéennes **France (Belfort)** // Daft Punk **14/07/06** Summercase **Spain (Barcelona)** // Daft Punk **15/07/06** Summercase **Spain (Madrid)** // Daft Punk **26/07/06** Global Gathering **England (Stratford-upon-Avon)** // Daft Punk **05/08/06** Festival Sudoeste **Portugal (Zambujeira do Mar)** // Daft Punk **12/08/06** Summer Sonic Festival **Japan (Tokyo)** // Daft Punk **13/08/06** Summer Sonic Festival **Japan (Osaka)** // Daft Punk **19/08/06** Pukkelpop **Belgium (Hasselt)** // Daft Punk **28/08/06** Marlay Park **Ireland (Dublin)** // Daft Punk **10/09/06** Summer of Music Festival **Poland (Warsaw)** // Thomas Bangalter **07/10/06** Nasa **Iceland (Reykjavik)** // Daft Punk **27/10/06** TIM Festival **Brazil (Rio de Janeiro)** // Daft Punk **29/10/06** TIM Festival **Brazil (São Paulo)** // Daft Punk **02/11/06** Sue Festival **Chile (Santiago)** // Daft Punk **04/11/06** Bue Festival **Argentina (Buenos Aires)** // Daft Punk **11/11/06** Bang! Music Festival **USA (Miami)** // Busy P & Thomas Bangalter **16/12/06** Showcase (Alors Les Filles) **France (Paris)** // Chilly Gonzales & Thomas Bangalter **2006** From Major To Minor (Rhythm) **France (Paris)** // Daft Punk **10/06/07** RockNess **Scotland (Inverness)** // Daft Punk **14/06/07** Palais Omnisports Bercy **France (Paris)** // Daft Punk **16/06/07** Wireless Festival **England (London)** // Daft Punk **17/06/07** Wireless Festival **England (Leeds)** // Daft Punk **23/06/07** Turkcell Kuruçeşme Arena **Turkey (Istanbul)** // Daft Punk **26/06/07** Arena de Nîmes **France (Nîmes)** // Daft Punk **29/06/07** Philipshalle **Germany (Düsseldorf)** // Daft Punk **30/06/07** Velodrom **Germany (Berlin)** // Daft Punk **04/07/07** 5 Days Off **Netherlands (Amsterdam)** // Daft Punk **06/07/07** Red Rock Festival **Luxembourg (Esch-sur-Alzette)** // Daft Punk **08/07/07** Oxegen **Ireland (Naas)** // Daft Punk **12/07/07** Traffic Festival **Italy (Turin)** // Daft Punk **21/07/07** Los Angeles Memorial Sports Arena **USA (Los Angeles)** // Daft Punk **27/07/07** Hearst Greek Theatre **USA (Berkeley)** // Daft Punk **29/07/07** WaMu Theater **USA (Seattle)** // Daft Punk **31/07/07** Red Rocks Amphitheatre **USA (Morrison)** // Daft Punk **03/08/07** Lollapalooza **USA (Chicago)** // Daft Punk **05/08/07** Arrow Hall **Canada (Mississauga)** // Daft Punk **07/08/07** Bell Centre **Canada (Montreal)** // Daft Punk **09/08/07** KeySpan Park **USA (New York City)** // Daft Punk **07/10/07** Louis Vuitton Spring 2008 Ready-to-Wear Runway Show **France (Paris)** // Daft Punk **27/10/07** Vegoose **USA (Las Vegas)** // Daft Punk **31/10/07** Palacio de los Deportes **Mexico (Mexico City)** // Daft Punk **02/11/07** Monterrey Arena **Mexico (Monterrey)** // Daft Punk **04/11/07** Telmex Auditorium Mexico **(Zapopan)** // Daft Punk **06/12/07** Kobe World Memorial Hall (dafunkfest) **Japan (Kobe)** // Daft Punk **08/12/07** Makuhari Messe Event Hall (dafunkfest) **Japan (Chiba)** // Daft Punk **09/12/07** Makuhari Messe Event Hall (dafunkfest) **Japan (Chiba)** // Daft Punk **13/12/07** Sidney Myer Music Bowl (Nevereverland) **Australia (Melbourne)** // Daft Punk **14/12/07** Sidney Myer Music Bowl (Nevereverland) **Australia (Melbourne)** // Daft Punk **16/12/07** The Esplanade (Nevereverland) **Australia (Perth)** // Daft Punk **20/12/07** The Riverstage (Nevereverland) **Australia (Brisbane)** // Daft Punk **22/12/07** Sydney Showground (Nevereverland) **Australia (Sydney)** // Kanye West & Daft Punk **10/02/08** 50th Annual Grammy Awards (Rehearsal) **USA (Los Angeles)** // Kanye West & Daft Punk **10/02/08** 50th Annual Grammy Awards **USA (Los Angeles)** // Busy P, Thomas Bangalter & DJ Mehdi **21/04/09** Cinespace **USA (Los Angeles)** // Phoenix & Daft Punk **20/10/10** Madison Square Garden **USA (New York City)** // Daft Punk **01/10/12** Saint Laurent Spring 2013 Ready-to-Wear Runway Show **France (Paris)** // Daft Punk & Stevie Wonder **26/01/14** 56th Annual Grammy Awards (Rehearsal) **USA (Los Angeles)** // Daft Punk & Stevie Wonder **26/01/14** 56th Annual Grammy Awards **USA (Los Angeles)** // The Weeknd & Daft Punk **11/02/17** 59th Annual Grammy Awards (Rehearsal) **USA (Los Angeles)** // The Weeknd & Daft Punk **12/02/17** 59th Annual Grammy Awards **USA (Los Angeles)**

COMPILED BY LUKE PEREZ

**Editors In Chief**
Paul Benney & John Burgess
**Editor**
Jim Butler
**Design**
Chris Jones, Jones Design Create
**Commissioning Editor**
Sean Griffiths
**Production**
Harriet Jones

**Cover photo**
Jake Curtis

**Writers**
Ben Cardew, Duncan Dick, Thomas Hobbs, Kate Hutchinson, Paul Mardles, Michaelangelo Matos, Kevin EG Perry, Alexis Petridis, Rod Stanley, Emma Warren

**Photography credits**
Page 4: courtesy of Dave Clarke/Soma; pages 6-7: Philippe Levy/Dalle/IconicPix; pages 8-9: RIP; pages 10-11: Luis Sanchis; pages 12-13: Matt Sayles/Invision/AP/Shutterstock; Page 14: courtesy of Dave Clarke/Soma; page 21: Aude Prieur; page 22: Daniel Newman; pages 25 & 27: courtesy of Dave Clarke/Soma; pages 30-31, 34-35 & 41: RIP; page 44: Mark McNulty; pages 46-51: RIP; pages 53 & 56-57: Louis Vincent/Dalle/IconicPix; pages 62-63: Cyril Villemain/Sipa/Shutterstock; pages 74-75: RIP; pages 100-101: Alice Hepple; page 119: RIP; pages 128-129 & 132-133: Seb Janiak; page 137: Antoine Le Grand/modds/Camera Press; pages 138 & 141: courtesy of Mark Gardner; pages 144-145, 147 & 148: Jake Curtis, visuals by The Light Surgeons; pages 171, 173, 174 & 177: courtesy of Pedro Winter; pages 180-181: Martin Philbey/Redferns; page 185: Frazer Harrison/Getty Images for Coachella; pages 190-191: Jason Merritt/FilmMagic; pages 196-197: Naki/Redferns; pages 199 & 202-204: Zach Cordner/IconicPix; page 209: Dan Burn-Forti/Contour by Getty Images; page 210: courtesy of Official Charts Company; page 221: courtesy of Luke Perez; pages 222 & 223: courtesy of Artem Medvedev; pages 225 & 227: courtesy of Ariel Anaya

**Illustration credits**
Pages 82-83: Matthew Green

**Special thanks to**
Photographer RIP of ripleyfineart.com for the first-ever 1996 cover shoot and the use of all his 90s photography; Luke Perez for the use of his extensive Daft Punk archive; and Dave Clarke and Glenn Gibbons for access to the Soma vaults.

**Thanks**
Erol Alkan, Ariel Anaya, Ashley Beedle, Richard Brown, Calvin Bush, Ben Cardew, Eric Chédeville, Dave Clarke, Mike Dearborn, Étienne de Crécy, Adam Dewhurst, Tony Gardner, Trevor Jackson, K-Alexi, Jen Kanas, Lauren Kreisler, Neil Landstrumm, Dorian Lynskey, Kevin McKay, Stuart McMillan, Artem Medvedev, Joe Mount, Chris Munton, Jim Muotune, James Murphy, Mylo, Luke Perez, James Pitt, Caroline Prothero, Shaun Roberts, DJ Rush, Soulwax/2manydjs, Jonas Stone, Surgeon, The Blessed Madonna, Pedro Winter

DISCO POGO

“Stop the music and go home.
I repeat, stop the music and go home.”